Where Is Knowing Going?

WHERE IS KNOWING GOING?

The Horizons of the Knowing Subject

———◆———

JOHN C. HAUGHEY

2009

GEORGETOWN UNIVERSITY PRESS | Washington, D.C.

Georgetown University Press, Washington, D.C. www.press.georgetown.edu

Library of Congress Cataloging-in-Publication Data

Haughey, John C.
    Where is knowing going? : the horizons of the knowing subject / John C. Haughey.
        p.   cm.
    Includes bibliographical references and index.
    ISBN 978-1-58901-486-2 (paper back : alk. paper)
    1. Catholic universities and colleges—United States.   I. Title.
LC501.H355   2009
378'.071273—dc22   2008043332

♾ This book is printed on acid-free paper meeting the requirements of the American National Standard for Permanence in Paper for Printed Library Materials.

15   14   13   12   11   10   09   9   8   7   6   5   4   3   2
First printing

Printed in the United States of America

*Dedicated to Monika K. Hellwig (1929–2005),
to whom American Catholic higher education
owes a great debt.*

Contents

Preface

This study is addressed to those who are educated enough to wonder whether they are really educated. It will be of interest to such people if they are curious about knowledge, particularly about its generation in the knowing subject, and not just about objects of knowledge or about being educated in some body of knowledge. Since this can seem very ambitious, let me explain where the particular ideas in this book came from, and why they ended up in a book with this peculiar subject matter, the knowing subject.

I started writing this book thinking about my experience in Catholic colleges and universities. I held chairs in three of them and taught in three others. In each of them there was a tension with Roman Catholicism, sometimes creative, but usually not. So, in a sense, my own experience is naturally narrow. My purview, however, is not, as I hope the reader will judge from the contents of this volume. I will start with the narrow and branch out from there. The narrow contents begin with the question of the Catholic identity of these institutions. Because, in my experience, very few of the personnel of Catholic universities were comfortable with the university's relation to Catholicism, there has been a general, largely unnamed strategy in these institutions "not to push the Catholic thing." The feeling was "why bother?" since so many, in fact the majority, of the university employees were not Catholic, and those who were Catholic were often not at peace with the Catholicism they had been exposed to by the press, their pastors, or the Church's spokespersons. To put it inelegantly, the unarticulated strategy now seems to have become "let sleeping dogs lie." Exceptions to that strategy have been infrequent, but even the best intentioned of these have caused tension or disharmony.

As a result, a general air of uncertainty tends to hang over these institutions, obscuring their identity. I say this with great respect for the administrators of such institutions, because it has not been clear what should be done. In sorting out an answer, I find that Catholicism has an interesting relation to the question posed in the title of this book. Catholicism is not the answer, but it does contain a reservoir that can help to answer questions the knowing subject has, about where knowing comes from in the subject and either where it is going or could go.

The more I have delved into this question, the more clearly I have seen that if Catholic institutions of higher education can sort out their identities in light of their tradition, they will be able to shed light on the challenges facing education itself. The whole knowledge industry, with all of its wildly disparate trajectories, is in danger of being reduced to an exercise with one goal, namely, a learn-to-earn purpose. That would make education a servant of the market economy, instead of having the market economy receive from the knowledge industry educated people who are able to determine the good and serve the common good.

The inquiring public does not tend to ask questions as abstract as the title of this volume. It usually wants to know what is distinctive about the education at a given institution. Satisfactory answers take much ingenuity. They have to be specific enough to attract, and general enough not to exclude the potential market. Descriptions can be too slick or too churchy. The population that is typically least moved by going in either of these directions is the faculty. The value of academic freedom is the most obvious reason for their resistance to the latter. This book, fully aware of these sensitivities, will seek to articulate a different way of looking at the knowing subject and at the teleology of knowledge. Catholicism will be the foil that will allow us to explore these questions.

Let me be clear about my relation to Catholicism in this book. The book is not an exercise in apologetics, a subtle argument that tries to get the reader to consider becoming Catholic. It might seem like that at times as the argument of the book develops, since I am a theologian who is Catholic. Because I am, the material I know best for making the argument is from theology. But the use of the material is based on two more foundational questions: what is entailed in knowing, and where is it going?

There are five chief assumptions at work in this volume. The first is that the pursuit of knowledge is usually moved by good will, by something approaching the pure desire to know. A second assumption is that the Catholic tradition, in particular its relation to education, needs to be rethought in order for this tradition to be of greater benefit to Catholic higher education institutions (and for them, in turn, to be of greater service to Catholicism). The third assumption is that revisiting this relationship can help to shore up higher education's rationale across the board. The fourth assumption is that change in educational institutions usually comes from below, frequently from faculty, who will change things only to the degree that they themselves have been changed. The ideas to be expounded in this volume will invite a change in understanding, both about what an education is and what Catholicism brings to the table. The fifth assumption is that there is an explicit or implicit spirituality operating in faculty members, though its existence is not adverted to in educational literature or in its institutions for many reasons, the main one being that it smacks of subjectivism.

There is more than one mind behind the ideas in this book, but all of us who have been involved in this project are especially beholden to the mind of Bernard Lonergan (1904–84), a twentieth-century Jesuit theologian, philosopher, and methodologist. We have been consistently impressed by his particular genius; we are also unanimous in our judgment that his gift has not been sufficiently plumbed to assist in answering the question about what it means to be educated in light of the Catholic intellectual tradition.

A faculty member's lot is an exciting and complex one. At a minimum it entails attaining competence in a particular area of knowledge and the ability to research and communicate this material to students. So it requires wit and wisdom. But for those who teach in Catholic institutions, there is an additional challenge, an additional level of complexity. Since the Catholic faith is the unique raison d'etre of a Catholic institution of higher learning, all those associated with the institution will be more at home in it if that institution can give an account of itself that includes them, whatever their faith or lack thereof. Such an institution is a peculiar type of academy, of course, and one that in its self-understanding is still developing. Its personnel will more easily be able to identify with its mission and tradition if they have faith in Christ and knowledge of the Catholic tradition. What about those who don't, since they usually make up the majority in these institutions? This fact makes it necessary to elaborate a theological rationale for their belonging. An educational rationale that is able to give an account of the operations in consciousness that yield knowledge is the other challenge. This volume hopes to address both of these challenges.

All educational institutions have mission statements that convey their own self-understanding in abbreviated form. But these usually elicit the thinnest of assents, because as was already said, they are developed with an eye to attracting as broad a market as possible. Since such statements typically leave a faculty largely disengaged from the university's articulated mission, a feeling of disconnection is likely to run throughout the entire ethos of the school. Because the faculty tend to be underwhelmed by the institution's stated mission, both students and outside observers will have the impression that faculty members are committed to their disciplines, their specializations, and, on a good day, to their students and department colleagues, and infrequently to the institution itself.

The development of a clear rationale for the distinctiveness of a school serves many ends, including: (1) the faculty member's own integrity; (2) the integrity of the institution itself, which promises all sorts of unique "excellences"; (3) the university personnel other than faculty, who thrive on finding themselves in a place with a sense of common purpose; (4) the students, who need to experience being in a place where there is a deliberate reflection on the ends of learning; and (5) for a Catholic institution, the relationship of the institution to the Church and its tradition. The market that the universities seek to attract has a keen eye for whether its purported distinctiveness is hype or reality.

There are two poverties that this volume will seek to address: One is peculiar to contemporary institutions of higher education, whereas the other is peculiar to Catholic higher education in particular. The first is a poverty not of educational theory, but more foundationally of cognitional theory. Another way of saying this is that there has been an almost universal inattentiveness to the spirituality latent in the act of coming to know. The second poverty, peculiar to Catholicism, is doctrinal; the ecclesiological mark of "catholic" has been undeveloped. Consequently, Catholicism's contribution to education itself is also largely undeveloped.

This book's reflection on these two poverties should be of interest not only to those who are involved in Catholic higher education, but to anyone who is invested in understanding *understanding*—their own, for starters, as well as that of those with whom they interact and seek to learn from or instruct. There is a further conviction that will simply be asserted here: There is a tradition that is in a continuum with the best of the past, and its openness to the best of the present is crucial for the future of human well-being.

Whatever the reader's faith or lack thereof, whether the reader comes from an academic or a nonacademic background, he or she will be invited to examine two topics: his or her own intentionality, and Catholicism's intellectual tradition. The claim is that one has something in common with the other; namely, that each has a heuristic character that tends toward a wholeness that is more future than past, more unknown than known, more implicit than explicit. They both seek a better grasp of reality than is already attained. Both have a past: The reader's own intentionality has a short history, whereas Catholicism's intellectual tradition has a long history, which, if revisited, will enable that tradition to deal better with a confusing present, and more clearly see into the aborning future, near and far. In analogous ways, each carries a distinct legacy, some moments of it more honorable than others.

My initial approach here is to understand the purpose of a given institution of higher learning from below, that is to say, from those who ply their trade in it daily. Presumably, every discipline and all those who labor in them play a role in accomplishing the purpose of an educational institution. In the case of a Catholic institution of higher education, there is seldom a feeling that one is part of an intellectual tradition, either receiving from it or contributing to it. In fact, it is very rare that there is even a conversation within these schools about a Catholic intellectual tradition, as far as I can tell. But the need for this—or for any kind of conversation about any intellectual tradition—grows each year because of the fragmentation of higher education. Its disciplines and its specializations within them keep increasing, while the amount of data that each person has to take into account to attain mastery of even one's own field is more and more daunting. So, intellectual traditions, such as they are, tend to be ad hoc, usually with a short memory span.

In Catholic institutions a peculiar source of fragmentation, in many cases even alienation, is the feeling that to be completely at home in such a place, one would have to be in consonance with the beliefs of Catholicism. We will look at beliefs in a later chapter, but suffice it to say here that a good education at any college or university does not depend on each member of the community having the same beliefs, but on whether the particular beliefs each has received from his or her respective families and religious or cultural traditions are warranted and worthy of continuing subscription. Since everyone necessarily believes in any number of things, nonbelievers are, in fact, nonexistent. The question is, what do we do with the inevitable plethora of beliefs we inherit from the plurality of cultures in each of our backgrounds? We cannot be educated until we can take responsibility for our beliefs, including recognizing that a given belief is unreliable or that we have been mistaken in the way we have understood it. But it is difficult to take responsibility for our beliefs when so many of them remain hidden even from ourselves.

We usually assume that most of the data we have received is believable until and unless some pieces of it begin to show themselves to be untrustworthy. If being an academic means anything, it means that one is ever ready to examine or challenge the received, believed contents of a legacy, whatever its source. This presumes that one is prepared to be critical about what has been generated by one's forebears or contemporaries, and is sufficiently competent to do so. The gullible are not competent to judge received beliefs, nor are the skimmers in a field, who don't stop to examine any of the components of their received lore—its source, its cogency, its factual accuracy, or its value. What is needed in educational and cognitional theory is a horizon that is both critical and inclusive of plural beliefs. Whether Catholicism can be capacious enough to supply this inclusivity is one of the challenges I address in this volume.

For a given discipline to settle for a quasimonadic identity is fatal for a university. A discipline that tries to forge its identity in isolation from communities and legacies and traditions, albeit unintentionally, makes a mockery of the very idea of a university. And universities that would aim at less than knowledge within a horizon make a mockery of the collective enterprise of human understanding that is the very reason for a university. It was this exigency for knowledge and intelligibility in relation to a whole tradition that first brought universities into being in medieval Europe and Islamic countries.

Since we have adverted to tradition here, it could be cogently argued that the reason for the inability of the early Protestant universities in this country to retain their religious identities historically—a fact that in itself needs no argument—was that the connections between reason and faith in Christ were not well worked out. It was precisely this weakness that eviscerated their institutional commitments to their religious origins in the face of the enlightenment and the primacy of reason. Faith commitments were relegated to the private sphere of the individual believer's preferred beliefs. In *The Soul of the American University: From Protestant Establishment to Established Nonbelief*, George Marsden presents much of the data that establishes this thesis.[1] At the same time and despite these institutional failures, it must be said that one of the great strengths of Protestant Christianity has been its emphasis on the responsibility of the individual believer to appropriate his or her own faith. While the strength of that kind of faith is to be admired, Catholicism need not go the same route Protestants did with their universities.

It seems obvious that an educational institution needs a holistic theory of education if it intends to educate whole persons. Without such a theory it will likely produce disconnected persons. Schooled in specializations disconnected from one another, and lacking in the wherewithal to know what becoming a whole person entails, the young are left with far too much on their shoulders. Forming "the whole person" has become an adage with great cachet in educational circles, one that requires significant clarification. All agree on the value of the intention: One aspect is to help students sort out their own questions; their courses might keep them from even knowing what these are. We can be sure that students desire more than knowledge, but what that *more* is for is both numinous and transcendent. A theory about forming such whole persons is hard to come by. The author's intention is to try to articulate such a theory.

One reason for pressing for a better theory and clearer rationale for higher education is the negative effect on students who have to opt early for a major that puts them on a career path on which they will find out more and more about less and less—maybe. Another reason is that making a living and becoming educated get conflated into one pursuit, with the more measurable goal becoming a clear winner and the less measurable a clear loser. Another is that the heavy burden of integrating multiple realms of meaning—intellectual, personal, vocational, familial, and religious—is loaded on young shoulders unlikely to be up to doing the job well. Institutions usually have services to help students do some of this work of integrating different spheres of meaning, but they typically have many fewer services than students need.

So clarity about the purposes or ends of higher education matters, or should matter, to all parties. The preferred Catholic way of dealing with ends is in terms of the mission of these universities in relation to the mission of the Church. Some voices insist that this relationship will become pristine when and insofar as there is a greater adherence to Catholic doctrine. This volume will try to show that this is an inadequate understanding of the options available to a Catholic institution of higher learning. Its greatest asset is a centuries-old intellectual tradition that has been and still is accumulating insights from the light of reason as well as the light of faith. It is this tradition that must be better understood for the distinctiveness of these institutions to be better understood. Doctrine is only one component of this remarkable tradition, whose contents include, through a process of accumulation over the centuries, the best of what constitutes an education. It is also the oldest of the intellectual traditions, as well as one that continues to appropriate learning, whatever its source.

The most common bias against the Catholic tradition is the impression that it is narrow or reductionistic. This merits a deeper look. The Catholic intellectual heritage is not static in its contents; rather, it is a dynamic, cumulative, and living heritage that has been developing throughout history. Some of its most important contributors have not been concerned with the tradition, but with naming what is or isn't so, and with what is or isn't of value.

Although this notion will be explained in depth in this volume, let it just be claimed here that the continuing tension within Roman Catholicism about whether it is or is not sufficiently universal will best be resolved by looking at how the knowing subject comes to knowledge. This tension about who is in and who is out, or who belongs and who does not, goes back to the beginning, as far back as when some of Jesus's devoted followers wanted to keep his inner circle narrow. On one occasion they voiced their desire to exclude someone "who is not of our company." Jesus said: "Whoever is not against us is for us" (Mark 9:40). Peter was converted from his myopia about universality when, from a vision he had received at Caesarea, his tribalism was confounded. "God has shown me that I should not call any person profane or unclean" (Acts 10:28). Having taken this to heart, he was able to say with authority that "God shows no partiality; rather in every nation whoever fears him and acts uprightly is acceptable to him" (Acts 10:34–35).

It is this vision of universality that is peculiarly germane to the relationship of Catholicism and its intellectual tradition to its universities. Catholicism's ability to embrace the pluralism that is its calling can be helped by an understanding of the operations of consciousness in all peoples within which God is at work. Making these operations of consciousness explicit will go a long way toward helping us to see the connections between the educational ends of higher education, of which there are many, and the mission of a Catholic college or university.

By now, the reader will wonder not where knowing is going, but where this book is going. Chapters 1 and 2 come from deep listening to faculty and reflections on their sharings with one another and with me. Chapter 3 delves into the dynamics of the change that can occur when one engages with others. Chapter 4 unearths a drive or notion at work in most human beings that explains their need to make meaning and wholes. Chapters 5 and 6 seek to describe the contours of the Catholic intellectual tradition. Chapter 7 gives a generic description of the dimensions of the Catholic intellectual traditions and invites the reader to examine whether it is operating on their campus. Chapter 8 looks at the teleology of knowing through three minds. Chapter 9 wrestles with the place of liturgical worship in connection with the Catholic identity issue in higher education institutions under Church sponsorship. Chapter 10 looks at the strengths and limitations of the most formal papal document ever produced on Catholic higher education.[2]

NOTES

1. Marsden, *The Soul of the American University.*
2. The most recent and most official effort at understanding the Catholic character of higher education has been the 1990 Apostolic Constitution *Ex corde ecclesiae.* It is this document that will be examined in the final chapter.

Acknowledgments

Hᴏᴡ ᴅᴏᴇs ᴀɴʏ ʙᴏᴏᴋ ɢᴇᴛ ᴡʀɪᴛᴛᴇɴ? Colleagues, friends, people who think your way and people who do not. This book is the result of many in-depth conversations. There were two groups in particular I want to mention. The first group was comprised of eight colleagues, from whom I had already learned much about their work and the wisdom they brought to it. So I invited them to come together over the course of the last three years, during which we had four in-depth conversations about the subject matter of this book. They are Patrick Byrne, chair of the Philosophy Department at Boston College; Cynthia Crysdale, School of Theology at Catholic University; Robert Deahl, dean of the College of Professional Studies, Marquette University; William George, director of the core curriculum, Dominican University; Fr. Patrick Heelan, SJ, Gaston Professor of Philosophy, Georgetown University; Msgr. Richard Liddy, Center for Catholic Studies, Seton Hall University; Fr. Gasper LoBiondo, SJ, director of the Woodstock Theological Center; and J. Michael Stebbins, director of the Ethics Institute, Gonzaga University.

The second group I am indebted to isn't really a group per se, but includes any number of faculty members from eight different schools with whom I have worked in some twenty different workshops. I do not list them by name because of their number, but their experience and insights are embedded in this book because they supplied much light to the subject matter. There are others who have also helped considerably at different moments in the journey. In addition to my colleagues at the Woodstock Center, who are supportive on a daily basis, I want to cite and thank Nelle Temple Brown, Peter Winter, Robert Heyer, William Walsh, Brittany Gregerson, Maria Ferrara, Nancy Swartz, Virginia Novak, and Martha Miller.

Finally, at a place like the Woodstock Theological Center, foundations are our bread and butter. The following foundations have been particularly helpful and are the major reason why my project on Catholic higher education at Woodstock has been able to operate: the Porticus Foundation, the Cushman Foundation, and the Sarita Kennedy East Foundation.

CHAPTER 1

◆

What the Mission Looks Like from Below

I HAVE ALWAYS ENJOYED and benefited from the poetry of Gerard Manley Hopkins. His sensitivity to words—in this case, the word *behold*—introduces the theme of this chapter. I don't think I would have noticed this word if Fr. Michael Himes, who teaches theology at Boston College, had not pointed it out to me. And after doing so, he commented that maybe a Catholic education is at its essence a training in beholding. I think this is true also of any education. The poem we were reading is called "Hurrahing in Harvest."[1] Hopkins wrote it looking down one autumn day on the long expanse of the Clwyd Valley in North Wales from St. Beuno's, a Jesuit house of study. I have lived in the same house, so the scene was very familiar to me. The occasion of the poem had Hopkins somewhat disconsolate because winter was coming and the delightful Welsh summer was over. He was not looking forward to a winter in North Wales.

But then he begins to become more attentive to what is before him: ". . . what wind-walks! What lovely behaviour of silk-sack clouds . . ." Though the leaves have fallen, he begins to appreciate their effect on "the azurous hung hills." Then he notices "the stooks," or sheaves of corn and wheat, that were being gathered and piled by the boisterous harvesters in the valley, which extends out all the way to the Irish sea. Hopkins is then struck that "these things, these things were here but the beholder—wanting." It is this line that has been so fruitful for me. As a beholder, how wanting I have been in what is there to be beheld! If the reader can identify with this, we will proceed.

WHAT I BEHELD

For the last few years I have worked with the faculties of many of our Catholic colleges and universities. In any number of workshops, about twenty-one as of this writing, the topic has been the good that each faculty member is attempting to achieve in his or her work at the school. I learned a few years before that if I had asked them about their research, though that is a major aspect of the good they do, the answer would get more complex, and the simple goodness of their academic

1

intentions and achievements would get lost on me and their colleagues in the workshop. The attention span of listeners is much shorter if the sharings are centered on intellectual endeavors, especially when these endeavors are outside the faculty member's field.[2] "The good" is easier to grasp than "the true."

These workshops have been exercises in beholding the "other." I will describe one recent workshop so that the reader might be able to get a sense of these kinds of events. I typically first ask the participants to pair up, and one describe to the other the particular good he or she is attempting to do at the school in and through their service, teaching, or research. Then, they reverse the process. When we come back together as a group, each person shares what he or she has heard from the other. Since the specific question the individual has addressed is the good he or she is seeking to accomplish, the listener's beholding is more attentive and their narrative about what they heard from the other is more engaging. Even when participants know each other, which isn't often, they learn what few of their everyday colleagues have ever heard about them.

One example of these privileged beholdings follows. This has no pretense of formal research, just what went on in the most recent workshop I conducted with faculty.

There happened to be twelve participants; no symbolism here. I will leave out the name of the university lest it distract the reader with his or her own associations about the university, and also because it was representative of many of the groups I have worked with in eight different colleges and universities. All were invited randomly and were convoked only to learn more about each other and to deepen a sense of their connection to the mission of the university.

Paul, the first of these faculty members, spent time in his early studies at Oxford in a student hostel with devout Muslims, whose fidelity to Islam reawakened him to his own Christian faith. He went on to do doctoral work in Islam and teaches students with the intention not only of informing them, but of forming them with a reverence for "the Muslim other" that they meet on and off campus and whom they are likely to encounter in various situations for the rest of their lives. The good he seeks to do is to make evident to his classes that the more visible world of Islam is only half of the story, and that the inner world of Muslims' faith can often be precious.

Dorothy's conversion, if I can call it that, came about from the work she did and saw being done in the Philippines, where she worked in a clinic as a nurse with the indigent sick. Her experience made her passionate about health care, in particular international health care. She now sacrifices both her leisure time and much of her research time to accompany her nursing students on immersion trips to countries in Africa and Latin America. She is deeply disturbed about the great disparities in health care around the world.

Elise has been attracted to dovetailing the life stories of people in prison with those of us, the innocent or at least uncaught, who have not been incarcerated. She does this work as a member of the English department, and through it seeks to show how the prisoners' humanity is the same as or at least very similar to ours. Between us and them, a connectedness is experienced that would not otherwise happen, had their stories not been known and told in greater depth at her behest.

George's story is more autobiographical. After a stint in graduate studies in math, he found that his questions were more philosophical than mathematical in nature, so he switched to studies in that field. His initial dissertation topic was "a philosophy of possibility." Gradually and unexpectedly, this developed into the question of the possibility of theism or of God. The result was a conversion to belief in God and to Christianity. His subsequent writings and courses show this linkage between philosophy and theology. He promotes an interaction between these two bodies of knowledge about which many in each of these fields are indifferent.

Barbara, whose field is nursing, has developed a program that enables forty of her nursing students to work in inner city Catholic schools. Nursing education entails learning skills to manage health and illness, while growing in knowledge about each. She has been inspired to connect her students' growth in these skills with attention to and personal care of a specific population whose behavior and worldviews are radically different from their own. The nursing students learn to deal with their own nascent or cultural racism, while encountering at times a certain prejudice against them on the part of some of the children in the schools. Since racism is divisive, its alleviation is Barbara's passion.

Alvaro, who is in the English department, had a very specific perspective on the good he seeks to do through his work: "What am I doing in and with the field of literature, to which I am devoting so much of my life?" This was the question that he had wrestled with in the early stages of his professorial career. His answer was simple and refreshingly succinct: "I seek out the Word in the course of savoring and teaching so many elegant words of the many literary artists of our time and those who have preceded them."

Just a pause at this point to name what I beheld in these sharings. The good these six people are doing is to link different elements, forming wholes that would otherwise remain disconnected: Muslims and non-Muslims, first- and third-world medical teams, prisoners and the free, philosophy and God, nursing students and the inner city, the words of literature and the Word. I will say more about what I mean by "wholes" in this book. Suffice it to say here that it was not what I was expecting when I launched these workshops, but it is what I found, with few exceptions.

Elizabeth's interviewer was balking at the assignment. He told us he didn't want to speak of her like she was a poster that could be described (a point that is well taken), since her distinctiveness was not something he could capture in words. But while he was distancing himself from the task, he actually furthered my agenda for the workshop by narrating the details of her decision to exit academia after the birth of her first child. This was still another angle of the good: the parenting and nurturing of life, in particular that of those most dependent. Now that her family is raised, she is back in academia and pursuing the peculiar good it makes possible.

Dennis, who specializes in foreign languages, goes about the good in a way that is more focused on the efficacy of prayer than is usual in the politically correct agora of modern university life. He begins his classes with a prayer. He is a proponent and devotee of a center on campus that emphasizes the nurturing of prayer for students and faculty on campus. He lets his students know the importance of prayer for both their present and future choices. Dennis's efforts help students discern through prayer how they will best serve others in their future lives.

JoAnn's specialty is history, so this matter of memory is in her bones. It speaks to and from another side of the good, that of institutional memory. To know what we are to become as an institution, we must be able to recollect the representative stories of which we are a part. Although the metaphor was not original to her, she is sure that better knowledge of the tracks that were laid out behind us, that brought us to where we are, will continue to guide us. Though the tracks before us are not yet laid, we will not lose our way unless there is amnesia about where we have come from as an institution.

Philip, who specializes in Asian studies, left a prestigious position in a state university because he felt an emptiness at the center of it. He came to this Catholic university hoping that he would find more of an atmosphere of contemplation in action, and apparently has not been disappointed. His scholarly way of going about this is to take the particular, secular matter that is the specific object of his research and splay it out on a larger canvas, one that is more attentive to the transcendent beliefs that guide his own spiritual journey.

Maxine, a language studies expert, had long suffered from the sexism that kept her institution unhealthy as far as gender fairness was concerned. As chair she found herself able to deal with this bias better than as a mere member of her department. Instead of acquiescing to it she forged ahead and broke as many glass ceilings as she could reach. She rose higher than chair with the same result, according to her interviewer, who was independently aware of Maxine's record at the university. Consequently, it is a much less sexist institution now than it would have been, had she accepted the unwholeness of sexism she experienced in her early career there.

Matthew, an expert in one of biology's many specializations, has a deeper challenge facing him and his department in this matter of the good than do the other eleven. Money in the form of grants threatens to erode whatever degree of collegiality there is among them. There is increasing competition within the sciences for scarce amounts of funding. Furthermore, there is a noncreative tension between research going in two very different directions—microbiology and cell biology. Matthew seeks to promote, with other members of the department, a research environment focused on the good of the group rather than the individual.

Again, this does not purport to be quantitative or qualitative research in any formal sense. It is an exercise in beholding, provoked by the question: "What is the good you are seeking to accomplish in your academic career?" I continue to behold wholes in these last six sharings similar to the previous six about the good. Wholes begin at home, are abetted by prayer, need to access memory, and are easier to fashion if there is a contemplative spirit within those forging them. Equality of gender is part of what is necessary for a team or an institution to be whole. Competition for money is a most unhelpful ingredient, and can be quite detrimental to a team's unity.

A THEOLOGICAL REFLECTION

What to make of all this? Granted, these twelve might seem too small a sample from which to cull any conclusions, except that their sharings were similar to those of faculty members at eight other Catholic universities where I have invited participants into the same process. The surprise I got from all of these was how often the question about the good was answered in terms of particular wholes, whether actual or aspirational, that the participants were seeking. I had the sense that there was something significant here, but what was it? Is there a larger pattern that might be operating here, one that is largely unnoticed by educators, Catholic or not, as far as I know? If these wholes—some distinct, some inchoate—are already operative in the school, they should be considered as building blocks for understanding and implementing the mission of the school. Not to notice them leaves something wanting in our beholding. I will focus my reflection on how these wholes might be interpreted.

There is some important work on the meaning of education being done "on the ground" in these colleges and universities. It is operating below the radar of those concerned with Catholic identity, but its implications are important for understanding both that identity and the identity of any institution of higher education, come to think of it.

Wholes do not arrive in a consciousness as such; one has to fashion them. There is an appetite for wholes that is built into human consciousness, and which accompanies its desire to know what is so or could be good. It is an appetite that is never satisfied. Whatever a school's Catholic identity, if these connections between truth-seeking and whole-making and the ethos of the school aren't pursued, its Catholic identity will always seem like an add-on, and remain extrinsic to its personnel. I will develop this whole-making drive further in chapter 4.

There are many people who are concerned that Catholic colleges and universities are losing their religious identity. Some parents, some priests, many bishops, some administrators, and some alumni can be counted among the concerned. There are many more for whom the loss of Catholic identity at these schools is not a particularly important issue. The majority of faculty and students could probably be counted in these ranks. But I am not at all sure that the Catholic identity of the Church's higher education institutions is the right problem to be focused on or the right question to ask. What is? The right problem might be how to understand the particular aspirations of the worker-bees of these institutions, which is how many faculty describe themselves. To approach the problem that way would be to think about Catholic identity differently than has been done in the past. It will have one think differently about Catholicism's presence or absence in a place. This approach could also be helpful for professional educators and the identity of educational efforts that do not have to deal with the question of Catholic identity.

It is a given that a school has plural disciplines in its curriculum, and that its faculty are developing something distinctive from their experiences, data banks, interests, and judgments. It is a given that each faculty member is playing host to the data for which they presumably have particular competence and responsibility. Their intelligence has been sufficiently trusted to employ them. But a denominationally Catholic school is not merely playing host to these pluralisms through its personnel who are intelligent about the intelligible. The wholes being sought by each of the players warrant closer attention, not to correct them as much as to connect them.

Typically, there are periodic spasms of concern followed by spasmodic efforts to shore up the identity of Catholic schools. While such efforts are admirable, the task would be easier if attention were given to the wholes being formed on the ground in these sites. Unmistakably, there is "the good under construction" going on, as Flannery O'Connor liked to describe it.[3] There are in these institutions any number of wholes being made at any given time, and the good can be seen in each of them. These should be recognized, prolonged, deepened, extended, shared, and named. To what end? To at least one end: that what is ungathered might be noticed and gathered, since it is grist for the mill of any effort to name the school's mission or its Catholic identity.

My own theological reflection is that an ongoing, self-giving action on behalf of the good is inexplicable if God is not its cause. Of ourselves we are morally and intellectually impotent to do the good in a sustained way, though we may be totally unaware of this. What explains why many people—in particular, academics like those described above—persevere and remain dedicated in doing the good and making wholes over many years? Granted, all are recompensed for the good that they do, and derive meaning from it and purpose and salary and maybe even appreciation, but does the accumulation of these benefits sufficiently explain the altruism needed for them to persevere? Granted, too, the experiential side of this perseverance—usually "love of the subject" or "love of my students" or "the thrill of the chase that knowledge incites"—is a further explanation. These sentiments are the most tangible evidence that there is indeed a built-in eros operating in the consciousness of those who continue to seek the good.

There are two theological poverties in some of us that keep us from being aware of how much we miss, from seeing that "these things were here but the beholder—wanting."[4] One of these poverties is a lack of insight, not into the good, but into its source. There seems to be an almost universal inability to see that the source of a persevering intention about the good is not self-evident. The conviction that finite good comes from infinite goodness can neither be proven nor argued to, but it has been attested to for centuries. It can be seen more easily in a colleague whose life and work demonstrate such remarkable goodness that one has a sense that this goodness does not originate with the colleague alone. Who among us has not experienced the impact on our lives of embodied good?

At this point I could pursue the theological route to examine the point of origination of the good, or leave that for the moment and go the cognitional route. How are this goodness and these wholes fashioned in one's intentionality? In the structures of consciousness there must be both the experiences and understandings that make for insight, as well as the subsequent processes for that insight to be verified, so that an objective judgment can be made about its viability. These operations can produce a sense of the good to be done both in particular acts and in career-launching or short-range wholes. So, part of the answer to the question of the origin of these wholes is that they are born of particulars attended to in the structures of one's consciousness.

Further, career-defining wholes usually have their foundation in and rely on human relationships, starting with spouses and families, friends, and the communities of which each person is a part. Wherever justice is being done to the demands of a given relationship, there interpersonal wholes are developing. But for academics, there are different kinds of wholes that are fashioned in relationship to the bodies of knowledge one has competence in and responsibility for. Academics have the added, unique responsibility to do justice to their data and subject matter. It is from this process that their wholes emerge.

CATHOLIC REVISITED

There is a second poverty, found in the Church at large, which is a poverty of insight into the meaning of its mark, catholic. As a doctrine it is underdeveloped. This impoverishes those who are committed to or responsible for preserving the Catholic identity of their institutions. One can accept that catholic, historically, has been taken to be a mark of the Church, but this mark is misconstrued if it is simply seen as something the Church possesses. This leaves beholding wanting!

Catholic as a mark of the Church is marked by the tension between the *already* and the *not yet*. The *already* is unmistakable: There is a church with its network of institutions, its doctrines, its compendium of moral teachings, its liturgical life, and its people, first and foremost! But the Church is so much more than its *already;* that more is its *not yet.* Catholic is an eschatological attainment that only God can and will bring about—a whole, a people, the parameters of which, at present, neither the eye hath not seen nor the ear heard. But instead of being passive about a mark it already possesses, the Church at large needs to see its catholicity as its ongoing challenge.

In a Catholic university this challenge is too narrowly focused if the university's concern with its Catholic identity is only in terms of its alignment with Catholic doctrine and morals. Equally or even more germane to the question of the mark catholic are the bodies of knowledge and whether justice is being done to the data of these fields. Bodies of knowledge are themselves an instance of an *already* and a *not yet,* an already known and an expectation of greater knowledge still to come. They are unique, always developing fields of endeavor or inquiry through which academics serve their students, their guilds, and their culture through their teaching and research. If anything keeps academics from being obliged by the data to which they are privy, or makes them biased in weighing it, then this does an injustice to those who have a right to expect objectivity. Insofar as such obstruction occurs and prevents academics from doing justice to the data in their fields, these academics will produce counterfeit wholes, if wholes at all. The effects of such blights are usually small and local, but not always insignificant, since misreadings and ignorance purporting to be right readings and accurate knowledge are cumulative. Trusting scholarship that proves to be untrustworthy leads the unwary away from paths they have relied on. The reader need think no further than the misreading of the data that has brought the United States to its recent international conflicts.

To the extent that the faculty members of a given school are competent and objective in dealing with their ever-developing subject matters, the good being pursued in that school will be of value. Academics value the good of the objectively true; they pursue it through new questions asked and answered, fully aware that there will always be questions yet to be asked and answered. Insofar as the educational movement is from intelligibility to intelligence, exercised out of a pure desire to know, the school will do justice to both its educational mission and, in the case of Catholicism, to its faith.

While concern about whether a school is retaining its Catholic identity is valid, I do not assume that the twelve whose work was described briefly above are Catholic, or that any faculty I met with in these twenty or so workshops I have facilitated were Catholic. I intentionally did not inquire about this. What I found is that each of those to whom I have listened intently through their narrator is working toward some entirety, toward a distinctive whole in the work they do, even though that particular description might not have occurred to them.

Academic specializations are like discoveries or landings on the outer edge of "being" between the unknown and the known. This knowledge, as it is appropriated by peers, can then become a part of a larger body of knowledge, gradually being arrived at over the course of the discipline's history of intelligent inquiry and verifiable judgments. Most of those who devote themselves to their disciplines and specializations see their work in terms of the good of their disciplines, usually with some sense, whether strong or weak, that their work also contributes to the common good of an educated public.

But a further question surfaces at this point. How do these discrete, particular wholes relate to one another? What adds urgency and poignancy to this question is that the personnel of the schools in which I have taught and facilitated workshops have seldom had a sense of belonging to an enterprise heading in a clear direction. Rather, the experience of disconnection is so pervasive, it is taken for granted as the best we can do, given the proliferation of disciplines and data. But is this the best we can do? Yes, each school might seem like a single enterprise at graduation or at freshman orientation, but in actuality it is more like an endless series of disconnected industries, each with its own stovepipe billowing its own smoke and heat, contiguous to other little industries, each with its own stovepipe.

Even faculty members from the same departments can have large distances between their specializations and methodologies. Some of the distances, of course, are created by personality conflicts, but that is the least of the sources of distancing. One of the frequent remedies proposed for this sense of disconnectedness is interdisciplinary research or study. That is not an errant idea, but even when it is successful, the yield of interdisciplinary study is localized around the few who cooperated on the work, rather than having an effect across the institution. The complex enterprise that is a modern university needs more than interdisciplinary research to come to a sense of a common work or to the experience of being in a common enterprise.

I do not apologize for seeing this data in theological terms, because I am a theologian and because the work of these schools is being done under religious auspices. It is unlikely that the intentions, motives, or ends of the university personnel have the eschatological character of catholic or the reign of God as part of their horizon. It is not essential that they do, or that their perspective be theological or that long-ranged, but that doesn't make the question of where their knowing is going irrelevant, nor its theological import insignificant. It can have great relevance to the reign of God.

AN EXAMPLE

What does all of this have to do with the above claim that there is a poverty of doctrine in this matter of being Catholic individually and institutionally? A brief autobiographical aside should help to focus the issue. As a Jesuit scholastic studying theology at Woodstock College in the late fifties and early sixties, I was privileged to have Fr. John Courtney Murray as one of my professors. At that time he was under a dark cloud that emanated from the Vatican, though the matches and wood for his incineration were shipped over there by two professors from The Catholic University of America in Washington. In brief, he was forbidden to publish. His research and writings were attempts to weigh the import of the experience of religious freedom in the United States against the Church's undeveloped doctrine about religious liberty. His insight, which was eventually accepted by the Vatican Council, was that religious freedom is a right everyone possesses, an inalienable right that comes from God. It seems simple enough to accept this now, some fifty years or so later. But, as the poet James Russell Lowell put it, "Thoughts that great hearts once broke for we / Breathe cheaply in the common air."[5]

By challenging the long-reigning conservative Catholic axiom that "error has no rights," Murray carefully crafted the idea, which eventually became doctrine, that everyone has the right to freedom in the matter of their religious commitments. Murray's classes often stressed the need for doctrinal development to play catch-up with human experience. In this case, he had become convinced that the American experience of religious freedom could supply the key data for the Church universal to understand this universal right, and for the Church to formally make it its own doctrine. By eventually doing so, it overcame a lacuna in its understanding of the freedom needed in being religiously self-determining.

The memory of those days is still vivid in my mind, partly because the candidacy of John F. Kennedy for president was being hotly contested at the time. Many non-Catholics feared that this and other rights and freedoms that Americans had enjoyed would be in jeopardy, because they imagined orders from Rome would constrain a Catholic president and therefore constrain them, too. I recall a number of our classes during which Murray was called out of class to take urgent calls from Ted Sorensen, Kennedy's advisor about matters of Catholicism. The Democratic candidate for president needed help in giving an account of the compatibility between American politics and what would eventually become Catholic doctrine.

We were then more than a decade beyond the United Nations Universal Declaration on Human Rights, but the Church had not yet caught up to that virtually universal moral agreement—the first of its kind in the history of the human race—about what was due to the dignity of each human being. Murray was grieved by his church's tardiness about accepting the world's insight into human rights in general and this right to religious freedom in particular. He wondered why the world had to teach the Church, and why the Church had to be such a slow learner. It is intriguing that the first draft of what would become the Vatican Council's doctrine on the universal right of religious liberty, *Dignitatis humanae,* was presented to the bishops for their deliberation on November 19, 1963, three days before President Kennedy was assassinated in Dallas, Texas.

This experience of how that doctrine of religious liberty developed is fresh in my mind as I think about the matter of the Catholic identity of these institutions of higher learning in America. Just as Murray found within the American political experience the data that was needed for that doctrine to develop, so I am wondering whether the kind of data being gathered here from the experience of listening to faculty could help the Church see that its doctrine of catholic as an ecclesial mark needs to develop beyond its present status. There is an understanding of catholicity developing here below the radar, so to speak. It challenges us to become better beholders so that what is latent in this ecclesial mark of catholic might develop a more eschatological depth.

SPIRITUALITY AND THE PROFESSORIATE

But I had a further question about these faculty wholes being reflected on here. So I tried a different tack in the last eight workshops I have done at the same universities, though with different participants. The invitation this time asked faculty whether their faith, whatever it was, was at play in their work, and if so, how concretely was it connected to their work? Interestingly, it was easy to get a positive response to that invitation, easier than to the previous one, which had inquired into the good. The surprise this time was to find out how a randomly invited group, whose religious background I didn't have any knowledge of, really welcomed the opportunity to speak about this seemingly verboten matter, and to hear fellow faculty, largely unknown to one another, reflect on it.

The outcomes I was looking for, which I outlined in the invitation, were met every time. These were for a more personal knowledge of one's colleagues; a valorizing of this kind of conversation about faith and work in the culture of the university; a deeper sense of belonging to a community of shared meaning; an appreciation of how different faiths have their believers approach the academic tasks differently;

and a hope that the sharings might help the individuals taking part in the workshops to bring the two parts of themselves closer together.

From what has been shared from both of these two topically different sets of workshops, something foundational has become more evident to me: There is a projective selfhood at work in faculty, much more than I had been aware of or anticipated. In looking at this more closely, I recalled a study done by Karl Rahner that underscored the fact that humans are the species that operates or "exists from out of our present 'now' towards our future."[6] Upon reflection, it should have been obvious how much of our energies are invested in the future—into what we want to accomplish or become—and in the relationships we want to cultivate and the wholes we want to birth. In abstract terms, futurology seems to be a constitutive part of our anthropology. In concrete terms, universities might do well to see themselves as birthing sites, places where wholes can be conceived and brought to birth.

Through an interesting study done by the Higher Education Research Institute at the Graduate School of Education, University of California, Los Angeles, I have been able to extrapolate from my own smaller experiences to get a national sense of the professoriate in this matter of spirituality.[7] Some 40,670 faculty members from 421 colleges and universities responded to questions about their own spirituality. Four in five described themselves as "a spiritual person." Over two-thirds said that they seek opportunities to grow spiritually. Nearly half of all faculty responding to the survey said that "integrating spirituality in my life" is an essential or very important life goal. When the category moves from spirituality to religion, the numbers are slightly lower but still very significant: 64 percent of this professoriate would call themselves "religious." About the same number, 61 percent, report that they pray or meditate. Given this material from so large a sample of secular higher education institutions, I wonder why academic institutions under religious auspices are, at least in my experience, uncomfortable with conversations about spirituality precisely in relation to academic pursuits?

The cascading number of objects that engage academics can make one overlook the blessing that is human consciousness itself, our own and others'. But for academics especially, what goes on in our consciousness is our bread and butter. How often have we marveled at our own consciousness and been grateful to God for it, especially as we learn about how slowly and how late in the evolutionary cycle the singularity of human intelligence came into this world?

John Henry Newman described one of the possible consequences of ignoring or being indifferent about such matters in *The Idea of a University*.[8] If an academic shuts out the transcendent dimension of his or her life and discipline, there is likely to grow a spiritual ignorance about what one knows in one's own area of specialization, because it is not located in a fuller horizon of reality, or seen as a part of a larger whole. But Newman also foresaw something more deleterious: The academic is likely to compensate for the neglected dimension by trying to make a fragment into a whole. Those who are familiar with Newman will know that this was not an effort to proselytize, but to keep disciplines from becoming occasions for idolatry.

Would it not be a strange school that met all the measures of being educationally excellent and met all the prerequisites of religious orthodoxy according to settled doctrine, while failing to instill in students and teachers a thirst for knowledge and its ensuing good? Two things that should be distinctive about Catholic schools are their insight into the teleology of human intelligence, and their awareness of the connection to the source of this intelligence, howsoever it is named. Enabling their personnel to make these connections should be foundational to the mission and identity of a Catholic school.

NOTES

1. Hopkins, "Hurrahing in Harvest," 273.
2. I learned the limits of sharings about research in sessions I conducted in a previous time. Cf. Haughey, "Catholic Higher Education."
3. O'Connor, *A Good Man Is Hard to Find.*
4. Hopkins, "Hurrahing in Harvest," 273.
5. Lowell, *The Complete Poetical Works of James Russell Lowell,* Part 13/21.
6. Rahner, *Foundations of Christian Faith,* 431.
7. This material can be found at www.spirituality.ucla.edu/; the title of the study is "Spirituality and the Professoriate."
8. Newman, *The Idea of a University.*

CHAPTER 2

---◆---

A Further Beholding

In the first chapter I looked at twelve individual professors, and each one's efforts to birth wholes in his or her work. This brings us to the question of how these twelve and other academics see the connections between one another's work. An image suggests itself for how these connections might be understood. The labor expended in bodies of knowledge, when linked, can be like building blocks of a vast cathedral. I think of the centuries it took to build the cathedral at Chartres, and the multiple skills of multiple craftsmen, generation after generation. Each did his or her part as the cathedral gradually rose to the sky to the praise of God, the Source of all their talents and of the materials they used, eventually bringing their centuries-long work to completion. The project gave all who were involved in the gargantuan effort purpose and meaning. On a down day, academics have to wonder what it is that they are building together, if anything. Could their combined efforts in any way resemble a vast cathedral that is being built to the praise of God, even though being able to imagine this might be a stretch? It would be easier to see the dignity and importance of the grunt work of marking and writing papers and teaching classes, if faculty members could see their efforts in terms of a holistic image such as the building of a great cathedral.

Less grandly, we should be able to agree that through the efforts of individuals and their colleagues who collectively have a sense of a common mission, something good is being constructed. A school is clearly a good under construction, but what is being constructed is not easily named. The body of knowledge that constitutes a discipline is like a plumb line, acting as a guide so that further levels of intelligibility can be built through the efforts of its certified laborers. But the connections between the plumb lines, the various disciplines, are poorly attended to. All disciplines, and all those who labor in them, are ever-developing works in progress. What constitutes completion, or what if any destiny do these fields of labor envision?

It seems like the best way to answer the question is in terms of value. Bernard Lonergan spells out the two horizons of value: "Without faith the originating value is man and the terminal value is the human good man brings about."[1] So, in this view, each component of the school represents a human good. The good under construction in a given school is any number of bodies of knowledge, each adding

13

the good of intelligibility and heightening the good of intelligence of those privileged to be part of the enterprise. But with faith, "the originating value is divine light and love, while the terminal value is the whole universe. So, here the human good becomes absorbed in the all-encompassing good."[2] It is in connection with this second articulation that the Chartres image appeals to me. The common good attained over the course of the construction is possible only because the builders share a teleology that transcends the here and now and the still-developing good of each discipline. Each laborer will have passed on before his or her part in the cathedral's construction is complete. What each one owes to the overall enterprise of education is to attain whatever degree of insight he or she can into whatever field that he or she has the competence and wit to contribute to over the course of a career.

These sentiments might strike some as naive. The skeptic who sits on my shoulder chirps: "Faculty believing that the academic experience can be imagined as a cathedral being built in the course of history, with foundations that stretch from time into eternity—how unreal can you get?" I resist this line of disparagement and feel supported in this proposal by the study mentioned in the previous chapter, in which more than 88 percent of the faculty answering the survey counted themselves as either "religious to a great extent" or "to some extent." Their schools presumably will not nurture the image of a cathedral being built, but there are sacred texts and sources that have grounded such beliefs for centuries. Of course, faculty members are of different faiths, and obviously there are different sacred texts and practices. But for faculty members who come from any religious background, the religions are fundamentally similar in having teleologies that transcend both the self and the world. Even humanisms have their teleologies.

Since I am addressing questions about what constitutes an education, and what Catholic schools have going for them in trying to answer this same question, I will mention some of the texts from the Second Vatican Council (1962–65), particularly those that relate to the "terminal value" of the Church's institutions. Since the Council presumes that the light and love that come from faith constitute the originating value of the Church's institutions, it describes their terminal value as "the future reign of God."[3] Lonergan's description is equally capacious: "the terminal value is the whole universe."[4] The Council states that the Church's mission is to try to make evident on earth the "initial budding forth of the reign of God."[5] I understand this to mean that each entity operating under the auspices of the Church is meant to strive in its own way to be a budding forth of the future wholeness that God intends for all peoples. But it was not the mind of the Council that the world was to become the Church; rather, the institutions under Church sponsorship are to try to be a sign to the world of what it could become. A glimpse of this holistic aspiration was set forth in *Gaudium et spes*, the document that articulated the Church's position in the world as one of service to it: "For here [on earth] grows the body of a new human family, a body which even now is able to give some kind of foreshadowing of the new age."[6]

If Roman Catholicism and the institutions that it sponsors are called to envision, anticipate, and assist in bringing about a new human family, where is the evidence that this is happening in Catholic universities? As I did in the previous chapter, I will try to seek an answer to this question inductively. Concretely, is there evidence of a deep desire in the minds and hearts of academics for a wholeness, to which they contribute within their own fields of labor? Though, based on the data of the previous chapter, the answer to this question seems to be "yes," we need to probe more deeply to see if we can find evidence of individuals trying to contribute to growing "the body of a new human family."

My method here is closer to qualitative research than it was in the first chapter, but maybe it would be more accurate to call it deep listening. Again, my sample is small and somewhat random, since I had only a slight familiarity with each of the five interviewees and no conception of their academic vistas before the interviews. I say this here lest the reader think I have corralled a group of "ringers" to prove a thesis I cooked up a priori.

BIOGRAPHICAL SNAPSHOTS

Here there are five biographical snapshots, taken of five scholars, giving us glimpses of their work in very different areas of expertise. It was obvious that all of them—in their efforts to become competent in their fields and to contribute to the world beyond them—lived for more than just themselves. In interviewing these five, the image of birthing continued to develop in my imagination. It is a helpful metaphor, since the experience of women in bringing their babies to term is paradigmatic for all who have committed themselves to the drama of birthing "the body of a new human family." For an academic, the process begins with a time of growing familiarity with the data, followed by the generation of an initial insight, akin to the fecundation of the ovum. Once implanted, the new life begins to call for attention; it takes room and time and nurture. As the new life begins to kick, the mother has to forgo more and more of her own agenda for the sake of the nascent insight, idea, or dream. For the life—the insight—growing in these minds to come to term, an institution must provide the necessary conditions for it to survive and thrive.

A university, among the other things it must be, is a birthing room. The new, emergent insight needs caregivers willing to forgo their autonomy, to suffer the enlargement of their consciousness and the transcendence of their own selves, without which the new insight will not see the light of day. This is how I see the persons I will now describe. All five would count themselves in the 88 percent of the population who consider religion to be connected with their academic pursuits.

I asked two questions of the interviewees: (1) Do you have a dream, a hope, or a long-term project that you are seeking to implement in and through your discipline?; and (2) Do you see your work as being of a piece with a larger whole?

(1) Paul Heck is a professor of Islamic studies. (He is the only one of the five that was introduced in the previous chapter.) As a young man in his early twenties, he

traveled from the parochial American culture of his native Massachusetts to Oxford in the United Kingdom, where he "lucked into" a close association with devout Muslims living in the same student hostel. Their devotion to and seeming familiarity with God awakened him to his own Catholic faith in a deeper way. Ever since then he has felt an affection for and an indebtedness to that tradition: "Islam is my friend" is the way he puts it. Since 9/11 he has realized that "[his] friend is in trouble." Paul's classes make evident his affection for his subject matter. He tries to help his students with what the Greeks called *paideia*, the refinement of soul. For him, this means forming in them a taste for the material they are studying rather than what too often can become information overload. Paul says that his goal in educating those who are religiously and culturally non-Muslim is to cultivate "an epistemology of friendship for the other."

Paul's research has focused on Muslim interiority, notwithstanding the huge amount of variation within it. At present, he is completing a book on the role of skepticism in classical Islam's approach to religious truth. His doctoral dissertation was also culturally focused: He examined the effect of state patronage on branches of knowledge in the Muslim world from the ninth to the eleventh centuries. The present international tension surrounding Islamic extremism has affected him, as it has the whole world, and has directed his focus to more immediate subjects than his pre-9/11 studies had, such as jihad, Sufism, and the moral implications of Islamic mysticism.

His long-range project focuses on the relationship between international law as the West understands it, and Sha'ria law as Islam understands it. At present, these seem to be hopelessly incommensurable, since "the will of God" is a very operative category in the Muslim mind, while rationality and precedent are sacrosanct in the Western approach to law. He sees this kind of research as having crucial importance, as the future well-being of the world is contingent on the development of mutual understandings between Islam and the West. Thus Paul throws his whole person into research and writing about his field, for the sake of encouraging a future political harmony between these two traditions. It became obvious in conversing with him that he has not graduated out of his Catholicism, but that it is the universality latent in Catholicism that drives him.

(2) Rita Rodriguez spent her childhood and most of her adolescence in pre-Castro, pre-Communist Cuba. She and her family immigrated to the United States less than two years after the Castro regime was installed, having lost everything to Cuba. Still a teenager when she came to the United States, her dreams changed from those she had had as a high school student in Cuba. Her early goal in America was not just to get "some kind of a job," but rather a "well-paid job" that would mean economic security for herself and her family. With the last of her meager funds, she applied to New York University. She registered for a smorgasbord of business courses, intending to find employment after one semester. In that first semester, as she developed a love for economics, the faculty became interested in her. She went on to receive her doctorate in international economics and finance there. At Harvard Business School, in her first teaching position, Rita's goal was to get her MBA

students to understand the importance of theory in the world of international finance, drawing them away from a fixation on the bottom line. After teaching at Harvard Business School and moving from there to the University of Illinois at Chicago, she eventually became a director of the Export-Import Bank, where she remained for nearly seventeen years.

As one of five directors of the Export-Import Bank, Rita found herself in the singular position of being neither a Democrat nor a Republican. Her politically nonpartisan role served both her and the bank well, since she was the swing vote on a number of occasions. She felt she had more impact at the bank than she had had as a teacher. As Rita explained, "In the classroom you can figure out whether what you taught was learned by what shows up on the final exams, but in government I could figure out what was learned by seeing the decisions I helped to shape." Instead of being judged by the referees of academic journals, she now had to judge an unending number of memos written by these referees. She found the regulatory atmosphere in the bank to be refreshing, because it allowed her to see and enjoy the doable good, in contrast to the relative indeterminacy of the good she felt while teaching business school students.

Rita became particularly attentive to and articulate about "the internals of her life," as she calls them: "my spiritual life, my spirituality or interiority." From her interiority, she reflects on her own work experience. "When I was careless about my spirituality I found that I was abrupt with people, coarse in handling issues, obtuse about the good that could be done." By contrast, Rita found that when she was "more centered, things went more smoothly in human relationships, and I think I saw more clearly into the policy questions as they might affect people." She described these two different states or conditions using the analogy of a machine. When out of touch with her interiority, for whatever reason, she always felt as if she were lashed to a high-speed machine, a juggernaut that sucked her in and propelled her on from one task to the next. By contrast, when she was centered in herself, Rita felt that she was able to determine the direction and pace of the machine from her own free will, rather than being determined by it.

Another analogy she used to describe these internals was that of two parallel lines, with one of these representing her professional life and the other her spiritual life. When and insofar as these two are virtually in synch, her sense of purpose and of the good to be done is clearer. When they are off-kilter, the tedium and burdens of daily work are much harder to bear. Academe and government tended to pull her away from her interiority, though in different ways. Each has its temptations, its promises of reward. Rita became convinced that if she were to gain the whole world of the rewards offered (by either of them), she could have lost her own soul, not in the sense of eternal damnation, but in peace of mind and sense of purpose.

(3) Philip Rossi is a sixty-one-year-old Jesuit who specializes in the ethics of Immanuel Kant. He entered the Society of Jesus just as the Second Vatican Council was beginning, and he experienced firsthand during his training one of the problems that developed as his professors moved away from the tried and true categories of scholasticism to an untested pluralism. Phil's interest had always been in the field

of moral theology, but it was in this area that he sensed trouble brewing by the late sixties. While he appreciated the insights of his Jesuit professors, he found their insights to be too piecemeal, and longed for a more systematic approach to moral thought than his teachers were offering. This generated a great desire in him to try to link moral theology more closely with philosophy.

Phil's most influential professor at the University of Texas, where he did his doctoral work, was a Dutch-American Wittgensteinian, whose genius was not in teaching his philosophy as such, but in getting students to know their own questions and appreciate the skills they would need to answer them. Luckily for Phil, he knew what his question was: How do the pieces of the moral life fit together, so that it can be unidirectional and coherent? To his surprise and great delight, he discovered that Kant was trying to answer that very question. In particular, Kant tried to combine the analytic way of philosophizing that was just coming into vogue with the more traditional way that philosophy had been done before him. The deeper Phil went into the Kantian corpus and mind, the more he appreciated the bridge-building potential that that framework suggested. He learned how Kant came to answer his own questions about being human, responsible, communal, finite, and imaginative in a way that made sense to him.

By way of contrast, the more Phil learned about David Hume (who was roughly contemporary with Kant), the more he saw how Hume's line of thought discouraged pursuing one's questions because of their tendency to produce unanswerables. In Phil's analysis, those who studied Hume eventually settled for less than the whole to which their intentionality would naturally move them. But if one's a priori assumption is that things just don't fit together, then there isn't much point in asking questions.

The work of Immanuel Kant had a seminal influence on Phil Rossi, as evidenced by the integrity of his research choices and his thirty years of teaching. As Phil intuited early, theology is more coherent when it is in conversation with a philosophy. In general, the rich material he has produced over the years all has to do with showing how the moral life does not consist in a series of discrete decisions that are made when confronting immediate quandaries, but in the knitting together of character within a community. Why was this basic conviction important enough for Phil to expend so much of his life on this particular area of study? He was convinced that if people make the right moral choices, then not only will the character of the moral agents be good, but their lives will acquire a certain wholeness and society will be healthier, merely for their being members of it.

(4) Charles Keely is a professor of international migration, a subject he has taught at several universities since completing his doctorate at Fordham and a postdoctoral stint at Brown University. In addition to his many articles, he is the author of several monographs on migration. But closer to the heart of the man, one finds that his passions are split between immigration research and teaching. The dream that has been motivating him since his early childhood in Brooklyn has been to help students at both the undergraduate and graduate levels to know what it means to be

free—free from demons like the ones that had infested his psyche in his youth—and thereby to be free to make a more mature contribution to the common good.

Charles describes his childhood, looking back at it at the age of sixty-two, as a formation in a fundamentalist Catholicism. This was not a scriptural fundamentalism, but one more determined by the Church's magisterium. Unfortunately, he experienced "a religion of judgment, not of joy." When I asked him what it was that had freed him, insofar as he now would consider himself free, he answered, with utter succinctness: "Free men freed me." His liberators were all Fordham-affiliated academics. Three of them were philosophers, and one was a sociologist, Fr. Joseph Fitzpatrick, SJ, under whose direction he did his doctoral work. Each of them had a breadth and a depth of understanding that enabled Charles to learn to think on his own, and escape from the confines of an Irish Catholicism that he experienced as hegemonic.

These free men gave Charles an example of how he could function in the classroom. His notable competence and accomplishments in the field of international immigration are evident in his classes and his curriculum vitae, but his focus in teaching is not as much on a specific content as on enabling students to make their own judgments and verify them. As he explains, "I ask them to examine on what basis they claim to know such and such about an issue, since how they answer that question has ramifications, not only for policy questions but also for their own personal decisions and choices." His hope as a teacher is that he can replicate for his students his own "experience of becoming free of servile fear and greedy hope."

It is worth commenting here on what drives men and women in academe. It seems as though whatever the particular gifts and academic competence they bring to their work and their classes, they themselves might be more shaped by suffering. In Charles's case, there were two kinds of suffering: One was the psychic damage already alluded to from a fundamentalist Catholicism, and the other was his deep compassion for refugees and immigrants, born of his work with these populations. Two factors from his Irish cultural heritage—the early disidentification of the Irish with the Protestant establishment, and a later deep identification with the underrepresented "little guy"—became elements that added passion to Charles's demographic studies and monographs about international migration.

An academic, among other things, teaches who he or she is. In this sense, Charles's most recent course is revelatory. He conducts a freshman seminar that he dubs "the journey." The journey is a way of getting students to enter into the drama of the immigrant, while examining themselves. Some of the readings are about the journey to somewhere, others about the journey from somewhere, others about interrupted journeys, and still others about the journey as liminal, focused neither on the "to" nor the "from," since a journey is what all of them are on. As he warms to the subject and to his class, he sounds more like a Socrates than a professor of international migration. He is a perfect example of how a childhood constraint often shapes an adult's sense of calling, or how a dysfunctional beginning can forge a sense of purpose in one's life.

(5) Maria Bettinotti is a forty-six-year-old Argentine scientist. She entered the field of genetics during her doctoral work in human biology at the Ludwig-Maximilians-Universitat in Munich. She specializes in immunogenetics; she came into that field at the same time as other scientists had completed the initial sequencing of the human genome, some fifty years after Watson and Crick discovered the structure of DNA. Maria's great goal is to help to bridge the distance between the pure scientific research being done in her field and the clinical medical research that is conducted in relation to specific illnesses. She judges that the distance between them is still too great. She dreams of helping them to narrow this divide.

The dynamics of her field, molecular biology, verges on the overwhelming. It is a field in tremendous flux, with clear progress and needless decline occurring at the same time. The decline is due to several factors. There is enormous pressure on scientists to continually come up with new knowledge, in order to meet society's expectations for advances in human well-being, expectations that have grown greater since the era of molecular biology began. Also, with the understanding of the chemistry of life still in its infancy, new data is being acquired at a simply torrential rate. Before the recent revolutions in biotechnology, robotics, and supercomputers, data was as scarce as gold; since then, data has been tumbling forth from labs in such volume that "it's like sand on a beach." Much of this data now goes unanalyzed because of deficiencies in processing capacity. The field needs expertise in designing new ways of interpreting data being acquired at such a high speed.

Given these conditions, scientists are faced with two different temptations. The first is to interpret the data prematurely, so as to be ahead of the pack in publishing one's findings. Yes, the steady grind of science can eventually correct the errors, and winnow the chaff from the wheat over time, but trustworthy findings would multiply if researchers were less opportunistic, less focused on personal advancement and credit in journals. There is an imbalance between production and reflection, with much more emphasis being put on the former. Thus, junior faculty are faced with the enormous temptation to publish as much as possible as soon as possible to obtain tenure.

For more settled scholar-scientists there is a second temptation, which is to change one's avenue of research to a line with better funding sources. As Maria explains, "One year it's HIV, the next it's SARS, the next it's obesity, and always, there's always cancer in all its various forms." Unfortunately, some researchers become opportunists, who are all too willing to slant their research proposals in order to get the grants. Maria contrasts the culture of scientific research in the United States with that of other countries, especially European ones. "There they do more with less. Their scientists also do not seem to have specialized as early as Americans so the range of knowledge they bring to the table is wider." She notes that pure research is getting hijacked or neglected for the promise of immediate results in the medical field. One of the elements in Maria's dream is to fight to ensure that the value of clinical research, which seeks short-term results, does not jeopardize the status of longer-term research, since that is where some of the deepest breakthroughs have come from in the past.

One of the more interesting of Maria's many trenchant observations focuses on the role the question has played in her own experience as a scientist. For example, when it looked like her specialization, immunogenetics, might have run its course, with many of the key unknowns having become known, a whole new area of discovery came into the field's purview with the simple posing of a new question. In the first days of the field, scientists were focused on the conditions necessary for transplanting organs. But new questions about the function of the molecules responsible for transplant rejection now have immunogeneticists investigating the role that those molecules play in all our cells, as an integral part of our entire immune system. Had the field not moved in that direction, it would have easily settled into a mechanical body of knowledge.

Maria's point in all this is that the deeper you go with questions about the findings in your own field, the more likely it is that your field will come into contact with other fields. Consequently, a synthetic approach to knowledge acquisition now often complements analytic approaches. The emergent field of systems biology seeks the integration of knowledge, for example, from experiments done *in vitro* (in glass), *in vivo* (in a living organism), and *in silico* (in a computer). The volume and complexity of this new biological data, coupled with new health threats (such as from bioterrorism), call for a much closer collaboration than ever before between biologists, chemists, engineers, computer scientists, and social scientists. The National Institutes of Health have been taking the initiative in facilitating these linkages by funding more projects in what it terms "team science," a new kind of interdisciplinary approach to medical research. In other words, wholes are the new desiderata.

REFLECTION

In the course of listening to these five people, the thought kept occurring to me that communities are constituted by shared meanings. These five do not know each other, nor are they from the same university. But even for colleagues in the same school, how are shared meanings possible? How, especially, can academic institutions that began under religious auspices, but that, as George Marsden has pointed out, have become institutions of "established nonbelief," facilitate shared meanings?[7] So my challenge here is how to reflect on these interviews, whose worlds of meaning are so disparate. Is there any way of seeing a commonality in their different horizons?

One thing the five scholars had in common was the Christian faith, though that was not the focus of our conversations. Although most American colleges and universities would confirm Marsden's description, the odd thing is that the majority of their professors have a very different view of themselves, if the already-cited "Spirituality and the Professoriate" data is trustworthy. What I will do, therefore, is to take the liberty to reflect on these biographical snapshots in light of a New Testament text, one I presume they would all believe to be inspired. That is one way to see if there is a common meaning latent in their personal self-understandings. For the 13 percent in the aforementioned study who are "not at all religious," they can read the following as a reflection on a text that is merely symbolic, or poetic, or mythical.

Parables were Jesus's preferred way of speaking about the connection between the present and the future that God intends to bring about, and which humans are depicted as having a part in bringing about. In other words, the text sees two laborers presently at work on this future: God and humanity. Since co-laborers and the future are the two main emphases in parables, perhaps the parables help one see how education could be understood, at least in Catholic schools. One could expect that there must be some common meaning between these five scholars and the horizon of the parable. Is there?

Between the end times (about which we know so little) and the present time (in which we are simply flooded with information), there are several things that can be known if one allows these parables to do what they were intended to do, which is to lift the curtain of obscurity about the relation between present and future, however slightly. In the parable about the talents (Matt. 25:14–30) (or "gold coins" in Luke 19:11–27), the one who has been given the talents is expected to be industrious about increasing their worth. The donor seems adamant about this. The reward for the good use of the talents is considerable: The industrious servants are made partners and are given greater stature as they share in the master's joy (verses 21–23). The lesson here is that there is a direct connection between conscientious work done in time, and the condition of delight one will enjoy in the mysterious future, which Jesus referred to as the reign of God. The parable can speak volumes to those who recognize and remember the source of their talents. It can also generate common meaning.

The story line goes like this: Before the master travels to a distant country, he leaves his goods with his servants, with the intention that the servants will increase the goods' worth in his absence. He gives to "each according to his ability," and in return expects creativity, energy, and industry, so that there will be an abundant yield. After a long time, "the lord of those servants" comes back to see what has been done with his goods and to settle his accounts with each of them. Those who have increased his investment are rewarded. The only one who is reprimanded is the one who completely misread his master's character, so he hid the resources he had received and had nothing to show at the moment of accounting. This servant seemed to project his own logic of scarcity onto the lord, who, as it turned out, was operating from a logic of abundance, to be generated through the servants' initiative. The cautious servant was cast into outer darkness for having neglected his relatively small responsibility to make use of his one coin or talent.

If we read the parable in terms of the tasks of educators, we might say that the initial talents are given to teachers so that they can enlighten themselves and share that light with others whenever possible. Teachers are to ply their trade in the area of knowledge by seeking to grow, by pursuing their questions, and by acquiring the knowledge needed to answer these questions, both to their own satisfaction and for the sake of others. They are to do all of this, hoping that when the Lord returns, they will have something to show for his having entrusted them with the precious ability to know and the responsibility to teach. The parable suggests that the Lord is passionate about this, and will reward those who match their industry with his passion by inviting them to enter into his joy.

An even more familiar parable centers on the sower whose seeds are strewn generously over the ground (Mark 4:3–20). Few of the tiny seeds are noticed, or given sufficient room to grow into a fruitful plant, and multiply thirty-, sixty-, or one-hundred-fold. When I apply this parable to the five scholars interviewed above, I see that each of them has noticed seeds, given them room to grow, and undertaken the unique task of nurturing them, thereby growing in competence, in fact, in mastery of their subject matter. For these five, growth in their respective competencies also produces a commensurate growth in their lives' meanings. These meanings are bound up with the noticed seeds—the insights—which are either nurtured, by giving them all the critical attention they need to be verified and grow, or pruned or dismissed. The seed is not strewn carelessly onto a field; the sower's care and attentiveness can produce new meaning for both the one who plants it and for those who are careful to attend to the seed's growth. Contemplating such parables invites us to connect the meanings of academic tasks with the pursuit of the good, which is God's agenda. We are invited to bring what we do with our talents in the work of knowing to a plane of meaning that includes the good of the discipline, the good of those who are informed by it, and the common good, which is part of God's plan for the world.

The process by which an individual chooses an academic field or a dissertation topic can also be likened to the growth of a seed, which comes to be sown in a mind or heart as an intuition that is often initially vague, but which causes one to notice something that has usually been overlooked by others. The individual attends to that seed, that initial intuition, and thereby eventually makes a contribution to his or her field. However imperceptible the nascent insight may be, cognitively or affectively, it sufficiently grabs one's interest as one senses its potential value. One can, of course, spend a lifetime of labor elaborating on that first intuition. (This is, of course, radically different from the student who just needs to find a topic, who just wants to prove him- or herself competent to examiners or peers, or is just seeking the needed credentials. Compare him or her to someone who is truly focused on proving the intrinsic worth of his or her insight or project.)

The parable of the sower prompts a further reflection. Some seeds are sown into shallow soil, so that "they wither for lack of roots." One can be too indolent to pursue an insight, or too busy or distracted by "anxiety or the lure of riches or the craving for other things that intrude and choke the word [seed] and it bears no fruit" (Mark 4:19). One might also be trying to do so many disparate things that they cannot be aggregated into any larger whole. Of course, one may also do ad hoc projects opportunistically and for selfish purposes, which end up benefiting few, if any. Granted, every research project is an opportunity, and we rarely have a single, pure motive, but the parable recommends that we be attentive to our own interior movements when we find ourselves attracted to something that is ever so slight at present, but that could be full of promise if attended to.

This parable, like all other parables, takes the soil of interiority seriously. Just as the Sower doesn't sow trees or full-grown plants, but seeds that need attention, so too must we be attentive to our attractions, our curiosities, and our questions. What is planted and cared for takes up more and more room, until the self has been to some extent transcended. The cost of full growth is that one loses something of one's own autonomy. There is an obvious analogue here, since most academics are also parents. Spousal care and childrearing probably take even more attention and nurture than one's academic work, but there is a parallel between the two responsibilities.

It seems that each of the five interviewees all made room for a seed and allowed it to grow, though, to some degree, "they knew not how" (Mark 4:27). Interestingly, it seemed to do so almost "of its own accord (so that) the land yields fruit, first the blade, then the ear then the full grain in the ear" (v. 28). And from this small seed "it springs up and puts forth its branches and becomes the largest of plants so that the birds of the sky can dwell in its shade" (v. 32). One might imagine a university as an arboretum or garden full of such plants, such insights, growing for students and for the culture at large. The plants may be planted by individual scholars, but they require the support of the institution to thrive.

THE PROFESSORIATE'S VIRTUES

There are approximately 675,000 professors in more than 4,100 institutions of higher education in this country.[8] What do they all have in common, other than their work as academics? There are three key elements that receive no attention, as far as I have read, in educational literature. Faith, hope, and love enter into the academic enterprise and energize it, notwithstanding the silence in the literature about them. Without these three, the academic enterprise would be flat, stale, and unprofitable. To elaborate, there has to be faith that the questions, one's own and another's, are worth answering or seeking to answer, and that a career at this is a worthwhile use of one's life. This is not faith in the sense of religious belief, but a belief in the validity and value of the findings of the field to date, and a trust in those who have amassed these.

Further, there must be hope, hope that the present and future work in this body of knowledge will continue to yield greater results. Scholars, if they are anything, are hopers. Their hope is that data can be discovered, or uncovered, or collated and communicated where it had not previously been, or that it can be construed in a new way. Their hope may not extend as far as the reign of God, the horizon that Jesus speaks of in the parables, but the more tangible the horizon of hope, the more certain there will be perseverance in the career which may only have knowledge as its reward.

And how is love an integral part of the academic enterprise? Without love—love of learning, love of one's discipline, love of one's areas of research, love of teaching and of one's students, indeed, love that can extend the subject matter beyond where it was before—the academic could too easily become one of the knowledge elites for whom learning is for oneself, for one's own advancement and security.

I have been speaking of these three elements of faith, hope, and love, fully conscious that they are usually associated with the theological virtues and baptism in Catholic theology. However, even as natural virtues, they have an immediate relevance in the academic enterprise. To confine these to the theological realm is to fail to see how important they are in the academy and beyond. For academics to participate actively and enthusiastically in the learning required to keep up with their respective fields, it would seem that faith, hope, and love in the natural sense of these virtues have to be operating in them. And so, while believing in the worth of the field and loving the field enough to commit a sizable portion of their lives to it, they also have to hope that their particular contribution will eventually make a difference to their discipline, to their students, and to others.

Only God knows whether these three virtues are theological and infused or natural in a given person. According to the Catholic faith and many Christian denominations, faith, hope, and love are infused in the baptized. But religious language cannot confine what is essential for the well-being of the human community. Faith, hope, and love are necessary for the formal pursuit of knowledge and its dissemination. Intelligence is essential, of course, but in learning and teaching, these three energies are paramount.

To bring others to horizons they would not be able to attain themselves is to be an agent in the intellectual conversion of individuals and societies. The public service that academics perform is to move their students along a continuum from ignorance to knowledge, from incompetence to competence, from being uninformed to becoming more informed members of their communities.

This might be too simple or too optimistic a reading of the complexity of the knowledge industry. There is the negative side of the industry, insofar as there is academic careerism. I think of when Jesus urged his hearers to be wary of "the yeast of the Pharisees" (Matt. 16:6). This is a condition in which knowledge puffs up the knower, in the egotistical sense of the term. There also can be very minimal faith, hope, and love, if these are all but stifled by concern for the self. In an academic setting, conceit corrodes community and prevents it from flourishing. Instead of faith, hope, and love as three virtues moving the person, there can be self-importance, with an eye on advancement or reputation or attaining admiration, rather than truth. Suffice it to say, however, that efforts at real scholarship usually have the opposite effect; sincere scholarship generates humility about how little one knows. The institution itself must make it clear that the function of the knowledge industry of which it is a part is to advance the condition of the many, not to benefit the few who have the privilege and opportunity of a life of scholarship.

If we were to ask the ancient Greeks about what makes for community, or what gives rise to the wholes that transcend individual strivings, they would tell us to look at the virtues. They spoke of four cardinal virtues without which neither community nor common meaning would be possible. These were prudence, temperance, fortitude, and justice, each of which was necessary in order for people to trust one another enough to grow into a community. These were called cardinal virtues (from the root *cardo*, hinge) because they were the hinges between peoples. Without these virtues, the doors that allow us to be in relation to one another couldn't swing open, and community wouldn't happen.

To imagine the importance of these virtues, we have to think of the vices they are meant to inhibit. Recall, possibly, the colleague who is so imprudent that you wonder what he will do or say next, so that distance is one's only protection. Or think of a colleague who lacks restraint in regard to food or drink or anger or lust or their own opinions; this intemperance can be poisonous to a department. The coward will stand for nothing in the face of a threat to his security or his advantage or position with the crowd. The many forms of injustice in a university—including favoritism, political maneuvering, inequality of compensation, sexism, racism, false witness, competitiveness—can wither whatever morale there is.

I bring up these cardinal virtues in part because of conversations I had with Monika Hellwig (1929–2005), to whom I have dedicated this book. She had a brilliant thirty-year teaching career at Georgetown, and was president of the Association of Catholic Colleges and Universities (1996–2005). In the course of these years she had any number of in-depth experiences on any number of campuses, most of them Catholic. That both her last book and the book she was never able to begin because of her untimely death were on the cardinal virtues testifies to her belief in the virtues' importance for institutions of higher education.[9] Universities must rely on the character of their personnel to make any progress in terms of mission and community. The virtues that make for interpersonal harmony and inchoate community are prerequisites of mission. What Hellwig does in her published book is to show the need for these virtues in the Greek sense, and to demonstrate how a Christian or religious commitment strengthens and completes one's understanding of them.

This brings me to one last note, prompted again by the responses from 40,670 faculty members in the UCLA study. About 69 percent of them said that they "seek out opportunities to grow spiritually."[10] One way to grow spiritually is to become sensitive to cultivating the virtues elaborated on here. If one associates growing spiritually with the Spirit, one might recall St. Paul's observation about the fruits of the Spirit. These are virtues like "love, joy, peace, patience, gentleness, self-control, and fear of the Lord" (Gal. 5:22). Since these qualities are not exactly ubiquitous, one might see them not as mere personality qualities. And by appreciating the need for these qualities and the aforementioned virtues, one might acknowledge the Source of spiritual growth, at least in the Christian understanding of it.

There is much more potential for commonality in academe than meets the eye. The parables can bring into focus a fuller meaning and higher viewpoint that can help academics see beyond their trenches. The genius of a parable is that it addresses persons individually and collectively about both their here-and-now and their fuller meaning. If a fuller meaning can be found, personal and communal, that could hardly be a matter of indifference to those who invest so much of their life's work with colleagues in a common enterprise. The academic profession grows in stature and dignity to the degree that it can see its contribution to the common good of the world. Faculty members need to be able to see their learning, teaching, and research as having more than an ephemeral value. The parables envision an eschatological scenario, the final reign of God, though of course the details of how and when remain unknown. What is comforting about the relation between now and then is that, according to the parables, our work is not merely of ephemeral value. This is also affirmed by Vatican II: "When we have spread on earth the fruits of our nature and our enterprise . . . we will find them once again cleansed this time from the stain of sin, illuminated and transfigured," when the kingdom of God, which is now only "mysteriously present," will appear in "its perfection."[11]

NOTES

1. Lonergan, *Method in Theology,* 116.
2. Ibid.
3. *Lumen gentium* (5), in Abbott, *The Documents of Vatican II.*
4. Lonergan, *Method in Theology,* 116.
5. *Lumen gentium* (5).
6. *Gaudium et spes* (39), in Abbott, *Documents of Vatican II.*
7. Marsden, *Soul of the American University.*
8. Cohen, "On Campus: The 60s Begin to Fade and the Liberal Professors Retire," *New York Times,* July 3, 2008.
9. Hellwig, *Public Dimensions of a Believer's Life.*
10. "Spirituality and the Professoriate," available at www.spirituality.ucla.edu/.
11. *Gaudium et spes* (39).

CHAPTER 3

◆

Engaging Otherness

WHEN A GOOD ACT becomes habitual, it becomes a virtue embedded in one's character. A strong virtue functions like a headwater, from which positive acts flow more freely. One virtue that can be seen operating in all the narratives of the previous two chapters is the virtue of hospitality. The interviewees have made room for the other, whether that other is other people's needs, other bodies of knowledge, other religions; in a word, they have made room for "otherness." The virtue that is most peculiar to committed academics is their hospitable disposition towards data, in whatever guise it comes or however uncongenial it might seem to be. Hospitality welcomes others—whether the others are persons or ideas—as worthy of the room one makes for them. Hospitality makes a common space possible, insofar as it is practiced collectively by a critical mass of the members of an institution. Schools would do well to formally promote this virtue of space-making, and reward those who do.

Because of the universality latent in the notion of catholicity, hospitality should be frequent, rather than rare. And yet common space is rare in modern organizations. Since hospitality can create such a commons, it deserves a closer look. For starters, hospitality presumes openness. Bernard Lonergan helps to get us started, with a tantalizing series of insights into openness. He sees three meanings of the word: openness as a fact, as an achievement, and as a gift that God can give.[1] As a fact, openness is the quality that makes people willing to find out what they need to know or want to know, from whatever source their knowledge may come. Openness is also an achievement, which brings satisfaction when we obtain whatever it was we were seeking. We must constantly struggle to be open and stay open; neither task is ever completed. Finally, to live in a condition of openness requires a gift, because without it, our natural inclination is to be open to a very limited range of people, things, and experiences. Without the gift of openness, we cannot be open enough to be hospitable.

Does the work of scholars—in particular their work with data—require the gift of openness? It would appear to, since the process of research requires one to be open to data, to successive enlargements of one's horizon of understanding, in order to develop and complete research projects competently. So openness as a gift seems necessary, since there is the ever-present temptation to "make do" before our inquiry is complete. Failure to take certain data into account, or to read all the relevant material; carelessness about ascribing to others what we have learned from them; rushing, skimming, guessing, and cutting corners—these are only some of the ways that a lack of openness affects research and scholarship. We need the gift of openness, argues Lonergan, because "the successive enlargements of the actual horizon of one's consciousness only too clearly lie under some law of decreasing returns."[2] It is the gift of openness, therefore, that keeps us from settling for the half-done, and from just making do. It enables us to challenge the law of decreasing returns, to enlarge our horizons in order to deal satisfactorily with the questions for which we are responsible.

These successive enlargements of consciousness are of two kinds: one that is within our own capacity to effect, and the other that is beyond our capacity, and therefore dependent upon something beyond us. On our own initiative, our consciousness can more or less master a specific field of inquiry, but by ourselves, we are not likely to remain open to further enlargements of consciousness. But the second enlargement of consciousness Lonergan would call a further gift, an elevating grace. It is this further gift that would enable the researcher to become open to the transcendental dimensions of one's field of vision, namely the good, the true, the beautiful, and the divine. Openness is a journey through the successive stages of consciousness, a journey with the potential to take one into a greater horizon of interest and perspective.

HOSPITALITY AND THE UNIVERSITY WORLD

How might these insights into openness and the virtue of hospitality pertain to the university culture? I believe that hospitality and openness would be more formally valorized if faculty members could see what they are already doing in these terms. Scholars show hospitality to data, to the work in their own disciplines, and to those competencies in other disciplines that can enhance their own insights, research, and teaching. The hunt for greater intelligibility never ceases. I have already suggested that there are wholes being birthed by academics that can be interpreted as parts of the larger whole that Jesus seemed to allude to and named the reign of God.

Awareness of a greater whole, and the ability to see others' work as pieces of a larger whole, can be consoling and sustaining in the slog periods of an academic's career. The image that occurs to me here is that of a stained-glass window: Each developing body of knowledge is a single piece of the window being crafted by the professoriate. Each piece is a part of a greater, magnificent whole. It is the whole that has integrity, not the individual pieces. In order to appreciate a stained-glass window, not only does it have to be constructed, there also has to be light coming into it from beyond, illuminating each of the panes. Each pane of the window is essential for the overall unity and beauty of the whole to be beheld, and there must be a transparency in each of the pieces. There is consolation to be had in having a sense that the pieces can be conjoined, but unfortunately that experience is rare in the academy. Interdisciplinarity is a start, but it is just a start. I have found that time spent together sharing one's work under the rubric of the good is a better way of beholding the stained-glass windows that have existed all along, if only we can move back from laboring on our particular panes long enough to see what the collective enterprise might look like.

"But there is so little time." Why don't we have time for hospitality? I want to suggest three likely reasons. The first is a lacuna in our expectations and our job descriptions; the second is technology; and the third is our collective lack of experience with the self-transcending value inherent in proactively hosting others and their fields of work.

First, there is a lacuna in our expectations and our job descriptions. Jesuit schools place a strong emphasis on the value of *cura personalis*, the personal care of the teacher for the individual student. (This may not be a particularly special insight into education, as nearly every teacher in nearly every educational system would likely agree with the emphasis). The lacuna is that we pay little or no attention to horizontal relations; we do not emphasize the importance of interest in and care for one's professional colleagues. Presumably, most faculty members assume that since their colleagues are adults, they can take care of themselves and, if they need help, will initiate whatever steps are necessary to get the help they need. All of this sounds sensible enough, and is an accurate description of how the educational system actually works. Department meetings are usually focused on business, new hires, tenure issues, curriculum revision, university committees, and reports on the same. The ruling virtue, if there is any, seems to be civility, rather than hospitality. Why not leave it at that? Because civility is far too thin a virtue to provide for mutual enrichment, or enrichment at all.

Universities do not typically value hospitality to fellow faculty members. But all academics should concern themselves with the behavior they model for their students. Whatever else students learn, what if they see the majority of faculty members burrowed deep in their own specializations without demonstrating much—if any—personal connection with their own colleagues, their interests, research, or findings? However unintentionally, faculty could be modeling for students a kind of individualistic careerism, and reinforcing a culture of autonomy and learning for the sake of self-advancement, contrary to the intentions they presumably had in becoming academics. We teach who we are; if we are isolated individuals, we teach students to be isolated individuals.

The second reason we have little time for hospitality relates to technology. Modern technology (and even more specifically, advances in communication) has radically changed the way people relate to one another. What is of particular interest here is how communications technologies have affected the interpersonal relationships of both faculty and students. In one sense, the effect has been entirely positive, since both can now access exponentially more information, far more quickly than was ever dreamt of in the print culture. This development has also transformed the teaching and research world into a place of immediate global connections, but there is a paradox here. On one hand, there is a new virtual universe, giving us access to data previously unknown or inaccessible to most seekers of knowledge, which is now open and taken for granted by the vast majority of learners at every age level. On the other hand, it is becoming increasingly clear that this technology can make those closest to us physically more and more remote psychically. Further, aided by new technology and torrential sources of data, one's growing competence in and familiarity with faraway matters can all too easily distance one from one's colleagues (and friends and family members as well).

Rather than helping to make a community more whole, growing up with cyberspace as a constant presence in one's life seems to be creating a population that is more informed but increasingly disconnected one with another. Linda Stone, a repentant cyberspace technologist, noted that "the disease of the internet is continuous partial attention."[3] The long-term effects of all this have not yet been sorted out—and may not even be knowable, since the internet and its relationship to society are still evolving—but it is not too early to be concerned about the social impact of so much information and exchange with virtual interlocutors, coupled with a serious decrease in faculty members' levels of identification and engagement with the people and the institution of which they are a part. One would have to agree that the results of internet-based collaboration are highly ambiguous to date. Can being married to one's monitor cut one off from the local community? Or perhaps the fault lies not with our tools, but with us, for allowing our tools to impoverish our relations with one another.

The third factor severely limiting our hospitality is an issue of value: We naturally spend our time on the things we value and avoid spending time and energy on persons or causes we deem of little worth. Since the minimum purpose of a school is to graduate informed people, it would seem that the more time faculty members and students spend becoming informed, the better. While accessing and processing information, as I argued earlier, is a form of hospitality towards data, the question remains: For what am I (are we) becoming more informed? When a faculty member spends more and more time getting more data, and less and less time being engaged with colleagues, he or she is making an implicit value statement. And to put this matter in religious terms, the fact that a school describes itself as Christian in its mission would seem to suggest that it places a value on love of one another. Placing a high priority on love of one's colleagues and students is one value that would make the enterprise of teaching and learning in this kind of school truly distinctive.

VALUING HOSPITALITY

For a virtue to develop in a person, that virtue must first be valued and then practiced. How does a virtue come to be valued? We ordinarily value virtues that are embodied by people we respect.

For generations, believers have been impressed by the hospitality of Abraham to the three strangers who came by his tent in Mamre (Gen. 18). On a visit to Turkey last year, I was reminded of how much emphasis Muslims—who also see Abraham as their father in faith—put on the virtue of hospitality, and how generous their hospitality is, in imitation of Abraham. That experience helped me to reflect on Jesus in terms of hospitality.

The more I thought about this, the more it seemed that the virtue of hospitality was a central theme in the life of Jesus and of his contemporaries. I am especially struck by his reliance on the hospitality of others, beginning with that of his own mother, who made room for him in her womb. And at the end of his life, there was Joseph of Arimathea, who made room for Christ's body in his own tomb. Think, too, of all the intervening acts of hospitality that made room for this man "who had nowhere to lay his head" (Luke 9:58). Think, too, of the cost he himself incurred when he availed himself of the hospitality of all "the wrong people"—the sinners, tax collectors, and prostitutes. This fomented a violent inhospitality towards him at the hands of "the right people." Think, too, of the number of his parables that highlight hospitality, the most familiar of these being the story of the Good Samaritan, a parable that answers the question about what one must do to inherit eternal life (Luke 10:25–37). At the last supper, in the room provided for him by an unnamed benefactor, he goes so far as to make himself food for his disciples (Mark 14:22–25).

The story of Jesus's life also bears witness to something paradoxical about hospitality. In any number of situations, the guest and the host seem to switch roles. As a guest, he ends up serving his hosts as if he were their servant (Luke 12:37). He washes the feet of the twelve; he provides the healings sought by the sick; he teaches the knowledge that he himself acquired, even though it endangers his life. It seems that Jesus's instinct for hospitality was especially triggered whenever he sensed any need or vulnerability. Think of the multiplication of the loaves after the disciples had thought it impossible to feed the crowds. But Jesus was usually the guest, rather than the host, since he did not have the resources that enabled him to afford to be a host.

While Jesus accepts hospitality and generates it, both of these roles are intrinsic to his mission of proclaiming and expecting the fullness of hospitality in the coming reign of God. Jesus understood present acts of hospitality in light of an expected future, a divine milieu of unconditional hospitality. Hospitality was enacted in the present and enjoyed in the present, but it was an act that anticipated a future that was never far from Jesus's mind since it was in-breaking. In fact this virtue makes the journey's end closer; its promise is experienced in the interaction between hosts and guests. Hospitality has a special meaning for those who come to realize that they are involved in the drama of salvation. Think of what the consequences would have been for Dives had he extended hospitality to Lazarus, who would then have become a sort of sacrament for him, had he bothered to make himself and his table available to Lazarus in his dire need (Luke 16:19–31). If strangers, when offered hospitality, can be like sacraments for their hosts, enabling them to arrive successfully at their own journey's end, then hospitality must be more central to the Gospel than I have previously understood.

Another text that underscores the value Jesus places on proactive hospitality is Matthew 25:31–46. Those who extend themselves to those who are vulnerable in varying ways are in for two surprises. The first is that "the Son of Man" identifies himself with these vulnerable people. And the second is the blessing the proactive "hospitalers" receive: They "inherit the kingdom prepared for you from the creation of the world" (v. 34).

THE DEVELOPMENT OF A DOCTRINE

The Church has in its entire history been continually returning to the Gospel to seek the truth and to grow in its understanding of who Jesus was and is. It would seem that there is still much more to be learned to appreciate fully the implications of Christ's openness and hospitality. The hospitality of Jesus is the best source of inspiration for this still-to-be-articulated doctrine of the catholicity of the Church. By revisiting and imitating the praxis of Jesus, a new understanding of the ecclesial mark of catholicity can also develop. Jesus's life was an open narrative that kept developing new insights. He was open to God, to his own Hebrew faith, and to growth in knowledge and love of God and neighbor, especially those neighbors who were in need. Foundational to all of this was Jesus's openness to, and willingness to be led by, the Spirit: first into the water of the Jordan, then out into the desert, and from there eventually to the cross, a journey not always undertaken according to his own will. Along the way he eked out intelligibility and his own meaning from the ground he was standing on and the people he was talking to.

Jesus's life is depicted in the Gospels as a learning process; he was even at times forced into widening his own religious horizon. A case in point—when the Syrophoenician woman begged Jesus to drive the demon out of her daughter, his response was, "Let the children [of Israel] be fed first. For it is not right to take the food of the children and throw it to the dogs" (Mark 7:27). When she replied, "Lord, even the dogs under the table eat the children's scraps," Jesus seemingly had a change of heart, whether it was because of her courage, the depth of her need, or the simple fact of his compassion. When confronted by the other's desperation, his boundaries widened. It seems as though the more "other" Jesus's dialogue partners were, the clearer his sense of himself and his mission became.

A new Christological and ecclesiological category, developed by Lieven Boeve, is "open narrative."[4] Open narratives develop from new encounters when we are fully prepared to take the alterity of the other seriously, especially when the other belongs to another faith or system of meaning. Having an open narrative enables the Church and its members to become more aware of the particularity of its own faith narrative. The encounter with the other can be pleasing or perplexing, strange or enriching. One cannot remain merely an observer, but must enter into the encounter prepared to meet an irreducible otherness of belief or value. The more that the Church is centered in its own belief system, the more it will be able to enter into a mutual bearing of witness with other meaning systems.

One of the fruits of these encounters should be the realization that there is more to this mystery of religion than might have been previously appreciated by all parties. The sacred texts of the religions were written centuries before the cosmological discoveries of the last 150 years. Just as there is so much more to learn of our place in the cosmos, so also there is so much more to learn about God. The same could be said about ethics and cultures. The more "other" the other with whom we are interacting, the more we can become aware of the uniqueness of our own narrative. It is through our interactions with and reactions to those different from us that we learn to see more clearly who we are, and what we believe. Interrupting settled boundaries can be enriching.

The question will inevitably arise about how open our narratives can and should be. If we think that we already possess the truth, then we will see any openness that might alter our thinking as dangerous, and reject it. This is particularly so of religious truth: If our faith has put us in touch with the living God, why should we be open to another's supposed faith? Wouldn't openness in that case constitute infidelity or syncretism? Turning to the Gospels, though, we find a different perspective. Although the Old Testament constantly warns against the faithful having truck with other gods, Jesus seems to have staked out for himself a different position on this issue, by ignoring it. Instead, his horizon was always oriented towards the in-breaking reign of God. He seemed to find God at work in contexts where others couldn't even imagine such a thing. His was an open horizon; for him, God was always greater—*Deus semper major*—than a perspective that had "already arrived" would have been able to see. The Gospels depict Jesus as learning about God from people outside of Israel. Recall what Jesus said about the centurion in the Gospel of Matthew: "[I]n no one in Israel have I found such faith" (Matt. 8:10). If Jesus himself was that open, are his followers not called to be the same?

Over the last fifty years, many theologians studying accounts of Christ's life have demonstrated a preference for a low Christology. Such an approach sees no problem with the idea that Jesus continued to learn throughout his life, even when the learning in question was about the God with whom Jesus had an unprecedented familiarity. Nor does this Christology have a problem with Jesus being a man of faith, and the pioneer for all who are never finished plumbing the mystery of God, or discerning where God is leading them. It might be difficult for those who prefer a high Christology to see Jesus as forging the way for us through his own faith and choices, rather than seeing him as divinely sighted from the beginning. Throughout his life, Jesus's own narrative was constantly getting interrupted and its boundaries widened, as was the narrative of the early Church, as the Acts of the Apostles so eloquently depicts.

FROM PRAXIS TO DOCTRINE

The Church develops its doctrine from the practices of the faithful, including their prayer. Technically, *lex credendi* flowers from and is moved by the Church's *lex orandi*. A doctrine of catholicity that is world-embracing, a doctrine that affects and is affected by human aspirations for justice, peace, international and interfaith harmony—in a word, aspirations for wholeness—must spring from the prayers and actions of small groups of believers. Prayer and praxis come first; reflections on this prayer and on the implications of this praxis lead to the second step, which is doctrinal development.

So the praxis of hospitality and the doctrine of catholicity are interdependent. They need each other. The praxis without the doctrine will be too spasmodic and voluntarist; the doctrine without the praxis will become doctrinaire. The Church has to learn how to host the work of God taking place not only within but also outside the borders of its own self-understanding and institutions. The work of God is both secular and eschatological at the same time; it is secular in the sense of being grounded in this world in its particularity, and it is eschatological in the sense of its anticipation of wholeness that will be attained through the particularities of work, nature, relationships, sufferings, and joys. This catholicity will be fully realized only at the end of history. But between now and then, there have to be partial realizations of it to stoke the hope for entireties that lie beyond our sight.

Maybe the needed doctrine has not yet been developed, because up until now, the Church has understood 'catholic' too insularly for the Church to open itself to the emerging world, and to understand its calling and its challenge accordingly. Although understanding catholic as "a mark of the Church" was a valid use of the term throughout its history, a purely ecclesial purview is now too small. The notion of catholicity must be freed, and allowed to be in dialogue with the world's peoples, with their many needs, plural belief systems, and their visions of the good and the true. This notion of catholicity must be free to be enriched or challenged by encounters with such different systems of belief and thought, and also able to critique them. The scope of the Isaiah text may apply here: "It is too little," the Lord says to his servant, "for you to be my servant, to raise up the tribes of Jacob and restore the survivors of Israel; I will make you a light to the nations, that my salvation may reach to the ends of the earth" (Isa. 49:6).

Most people grow up and out of the restrictive notions about "the true and the good" that they are taught as children; as they mature, they are privy to a whole range of new information and encounters previously undreamt of. The Church, too, as a people, has shed outdated categories and modes of thinking in the course of its history. If the ecclesial mark *catholic* became a challenge both for the Church and the academy, room could be made for many of the enlargements of consciousness all people are daily invited into.

The Church needs the academy in order to be open to these enlargements of consciousness, and the academy needs the Church to teach it the importance of the wholeness that an eschatological worldview supplies. In a sense, the academy is expected to do much of the Church's thinking. With a more expansive understanding of the doctrine of catholicity, consciousness could be caught up into a heuristic that keeps minds and data from being so anomalous and nomadic in the world of human meaning. There is so much more than what now counts as "Catholic" that could be elucidated by such a doctrine.

Unfortunately, it is not hard to find the opposite of the hospitality I am describing here. Think of the inhospitality within the academy and the forms it all too easily can take: competition, jealousy, insecurity, or lust, among others. Disciplines and academics all too often can grow enclosed within their data, settling on certain theories and mindsets as sufficient, and staying within the range of questions that their own fields reward. There are many forms of inhospitality in the academy, and they all lead to poor scholarship. There is the simple refusal to entertain a question, or to inquire about the findings beyond one's own horizon of interest or competence, or to be open to methods other than those one has grown comfortable using; not to mention the virus of disdain that a particular field of study and its adherents often develop toward other disciplines. As with any other institution, antipathies—interpersonal, interdisciplinary, inter-institutional, and political—can generate a beehive of hostilities and drag a school farther and farther from its claimed identity. Inhospitality is a certain recipe for ignorance. We are all ignorant in various areas, of course, but as our access to knowledge grows, the range of allowable ignorance, especially for academics, for whom knowledge is a primary responsibility, can become extremely small.

There is one other thing to be mentioned here, namely the growing inhospitality of hyperspecialization. It is not always true that specialization is more beneficial than generalization when it comes to fields of study. One of the negative outcomes that can result from the balkanization of academia is a fragmentation of meaning and purpose, which runs contrary to the unitary purposes of academic institutions. If the term *uni-versity* means anything, it must be vectored toward the unitary. Catholic universities in particular must be institutions that have time for otherness, whatever form it may take, and be open to learn from the guests they have chosen to host.

GLOBAL CONTENDERS

One would have to wonder whether there are any worldwide institutions that might eventually be able to qualify to play the role of hosts to the world's pluralism. By way of answering this, I think of Catholicism, or possibly Islam (in some form still to be determined), or an international scientific or political authority that could commandeer common action *ad bonum commune*, though each of these entities has a long way to go before any one of them might be up to this challenge. We might come to a time when all three have a host-guest role. Meanwhile, a Catholicism that grasps the challenge of being catholic should ask itself: If not us, who? If not now, when? If not here, where? The "where" question, as it is answered in this book, starts with the universities that call themselves Catholic.

Once one appreciates how dynamic the term *catholic* can be, one understands the challenge the Church faces in this age. A place to start is with people who spend their lives enlarging their consciousness with more and more knowledge, such as the twelve professors we met in the first chapter and the five in the second. They contribute what they can, with competence, insight, and energy, to bring about the good of the verifiably true. Intending to produce something of value, these scholars, and others like them, are collectively focused on a further good, a future good, and a greater good. These kinds of aspirations, and the perspiration and productivity that accompany them, merit attention from colleagues, for starters, and from those who are concerned with a Catholic identity in their institutions. Without such attentiveness, we will fail to notice the good of otherness, and will continue to sponsor what becomes more and more fragmented.

As catholic, a Catholic university inevitably houses many worldviews. It can do this in several ways. One is simply to make room for those who hold these plural worldviews. This is a negligent or, at best, a merely tolerant hospitality. A second way a university can house plural worldviews is by hearing them, taking them seriously, engaging them. This second form of hospitality can lead to a real growth in understanding on the part of both hosts and guests.

But there is also a third possibility, a form of patronizing in which the host only seems to be exercising hospitality. The example I have in mind is from a pericope in the Gospel of Luke, in which a Pharisee invites Jesus to his table, but has his own agenda in issuing the invitation (Luke 7:36–50). The story reveals much about what a hospitality that really welcomes guests looks like, in comparison to a hospitality that serves the host's own needs. After Jesus arrived, he "reclined at table," which was the normal posture of diners and guests. Traditionally, this kind of an occasion would have included rituals of hospitality, such as greeting the guest with a kiss, providing water for him to wash his feet, and anointing the guest's head with oil. The host did none of these things. It is unlikely that Jesus expected these treatments, knowing as he did that the true motive behind the Pharisee's hospitality was to provide an occasion for himself to be proven right about godly matters, and for Jesus to be proven wrong. The thoroughly unwanted, uninvited "sinful woman," the perennial "other," who brought an alabaster flask of ointment, bathed Jesus's feet with her tears and wiped them with her hair, is the one who shows up the host's self-serving hospitality. The Pharisee, seeing all this, was confirmed in his bias: "If this man were a prophet, he would know who and what sort of woman this is who is touching him" (v. 39). Jesus, however, saw her "great love" and bade her farewell, saying, "go in peace; your faith has saved you" (v. 50).

A host who is out to win is actually more like a would-be conqueror than a host. A host who claims to know what the other should do or be has already failed a basic test of hospitality. A host who invites in order to instruct is not really a host, but at best a lecturer. On the other hand, a host who listens to otherness and engages it learns both the reward and cost of hospitality. The costs of listening can be considerable. Deep listening is seldom seen as worth the effort, hence the strategy of "letting sleeping dogs lie." Bare civility costs very little, and is the law obeyed by most institutions, or the unspoken *modus operandi* for most campuses, including Catholic ones.

Briefly, then, the challenge of the Church is to go where it must and become what it has to, resisting the temptation to remain as it is. It has the example of Jesus's own life as its model. Traditionally, Catholicism has emphasized the *already* element of what it knows, to the detriment of the *not yet* of what it has yet to learn.

The empirical evidence that the Church is beginning to meet this challenge is the hospitality shown by its members and its institutions to other worldviews, faiths, disciplines, and convictions.

Granted, we have addressed and imagined a large panorama here, but this has been done to underscore the need that the world in all of its locales has for some kind of institutional hosting capacious enough to embrace the extant diversities that otherwise can remain distant, perhaps even alienated from each other, and in some cases dangerous, as the world today knows all too well. That host would have to be both local and transcendent, secular and eschatological, open and coherent. The Catholic university or college would seem to be a good candidate for playing this kind of role.

The Church is a good candidate for the task of hospitality, but it may be unprepared or unwilling to take up this new challenge. It needs to see the task that must be done, want to do it, and figure out how to go about doing it. In this, Catholic universities and colleges could be particularly useful, if they gave more attention to the particular wholes that God seems to be co-creating right before their eyes. These local, immediate pluralisms are grist for the mill of catholicity.

Hospitality is multilayered. First, there is the hospitality the faculty member offers to his or her data. It has become a truism in hermeneutical circles that we must let the text interpret us, not the other way around. Students should be able to see the difference between making data do one's bidding, and allowing it space to marinate in the scholar's mind and heart. One cost of hospitality, then, is an intellectual self-transcendence. The quest for objectivity presumes that the researcher or student is not so blindly self-interested as to be compelled to mangle the evidence in his or her favor. Another cost of hospitality, then, is a moral self-transcendence.

The second level of hospitality is interpersonal. One party must take the initiative to host another party, so that a meeting of minds may take place. An engagement between scholars with different understandings will not necessarily lead to agreement, but at the very least it will give them space in which to voice their convictions and listen to the counter-positions. Without these kinds of initiatives, however brief, the school becomes a place where groups of individuals interact without any real experience of community developing. In this sort of culture, chance interactions usually do not accomplish much. Engaged hospitality has to be intentional.

There is also a third level of hospitality that must be made explicit, though it can be operating in the first two as well. This is engagement with the Catholic intellectual tradition. I will address this issue in chapters 5 and 6. Suffice it to say here that for this third level of hospitality to flourish in an institution, it would be helpful if there were a centralizing, animating force to which the interested parties could repair in order to be in dialogue with this living tradition. In the past, it was expected that this third level of hospitality—engagement with the living tradition—would be animated by the theology or the philosophy departments. But in most Catholic institutions of higher learning, these have become so highly specialized and multidisciplinary that they cannot readily serve the heuristic dimensions of this tradition. Thus, Catholic institutions need to create processes that connect people and disciplines to this living past with a future, to which they can contribute and of which they can feel themselves to be an integral part. As I suggested in the first two chapters, such processes can develop organically if the spirit of *cura personalis*, especially at the level of the faculty, becomes embedded in the culture of the school.

NOTES

1. Lonergan, *Collection*, 185–87.
2. Ibid.
3. Friedman, "The Taxi Driver," November 1, 2006.
4. This category of the open narrative comes from Boeve's *Interrupting Traditions*.

CHAPTER 4

◆

Catholicity: Its Scope and Contents

Eᴅᴜᴄᴀᴛɪᴏɴ ᴍᴜsᴛ ʙᴇ something of great value, since everyone wants to "get" one. Superficially, what people want is the knowledge and skills to make a living. More trenchantly, what people want, I believe, is a deeper grasp of what is so and what isn't so. But the more informed one becomes about the "is so," the more complex matters get. In this chapter I would like to enter the discussion about the purposes and ends of education through the lens of catholicity. That will take some explanation, since it could sound like I am going to be hawking my Catholicism here. But what I hope to make evident is catholicity's potential to show us how we are better equipped to educate ourselves than we realize.

All that I have established so far is that faculty members have a special proclivity for connectivity or for making wholes, and that hospitality is crucial to the process. But these various wholes need a further explanation that indicates where they are coming from. It is this source that I want to explore in relation to the still-unexplained term *catholicity*. I will address four key components of this notion: its etymology, Bernard Lonergan's understanding of it, its relation to Jesus's understanding of the reign or kingdom of God, and the experience of catholicity in the Second Vatican Council. I will then apply these reflections to the context of the university.

ETYMOLOGY: THE MEANING OF "CATHOLICITY"

Right out of the blocks, there is something engaging about the term *catholicity*. It connotes openness, in contrast to what is incomplete, partial, sectarian, factional, exclusionary, tribal, and selective. (Unfortunately, ecclesial Catholicism is often tarred, however unfairly, with these brushes.)

The term *catholicity* etymologically promises a worldview that is universal. In classical Greek, *kata* (a preposition) and *holos* (a noun), when coupled, become *kath' holou*, an adverb meaning "wholly," and *katholikos*, a substantive that is best rendered "catholicity" in English. The word connotes movement towards universality or wholeness.

Walter Ong has made a substantial contribution to our understanding of the term, which he translates as "throughout the whole."[1] Ong spells out the implications of this translation concretely by citing the parable about the yeast that a woman takes and kneads through a batch of dough until the whole thing is leavened (Matt. 13:33). We will return to this translation and its implications in a subsequent chapter. At this point I only want to tantalize the reader with the question: What in this analogy constitutes the yeast that is kneaded through the dough so that leavening takes place?

Because the term *Catholic* is invariably associated with the Church, I will briefly describe its initial use in that context. Ignatius of Antioch (d. AD 110) introduced the term as an adjective: The Church was *katholikos*. But soon a tension developed about the term as applied to the Church. The tension was between a tribal ecclesiology and a more global one. For example, Justin Martyr (d. AD 165) believed that wherever right reason had prevailed in the pre-Christian world, there the Logos had been operating and enabling people to find truth. In other words, Athens had something to teach Jerusalem from the beginning. The opposite tack was taken by Tertullian (d. AD 222), who was adamant about the complete discontinuity between the two "cities." So Tertullian's ecclesiology was over against the world, while Justin's was in a continuum with the right reasoning that Greek thought had achieved.

After the term's usage spread beyond classical Greek, writers in the patristic age employed it adjectivally to describe the Church, which at the time was beginning to develop congregations throughout the whole known world. Cyril of Jerusalem (d. AD 386) used the term both to convey the Church's virtual universality and to connote its possession of saving truth, abundant virtue, and spiritual gifts. Augustine (d. AD 430) used the term to contrast the Church with the parochialism of the sects. In the thirteenth century, St. Thomas listed catholicity as one of the marks of the Church, not only because it had extended itself throughout the known world, but also because he saw the Church as having existed all the way back in time, all the way back to the sacrifice of Abel, as well as forward into eternity.

It is not hard to see why the early Church found this term so pertinent, nor is it difficult to understand how the Church, by appropriating it, has virtually arrogated the term to itself for the rest of history. That so many leading Catholic thinkers would see this term as appropriate for the Church's own self-description was inevitable, but that should not keep us from noticing the irony in its use. Think of the multitudes—all who do not profess the Catholic faith—who are excluded from this purported universality. Think of the countless numbers even of faithful followers of Christ who are not included in the term insofar as it is used narrowly of the Church—members of other churches across the globe. Think of the places to which the category of "catholic" doesn't extend, where "catholic" is understood as belonging to Roman Catholicism—much of our world.

It was not until the Reformation that "catholic" came to be engulfed in apologetics, at which time it lost the more expansive connotation it had usually enjoyed in earlier centuries. Once one understands the etymology, it becomes obvious that a sectarian catholicity is a contradiction in terms. Assertions like "The Catholic

Church is the one true Church," or "Outside the Church there is no salvation" understandably cause irritation or become the butt of jokes. The Second Vatican Council marked a turning point in the breadth of the Church's perspective. In that event the Church was able to grasp the scope its sources were alluding to all along, sources pointing to the universality it aspires to and is challenged to attain.

LONERGAN'S INSIGHTS INTO CATHOLICITY

Having considered its etymology and its evolution, a second tool we can use to understand this theme of catholicity is Lonergan's reflection on the nature of "being." Here Lonergan relied on the insights of a school of thought known as transcendental Thomism, which contrasted Aquinas's appreciation of the dynamic nature of the mind with Kant's more static understanding of it. The contrast between these two approaches is invaluable for clarifying how the university might be understood as a host of plural worldviews.

Every discipline invites its students to seek more knowledge. But what do students seek knowledge of? We might, presumably, say "reality," but the centuries-old, classical answer would have been "being." An investigation of why that term lost its cachet could serve to introduce us to Bernard Lonergan's contributions in this area, since with the loss of insight into "being," education itself lost its horizon. It is due to the unlimited character of "being" that there is a human urge called "research," an urge that only grows stronger the more one attends to the capaciousness of "being."

Several surprises await one who turns to Lonergan in this context. He makes many claims that seem counterintuitive; first among these is the claim that the best route to knowledge is to develop a strong grasp of one's own subjectivity, and of the operations of one's own consciousness, rather than seeking more and more information about stuff "out there." Unless our universities pay more attention to subjectivity and consciousness, they will continue to become di-versities, places where bodies of knowledge develop independently of each other, rather than universities, places where the connection among different branches of knowledge is fostered.

Lonergan mapped an invaluable cartography of subjectivity, showing how one can traverse the murky terrain of subjectivity by focusing on the cognitional operations we all use, though usually inadvertently. His careful attention to the subject in our operations made it more likely that objectivity could be obtained. In brief, Lonergan's advice was: If you ignore experience, you will do an injustice to your subjectivity; if you are cavalier about the understandings available to you, your judgments will be untrustworthy; if you assume that your insights are correct without verifying them, you will be relying on hunches, rather than making an accurate judgment. Lonergan has been like a Columbus to many, in that he helped them to discover a "new" continent by mapping out the operations of their own consciousness. One can ignore his map and go on thinking that knowledge is gained by looking at objects, howsoever intensively, while ignoring the inquiring subject and the compound character of the act of knowledge.

It was through his exploration of scientific methods that Lonergan's attention was drawn to his own and our subjective operations. At the same time, he became increasingly sensitive to the fact that our consciousness is historical. Through these realizations, he came to see the roles that pre-understandings and interpretative filters play into the cognitional process. As a result of these discernments, Lonergan began to prize authenticity highly: not only authenticity in a person, but also authenticity in a tradition. Rather than despairing that we will ever understand one another because of the increasingly differentiated universes of discourse developing in the world, Lonergan became convinced that mutuality and fruitful dialogue are best achieved where authentic personal subjectivity and collective intersubjectivity are operating in a more explicit manner. Why? Because of the fact that the cognitional operations we all are equipped with are invariant, hence universal.

Once responsibility for authenticity is located in the need to be attentive to the operations of one's own consciousness, this will help to clarify what responsibility entails and how irresponsibility starts with carelessness with these operations. This is not an invitation to self-centeredness that Lonergan is extending, but to self-knowledge. In the course of his intellectual career, he entertained a number of holistic visions of what is to be pursued by humanity. These were, successively: wisdom, the body of Christ, the notion of the one, the dogmas of the Church, cosmopolitanism, the universal viewpoint. Along the way, however, each of these came to be seen as less than satisfying. Instead, he focused more on responsibility, on where and how it was generated in the subject, so that what subjectivity produced could come to be more objective and trustworthy.

Lonergan was convinced that given the operations we all have in our consciousness, everyone can potentially contribute to progress in the human enterprise, just as surely as we can contribute to its decline through our ignorance of these operations, or by taking them for granted. Decline is seen most easily with criminal acts perpetrated on a grand scale, but we too easily miss the little crimes of inattention that generate small degrees of disunity and disconnection between people. Because we take the operations of consciousness for granted, or fail to notice or use them attentively, we do not achieve right reasoning or accurate judgments. Since our consciousness is invested all the time, every day, every hour, we cannot afford to overlook or take for granted its immanent operations, or simply allow them to remain implicit. Without explicit attention to these operations, it becomes more and more difficult to make connections between and among ideas, the people who have them, and the communities they form.

One surprise in Lonergan's analysis is the invaluable way he extricates us from the thicket of conceptual preoccupation. By conceptual preoccupation, we let concepts spawned by other minds do our thinking for us. Lonergan gets at this flaw by looking at the notion of a notion in contradistinction to a concept. Notions birth concepts. Notions are the triggers in intentionality that produce concepts. Let me start with the daddy-long-legs of notions, "being." Those who have only thought of "being" as a concept usually lose sight of its value. Conceptualizing "being" makes it the most abstract of all abstractions. "Being" as a notion, on the other hand, is omnipresent, free, unconfined, dynamic, and imageless. Lonergan shows how we can grasp the difference between a concept of being and the notion of being by seeing how being appears in all questioning. "Being is the unknown that questioning intends to know, that answers partially reveal, that further questioning presses on to know more fully."[2] It is omnipresent, in other words, without being adhered to as such. This is an extraordinary insight into the omnipresence of being, but to attain it, one must be willing at some point to set aside empirical categories, and to wonder, to be contemplative for the moment. Then one can return to the quotidian tasks of working within categories, concepts, images, and immediacies, with a new level of awareness of being's omnipresence in all of these.

But being is not, of course, the only notion; value is also a transcendental notion. "Just as the notion of being intends but, of itself, does not know being, so too the notion of value intends but, of itself, does not know value."[3] Look at the scope of each of these notions. Each is extremely dynamic; they keep one moving, either "toward ever fuller knowledge of being" in the first case, or toward "the fuller flowering of the same dynamic principle that now keeps us moving toward ever fuller realizations of the good, of what is worthwhile" in the second.[4] Life would be extremely dull without these two notions driving us. In the first two chapters, we found many examples of these dynamic notions at work in people, moving them toward an ever-fuller realization of the good and the worthwhile, always concretely. Naming these dynamic principles or the sources of our intentionality in terms of the notions of being and value is rare; also, we tend to be unaware of the different operations in our consciousness that trigger our intentionality.

A FURTHER NOTION

I would also like to argue that there is a third notion. Its scope is as broad as being and as deep as value, and it is latent in both notions. Like both of them, it intends wholeness, but of itself does not know the contents of the wholeness it intends. Like them, its dynamic is always moving us towards an "entirety." Like them, it is a heuristic notion, sufficiently known to give direction to the unknown. Like them, it gets concretized, in this case into meanings, but retains its heuristic character beyond its concretizations. It is distinctive in the family of notions insofar as its thirst is for meaning: the meaning of the known and the good as those other two notions undergo their concretizations. It is distinctive, too, in that it anticipates an entirety, the ecstatically meaningful, and thirsts for a future fullness. Like them it is patient; therefore, *this* is so, *that* is good, *this* has meaning. All three notions are heuristic, hence known unknowns that keep consciousness moving asymptotically toward an ever-greater grasp of the true, of the good, of the most meaningful: *Deus semper major!*

For want of a better term, I will call this the notion of catholicity. Like the heuristic notions of being and value this notion is best detected through its concretizations. It belongs to the family of notions, and like them it refuses the confinement of definition. To try to define it would be to force this notion to go the route of denotation and direct signification rather than connotation. If allowed to remain an undefined, nonobjectified, nonconceptualized notion, catholicity will have a better chance of approximating and including the anticipated "entirety" it connotes and seeks.

We are all hopers about any number of things, but howsoever varied these hopes are, they all seem to come down to the true, the good, and the meaningful. There is the ever-present need and hope to move from obscurity to clarity about what is so and about its value, and to see the fuller picture. When we are able to extract ourselves from our importuning immediacies, we should be able to appreciate the fact that we are scripted to pursue some kind of a *pleroma*—a completion, a fullness—just as surely as we are scripted to know what is so and what is good. Catholicity as a notion keeps beckoning us on to a more, to something yawning out before us, leading us on to something that is in the genre of the "is" and "is good," but also is meaningful.

There is a slow deterioration of the desire for this more when our élan is stymied by busyness, by immediacies that are too prepossessing to enable one to plumb one's deeper hopes. At this point I can appreciate the exasperation of an Aristotle, because he tried to understand justice and *eudaimonia* (happiness; the human good) by conceptualizing them. He solved his definitional problem by pointing to embodiments of justice and temperance, saying: "Actions are called just and temperate when they are such as the just or the temperate man would do."[5] I reflect on many academics I have known who embody the notion of catholicity in their lives, by their dot-connecting. By way of contrast, I also know embodiments of the opposite: people who are quite satisfied with the conceptualizations that they or their culture or their field have amassed. I appreciate how important unimpeded, unbiased intentionality is, and, when followed, how it can help to make a person, a school, a church, or a culture more whole.

Catholicity is intrinsic to knowing. The term came to be swallowed up by its association with an institution, the Catholic Church. This is unfortunate, since the term is more pregnant with meaning than it should be by being confined to that one usage. Catholicism, with its already articulated and established doctrinal tradition, can seem to the untrained eye to be a work no longer in progress, whereas the scope of catholicity, like the scope of value, is coterminous with being itself. The dynamism of catholicity is toward a fullness it never possesses; it awaits a wholeness that beckons rather than materializes. The notion of catholicity is the totality that accompanies and completes the notions of being and of value. Just as the totality of being would be attained only through a totality of correct judgments, so catholicity is a heuristic that is never completed, but remains an orientation, a drive, an undertow that anticipates a transcendent entirety.

What would the contents of the whole be if its promise were to be fulfilled? To answer that question, we must remember that while a concept has a known content, a notion does not, though we may be all too ready to assign it one. "Being" is a perennial example of this mistake. Being has too often been made to take its place alongside other concepts, thereby becoming the most abstract and useless of these. But we know that there is such a notion through its conceptualizations; it can be detected in each predication of "*is*," "*is* so," and "*is* true." So the *notion* of being can then be known to be operating in one's consciousness by its predicating *is*-ness of a near infinite number of realities. It is the passionate nature of being that triggers the human spirit to know anything and everything. The knowledge attained is always concrete, arrived at through a self-assembling structure of operations: experience, understanding, judgment. "Human knowing is formally dynamic. It puts itself together, one part summoning forth the next till the whole is reached."[6] The whole reached can be the predication of *this* "is" or that, *this* value or that, *this* meaning or that.

Catholicity conceptualized would suffer the same disfigurement as being has suffered from, which is why they must be allowed to remain notions. Catholicity as an exigence of consciousness accompanies the unrestricted desire to know the true and the good, but it goes further, with the desire to connect the already knowns. It is triggered by the desire to come to a higher viewpoint. Yes, we have a pure desire to know, but we also want to attain a sense of the connections between this known and that; we are bundlers, not just knowers. We are meaning makers, not just meaning receivers. Trying to conceptualize the notion of catholicity will inevitably make it something confined and tribalized, thus stripping it of its distinctiveness.[7]

There is an interdependence between the notions of being, value, and catholicity in human intentionality. As notions, each has an infinite capacity while our lives continually have to develop serial, concrete judgments about what is real and valuable, and about the meaning of a given connection. We live in a world in which meanings are made for us (received) and by us. Catholicity drives us to make dots connect, and until we do so a whole is wanting.

It seems obvious that all people have an orientation to and a desire for meaning. We know we cannot live without meaning; we are either meaning-hungry or find that what we are about is the bearing of meaning; more likely both. Lonergan does not posit a distinct notion of meaning or the whole as I am doing here. For him, "the notion of being is unique; for it is the core of all acts of meaning and it underpins, penetrates them and goes beyond all other cognitional contents."[8] He goes on: "The core of all acts of meaning is the intention of being."[9] I agree with both of these statements, but it seems that meaning, like being, is always concrete and the concretizations of these notions are not always identical. What I judge to be true is not always meaning bearing, and the concrete good is also not always meaning bearing, though they are both potentially so. The contents of all three are slightly different one from another. The reader can decide whether his or her acts of meaning are sufficiently explained by the notion of being or the good.

It would be a shame if one were not able to make the leap into self-knowledge that becomes possible when one is able to grasp the difference between a concept and a notion. One could object that clarity about such a distinction is impossible because of the extremely abstract nature of these notions. On the contrary; they are not abstract but so comprehensive, pervasive, and fundamental in our intending that they are easily and almost universally overlooked.

Since the notion of a notion is elusive, Lonergan supplies an image of what a notion is that might help. He asks, "How can an orientation or a desire be named a notion? A fetal eye is oriented towards seeing; but a fetal eye does not see, and it has no notion of seeing; a notion arises only insofar as understanding discerns future function in present structure."[10] So our understanding can discern future function in present structure, or go from a present act back to the innate orientation that explains the act. So, simply, one has to ask oneself whether he or she can discern that there are, in the present structure of our consciousness, drives to know being and the good, and to seek meaning or wholes.

JESUS'S CATHOLICITY

The previous section is difficult because it tries to explain drives so pervasive and comprehensive we are likely to not notice them. It might be a relief, therefore, to focus our attention on the concrete instances of a life, and to try to understand these drives, especially the drive to wholeness or catholicity. One could do a similar exercise with other figures from other religions, but here I will use the figure of Jesus of Nazareth to make this material more clear.[11]

The synoptic Gospels depict a Jesus nurtured in the Jewish faith by his parents, relatives, and teachers, as well as by his own prayer. His initial understanding of God, if one understands his humanity developmentally, was the God of the Hebrew scriptures. Without ceasing to be a person of faith—the same faith his contemporaries had and practiced—Jesus began to rail against its confined purview, possibly as early as his twelfth year, when he is described as astounding the temple's teachers with his probing, incisive questions. He was trying to connect dots that were not being connected back in Nazareth.

From the start of his ministry, Jesus chose the term *basileia tou theou*, the reign or kingdom of God, to connote the whole for which Israel was yearning. He proclaimed that Israel's waiting was coming to an end: "This is the time of fulfillment. The kingdom of God is at hand. Repent and believe in the Gospel" (Mark 1:15). This kingdom or reign imagery did not originate with Jesus, but his insistence that the kingdom was even now in-breaking did. His cousin John had introduced people to the kingdom's immanence by baptizing them in the Jordan, a rite of repentance that would prepare them for this epoch-changing event, which had been foretold in their scriptures. Their expectation was that this event would inaugurate their long-awaited freedom from their oppressors. They fully expected that it would usher in the fullness of time, eventually leading all the nations to come to Zion and adore the God of Israel. All of this hope centered on an awaited Messiah. Thus, the notions of wholeness and meaning were concretized definitively in this imagined messianic figure who was to come. He would make Israel whole. Meaning for Israel was made present by hope.

The Gospel of Mark's rendering of Jesus's opening salvo about people's hoped-for fulfillment might be read as follows:

> Repent of the constrictions of the faith you have been taught and practiced. It has become too full of your own activity, as if through your observance of the law, you could save yourselves. Repent of the narrowness of your faith. Rather, the good news is that righteousness is God's gift to give, not your burden to earn. The good news is that your salvation is a receivement to be believed, not an achievement to be attained!

Jesus preached what he himself experienced: namely, that God was much nearer than their emphasis on the law had led the people to believe.

Jesus did not claim to know more than he knew, hence the "known unknown" quality in his preaching about the reign of God. Jesus proclaimed and inaugurated this reign, but this did not mean that it was fully known to him. When asked about the when and how of it, he chided his disciples: "It is not for you to know the times or seasons that the Father has established by his own authority" (Acts 1:7). Or in Mark, when provoked by the same question, Jesus responded: "But of that day or hour no one knows, neither the angels in heaven nor the Son but only the Father" (Mark 13:32).

It is clear from the Gospels that Jesus was highly attuned to the false ways of going about making oneself whole. Thus he began to differentiate between the two kinds of minds he found in his contemporaries. One of these was a compartmentalizing mind, the other a notion-nurturing, kingdom-oriented mind. The former mind mistakes parts for wholes, investing the proximate with ultimacy. One of Jesus's symbols for this categorical mistake was mammon. Mammon is poorly understood if it is reduced to "money." A better definition of this Aramaic term is "that in which you put your trust." In one of the few stark black-and-white, either-or choices presented in the Gospels, Jesus warns against trying to serve two masters, God and mammon. Those who try to do so will increasingly attend to one master, while the other begins to recede from their attention and affections, perhaps even to the point of being despised (Matt. 6:24). The danger is that mammon will gradually fill one's horizons with what eventually will leave them empty. Jesus perceived that his hearers' minds were preoccupied and anxious over whatever form of "riches" was operating in them, so that their faith in God had shrunk to a mere vestige of the faith of their devout forebears. By contrast, Jesus often repeated his amazement at the strength of deep faith, presumably starting with his own (Matt. 11:23).

The primary examples of the compartmentalizing mind in the Gospels were the scribes and Pharisees. According to the stereotype, scribes and Pharisees taught that the better one knew and practiced all the religious precepts, the surer one could be of finding favor with God and obtaining righteousness through one's own doing. But Jesus knew that those who trust in their own adherence to the law to produce righteousness of the kind that Israel sought will not be open to the whole Mystery, nor to how its Otherness will reveal itself. Instead of the notion of the whole remaining receptive, they begin to crowd it with a composite of their own constructs.

The point is that once the notion of catholicity becomes static, it does not make a whole person, nor does it make a faith whole. The icon becomes an idol. Any faith, including Catholicism, can generate a series of concepts that in turn entail practices requiring our adherence. Meanwhile, God remains more and more unknown, and located on the other side of history. Suffice it to say that Jesus insisted that God would not be glorified by those who had constructed a religious system, the observance of which effectively and paradoxically made God superfluous.

Think of the two men who went up to the temple to pray (Luke 18:10–14). One was so sure of his faith constructs that his prayer was really no prayer at all, but only a soliloquy spoken into the air about his own righteous deeds. Thus, he did not go away righteous in God's eyes, but only in his own. The other man never raised his eyes upon entering into the temple, but only called out to God to be merciful to him. And God, whose greatest work is mercy, heard the prayer that came from the man's heart and understood its neediness, and made him righteous in God's eyes. To be whole before God, one must be open to the work of God, faith in whom makes one whole.

Or think of the elder son in the parable of the prodigal son. Though he had never left home, he did not really know his father, only his to-do list or not-to-do's. He was clueless about the heart of his own father, who at this moment simply "had to celebrate and rejoice because [his] brother was dead and has come back to life again; he was lost and has been found" (Luke 15:32). Jesus's description of the heart of the father of the prodigal son reflects what he had come to know of God's heart.

Jesus's own drive to his meaning and the meaning of Israel was deepened by the Spirit that rested on and led him "without ration" (John 3:34). It was through the Holy Spirit that he found the meanings he lived by and articulated. A unique dimension of the wholeness he came to proclaim was the relationship between being right with God and being connected with the least, the lost, the little, and the left behind. Hence Jesus cared for and embraced such people in his fellowship. His table companions were frequently the marginalized of their society. Finally, he connected salvation and definitive wholeness with one orthopraxis, that of time spent with and care given to those in need. In Matthew 25:31–46, the eschatological judge blesses those who showed mercy to those with whom Jesus identifies himself. Obviously, if Jesus is a trustworthy messenger, assisting in the task of wholeness for the broken is central to God's plan for humanity.

AN ECCLESIAL EXPERIENCE OF CATHOLICITY

One of the most important events in my lifetime and of many of our contemporaries for fleshing out the idea of catholicity took place during the Second Vatican Council (1962–65). I had been ordained the previous year, and found myself absorbed in anything I could find written about the Council, its tensions and breakthroughs, its conservatives and liberals, and all the issues it had to face. The Council itself evolved and grew, from the time of the creation of its preparatory documents, which were doctrinally wooden, to the publication of the final documents. The preparatory documents did not have the spirit of Pope John XXIII, who in his opening address envisioned the Council "as preparing and consolidating the path toward the unity of humanity itself . . . in order that the earthly city may be brought to the resemblance of that heavenly city where truth reigns, charity is the law and whose extent is eternity."[12] The scope of the rhetoric was breathtaking! However, from the very beginning there was a tension in the Council between Catholicism and catholicity, between those who were comfortable merely tweaking the doctrines already conceptualized in the past, and those whose horizons were more universal. These latter were driven by the heuristic notion of catholicity, though few would have put it in these terms. Cardinal Leon-Joseph Suenens voiced the need for catholicity at the end of the first session because of his restiveness with the conceptually tidy ecclesiology that had been in the ascendency until that point. He had gone to the Council with a vision of the Church "as a people on mission at all levels—laity, religious, clergy, bishops and Roman congregations! It would indeed be a magnificent Pentecostal grace for the Church."[13]

What was this "it" he was seeking? He felt that the Council up until that point lacked an overall structural theme, and he recommended that the Church construe itself as being on mission in and for the world.

He had made himself familiar with the work of the theological pioneers whose writings preceded the Council: theologians such as Yves Congar, Karl Rahner, M.-D. Chenu, Henri de Lubac, J. Jungmann, John Courtney Murray, Pierre Teilhard de Chardin, and many others. Through his studies, Suenens was also indebted to the social teaching of Leo XIII, the renewal of patristic studies, the openness of Pius XII's encyclical on the study of scripture, and his own experience of the movement of God in the hearts and minds of the faithful of Belgium whom he had pastored for so many years. The consequence of Suenens's intervention was a three-year drama involving many minds and hands, some of them wringing, some of them clapping.

The catholicity of the final document, *Gaudium et spes*, which was a Pastoral Constitution rather than a doctrinal one, is emblematic of the change that took place in the overwhelming majority, since it passed with almost unanimous consent. It was the only major document born from a floor suggestion at the Council, and it represents a leap in the Church's self-understanding on many issues. Its perspective was global, post-European, open to and identified with the joys and hopes of the whole world. It was optimistic in nature, in contrast to the suspiciousness and fear of the world that had been developing within the Church for centuries, and that had been formally articulated a century before in Pius IX's Syllabus of Errors.

Gaudium et spes was addressed "not only to all who invoke the name of Christ but to all humanity" (2). "Hence the pivotal point of our total presentation will be humanity, whole and entire, body and soul, heart and conscience, mind and will" (3). It set out to "scrutinize the signs of the times" in the light of the Gospel as the Council fathers understood it. Its scope was as wide as creation and as particular as history (4). For the bishops, one unmistakable sign of the times was the inclusion in the Council itself of non-European bishops; indeed, the whole world was represented. Catholicism had long since left the womb of Europe, but the geographic "newcomers" had much to say that the Europeans had not yet heard. *Gaudium et spes* was attentive to the feats accomplished by "the human intellect for broadening its dominion over time: over the past by means of historical knowledge; over the future by the art of projecting and by planning" (5). The bishops explicitly praised science, technology, biology, psychology, the social sciences, and history. They also noted that "the human race [has] passed from a rather static concept of reality to a more dynamic, evolutionary one" (5).

The whole document culls its insights not only from the Gospel, but from "right reason" and from natural law, and applies these to discerning what would be for the common good. For example, in dealing with the question of war, the Council fathers "recall first of all the permanent binding force of universal natural law and its all-embracing precepts" (79). This being said, the Council was not shy about insisting that at a basic level, the mystery that each human being is can best be understood in relation to the mystery of the person of Jesus. His incarnation united him "in some fashion with every human being," and in every human being of good will "grace works in an unseen way"; furthermore, "the Holy Spirit in a manner known only to God offers to everyone the possibility of being associated with the paschal mystery" (22). That mystery, of course, consists in Jesus's death for our sins and his resurrection from the dead. The universality of these assertions is both thrilling and challenging, though it is not at all evident that they have been understood or taken to heart by many Catholic Christians since the Council.

Rather than spell out the myriad insights and concerns of the whole document, what I want to do here is to comment on the excitement it generated in a number of us at the time. There was the experience of the bishops, who themselves had come to face the steep challenge of catholicity, some of them for the first time. This challenge did not make an ecclesial triumphalist of any of the bishops. Quite the contrary! The assembled bishops and many in the Church saw the breadth and depth of the task to which God was calling the Church at that moment in history, which was to be servants of the *not yet*. The *already* had to be retained, of course, but not preserved in formaldehyde. As the official title of the document conveys, the reflections of *Gaudium et spes* were on "the Church in the Modern World." Unlike previous papal and episcopal reflections about the world, it had a positive reading of the Enlightenment, the American and French revolutions, industrialization, the achievements of science, academic disciplines, freedom of religion, and freedom of conscience: "By the autonomy of earthly affairs, we mean that created things and societies themselves enjoy their own laws and values which must be gradually deciphered, put to use, and regulated by men (sic)—such (autonomy) is not merely required by modern people but harmonizes also with the will of the Creator" (36).

One year before writing this remarkable Pastoral Constitution, which put the Church at the service of the world, the Council had produced its Dogmatic Constitution on the Church, *Lumen gentium.* There the bishops describe the Church as "a kind of sacrament or sign of intimate union with God and of the unity of all humanity" (1). The theme of universal connectedness was already present in that first document. One section in particular, section 16, connects every conceivable population in the world through the understanding of the Church as a sign and sacrament of union with God. First, the Church sees itself connected to the Jews, or "the people to whom the covenants and promises were given . . . this people remains most dear to God for God neither repents of the gifts He makes nor the calls he issues." Next, the Church is linked to "those who acknowledge the Creator . . . in the first place the Muslims." Further, it claims its relationship with all those seekers who have not yet come to believe in God: "Nor is God far distant from those who in shadows and images seek the unknown God." Then there are those righteous people who "sincerely seek God and, moved by grace, strive by their deeds to do His will as it is known to them through the dictates of conscience." Finally, the Council is sure that "divine Providence supplies the help necessary for salvation to those who, without blame on their part, have not yet arrived at an explicit knowledge of God, but who strive to live a good life, thanks to God's grace." In brief, the Council exhibits the collective effects of the drive of catholicity, superceding what the Church had fractured or suppressed by its narrowness of vision in previous centuries.

CATHOLICITY AND THE UNIVERSITY

In our more or less postmodern culture, wholeness can sometimes be considered a toxic concept, or looked on with suspicion. Many academic circles prize deconstruction, and no longer aspire to wholeness. There is some value in this view, since the heuristic character of catholicity should keep a Catholic institution of higher learning from being tarred with the brush of an ideological past or an over-determined future. But as noted by many, one of the ironies about postmodernism is that more narrow wholes begin to emerge surreptitiously from what has been deconstructed. The more specialized academia becomes, the more likely academics are to be immersed in and absorbed by their fields. Specialization can be a way of demanding a virtual totality. Those who receive knowledge of specialists, such as students, or even members of the scholars' families, can, of course, benefit immensely from specialization or at times be jeopardized by the totality increasingly demanded by it.

An anecdote recently brought the shortcomings of specialization home to me. A friend of mine was admitted to a psychiatric unit at a prestigious hospital in Chicago. She was visited daily by six different specialists: a doctor, a nurse, a psychiatrist, a social worker, and two different therapists, one occupational and one physical. While each of them was somewhat aware of the others' efforts, none of them had a sense of how to treat this patient in order to allow her be a viable member of society once again. Their training only allowed them to be knowledgeable about a part of what she needed, and because of this, they came close to losing her, rather than healing her. Each specialist had spent years of training becoming more and more knowledgeable about less and less, and the effect on this patient, at least at this time in this one facility, was a well-intentioned series of failures. They were attentive to her symptoms, but their knowledge of these symptoms did not help her broken self to become whole.

I do not want to extrapolate from this one case to deprecate the entire health profession, since I am alive because of its specialists. I only use the case to highlight one of Lonergan's key insights, which is that "looking at" reality does not produce knowledge of reality. Knowledge is a compound act, which starts with paying close attention to what one is experiencing in one's intentionality. The experts in this particular psychiatric unit were not as attentive to the entirety of this patient as she needed them to be; they saw her through the prism of their specialties. Specialization alone, oddly enough, can make for inattention rather than insight. There is, no doubt, a growing role and need for specialization, but it is also important to realize that knowledge is best attained by attention to all the operations of consciousness, beginning, in this case, with an experience of the other.

To put it more into our context: What can we imagine that God sees when God looks at a university? Prima facie, much activity, industry, effort, and good will, and presumably much knowledge being attained. But all of this being done disjointedly, as if the university were a series of stovepipes. The stovepipes connote autonomous departments, intense enterprises that neither aspire nor pretend to aspire to nurturing a unity. The heuristic character of the notion of catholicity is a useful way of examining the value and the limits of this imagined God-view of the autonomy of the disciplines.

What would it look like if faculty were inspired to work more closely together, without losing their depth of knowledge in diverse fields of study? Are there not new ways of thinking about cooperation among the disciplines that would make its practice more frequent and more effective across the university? I could also frame the question in terms of the search for a holistic educational theory that takes into account the cognitional theory inherent in these ideas about the drives described in this chapter. While there are plural ends of bodies of knowledge, the common good has to take primacy among them.

The function of a university is to know and teach that which can be known and taught. But is it not obvious that universities and individual faculty members need to approach the pursuit of knowledge more holistically and with greater expectations about a wholeness that is even now able to come about? The resistance to this kind of vista in educational circles—the fear that such holism would homogenize what is irreducibly different—is understandable. This is where the notion of catholicity has its importance for education. (Notice once again that I am not speaking about Catholic education here, but about education as such.) I have posited this thesis about the notion of catholicity, not because I think of it as another requirement to be added to what education should be doing, but because a basic understanding of catholicity is imperative if we are to understand both what understanding is and where knowing is trying to go. Together with the classical notions of being and value, the notion of catholicity can help us to bring into focus what otherwise can be so disparate as to verge on the incoherent.

A university, ex hypothesi, prohibits no question, nor is any pursuit of knowledge extrinsic to its reason for being. By the same token, it should not simply applaud the pursuit of unlimited questions, and then be satisfied with a collection of disjoined answers. A school must seek to go further, in order to have the plural efforts converge into a more coherent whole. The suggestion being made in this text is that this further step will become possible in a university if a critical mass of its faculty can better understand their own understandings and see that the operations of consciousness are universal. This realization would also give educators some degree of confidence that they are not erecting a tower of Babel that will eventually collapse. Rather, with the authentic use of subjectivity accounted for, converging judgments can be weighed or diverging judgments can be argued in a court of appeal that understands the compound character of the birth of knowledge.

Converging judgments, accumulated over time, make for intellectual traditions. One conversation that needs to take place at Catholic universities is on the question of which intellectual traditions are operative on their campuses. The usual way of ensuring that the intellectual traditions on a campus are not discordant with Catholicism is to examine the doctrines being taught there. A different approach is to take the measure of the place according to the prevalence of Catholic practices. This is largely extrinsic to the intellectual life of the campus, and puts too great a burden on too few of the actors in the educational institution, typically campus ministers or administrators, who then seem to be the only ones responsible for carrying out the school's mission. To focus on Catholic practice is to circumvent the intellectual issue, which has to do with the intellectual traditions being promoted on campus and the curricular offerings and class syllabi.

The heuristic character of catholicity as a notion is concretized in two different ways. One is by particularizing the wholes we seek to confect; the second by particularizing that which we choose to believe. In this latter category, we have the official doctrinal teachings of the Church, which are its articulation of the whole, both immanent and transcendent. Its doctrinal tradition has been one of the strengths of the Church, orienting believers to a whole, while allowing the unknowable dimensions of the mystery to remain a mystery. Insofar as one fails to understand the dynamic between known and unknown, Catholic doctrines can be misunderstood. How? Doctrines are starting points, rather than final words; if taken as the latter, they will over-determine what is still mystery. They are invitations to belief and contemplation. They are not the last word. This is not said out of any lack of belief in the doctrines of the Church, but to underscore that mystery remains mystery, even after a doctrine articulates it. Such an approach allows us to grow in appreciation and in knowledge of the mysteries of God, while letting God remain God.

There is one doctrine that is central to the very existence of Catholic educational institutions. I have in mind the Christological doctrine of the two natures in the one person of Christ. A Catholic institution of higher learning that is uninformed about this doctrine is seriously deficient in its self-understanding. It will then be unlikely that its personnel will know why the school and others like it have existed since Catholic universities were born in the Middle Ages. The following box contains material that I distribute in my workshops with faculty to describe the foundational rationale for the existence of Catholic higher education.

Is There a Doctrine in the House?

One will make little headway in trying to understand the relation between the Church and a Catholic university by posing the question in macro terms, that is, in terms of the relation between the two institutions. It might be better to start with one's own field of knowledge, and through the questions that can be posed by and about this field, to come eventually to questions of its value and its nexus with ultimacy.

The doctrine articulated at the Council of Chalcedon in 451 supplies a definitive understanding of Christ as Christians understood him then. It takes seriously the humanity of Jesus, not allowing this to be absorbed by his divinity. It holds that, in the person of Jesus, an uncreated divine nature and a created human nature came into a wholly unique ("hypostatic") union. This sublation of these two natures into Christ's unique person took place without either being annihilated. Hence, the humanity of Jesus is completed by his divinity, without his having ceased in any way to be human; he became one of us in the incarnation and is so now. Catholicism teaches that it is through this union that God intends to bring all created reality to its completion and fullness.

Knowledge of this doctrine is necessary if faculty members and other university personnel want to know why Catholic universities were born historically *ex corde ecclesiae,* and why the Church continues to be committed to such institutions. This doctrine is also the key to understanding the radical difference between the rationale for these schools and that of their secular counterparts.

This doctrine, moreover, can also be understood analogously as the foundation of academic freedom. Each field of knowledge must be allowed to develop freely, as Christ's human nature developed freely. A school that traces its raison d'etre to this understanding of Christ must be academically up to

continued on next page

---

continued from previous page
date with the scholarship in the fields of study it teaches. It must do justice to each field without preempting them either with piety or with carelessness. "A second-rate Catholic university," writes Bernard Lonergan, "is no more acceptable to God in the New Law than was the sacrifice of maimed or diseased beasts in the Old Law."

So the Catholic faith's analogue for understanding the union between a field of knowledge and Christ is the union of Jesus's humanity to his divinity. These are not to be conflated. By the same token, if there is a complete separation between these two, then the telos of knowing, as understood by Catholicism, can too easily become obscure, or positivist, or commodified. But wherever there is a conjoining of the divine and the human, or a connection made between faith and academic discipline by an educational institution, that institution can expect to become just as anomalous to its secular counterparts in the present age as Christ was to his contemporaries.

Since the connection between any discipline and the Christian faith can be helped by knowledge of this doctrine, those who teach in Catholic schools should understand its foundational character. They, of course, are not required to believe in it or subscribe to it. Whether they do or do not is not the business of the institution. What is its business is letting its personnel in on why these institutions have been and still are of interest to the Church.

There are five ways in which a school's praxis can be at odds with this Christological doctrine. The first is for faculty to deny outright that a field of knowledge taught in the school is connected to faith in any way. The second is to connect the field to Christ piously, without doing the hard work of being competent in the field. The third is to attempt to control the findings of a field a priori through the imposition of an external authority, either ecclesiastical or academic. The fourth is to allow faith to be merely extrinsic to learning, such as by relying on the office of campus ministry to provide reflection on the faith. And the fifth is to leave students without any assistance in integrating their faith, whatever it might be, with the bodies of knowledge they study.

This doctrine puts knowing into a centuries-old framework that connects faith and reason. Such a framework for meaning and wholeness leaves students and faculty the choice to subscribe to it or not. It is a faith framework, and as such, cannot be required.

One of the values of the notion of catholicity is that it gives direction to both faith and reason without requiring that they become conjoined. There will always be, in every human being, a drive for meaning and wholeness anyway; what both faith and reason contribute to this drive is an orientation to, and a relationship with, the known unknown that we call Mystery. An education is valuable in making knowledge available to the student. And a tradition that has given room to both faith and reason is an invaluable added source of knowledge. Reason alone can become more and more weighty; faith alone can become more and more narrow; the notion of catholicity alone without an orientation can become amorphous. The three together can complement one another. This is not a promotion of the Catholic faith, but of the value of some faith.

LONERGAN'S UNNAMED EMERGENT

After finishing this chapter, I had the great luck to read a tome by Ivo Coelho on the subject of "the universal viewpoint" in Lonergan.[14] It was a delight to read not only because his scholarship was so good, but because it confirmed for me that the direction I have taken in this chapter on catholicity is right. Under the rubric of the "universal viewpoint," Coelho tracked Lonergan's mind through all its peregrinations. The universal viewpoint is the goal of what I have been calling the notion of catholicity. In *Insight*, Lonergan describes his hunt for such a viewpoint as "intellectualist, open, factual and normative."[15] Instead of working with "determinate conceptual contents," he described himself as dealing with "heuristically defined anticipations. So far from fixing the concepts that will meet the anticipation, it awaits from nature and from history a succession of tentative solutions."[16] (For me, this is a perfect description of the way the notion of catholicity operates. It seeks and anticipates wholes, rather than fixing them conceptually or arriving at "determinate conceptual contents.") In this context Lonergan is contrasting his own method with that of Hegel, whose dialectical method Lonergan describes as "conceptualist, closed, necessitarian and immanental."[17]

At this point in his study, Coelho examines what Lonergan calls "the universal viewpoint," and describes it as "simply a heuristic structure that contains virtually the various ranges of possible alternatives of interpretations."[18] The pure desire to know is triggered by the notion of being, and the operations of consciousness deal with whatever data is brought to the subject. Coelho puts it this way: "The universal viewpoint is the structure of the notion of being as protean . . . Grasp of the universal viewpoint is grasp of the structure of the protean notion of being, for once the structure is reached, the potential totality of viewpoints is reached."[19] (Again, for me, this description could be improved by differentiating the notion of catholicity from the notion of being. What consciousness grasps is protean being. But its grasp is for "the universal viewpoint" or "a potential totality of viewpoints." This seems to me to argue for something operating in human consciousness that is slightly different from being as such. This is why I posit a different notion: catholicity, the drive for a sense of the whole in the "potential totality of viewpoints.")

The heuristic notion of being is distinct from its goal. According to Lonergan, the goal of the pure desire to know is the universal viewpoint, but it is "a high and distant goal."[20] And what exactly is being sought with this goal? Meaning! "The universal viewpoint as a heuristic structure for meaning envisages both insights as well as judgments."[21] Before writing *Insight* (1957), there was *Verbum* (1946), in

which he envisioned the goal of the notion of being "as inchoate wisdom or a rudimentary view of the whole." This insight about inchoate wisdom then migrated to
the universal viewpoint, "as a type of wisdom insofar as it is a grasp of order in
the universe of meanings."[22] So being without meaning is incomplete. (All of these
reflections support my contention that in addition to the notion of being, a distinct
notion of catholicity is operative in human intentionality. This would explain the
"grasp for order," or the desire for "a view of the whole," in the face of a universe
of meanings that otherwise lack order or a sense of the whole.)

Wisdom cannot be possessed, any more than being can be. Wisdom belongs to
God and is God's to give as gift. It seems to me that this gift is usually given gradually, and is helped if one becomes familiar with and attentive to the operations latent
in one's consciousness and conscience. Insofar as one is attentive, one's wisdom
grows, slowly, as a rudimentary view of the whole emerges and one's knowledge
increases. Commenting on St. Thomas, Lonergan describes knowing as a participation in the light of wisdom. Thus, according to Thomas, "the intellectual light itself
which we have within us is nothing else than a certain participated likeness of the
uncreated light."[23] "Our intellectual light derives its efficacy from the *prima lux*
which is God."[24]

At this earlier point in his thinking, reflected in *Verbum*, Lonergan was focused
on wisdom, and saw it both as epistemological and metaphysical. But in *Insight*,
wisdom transmogrified into the general empirical method and the universal viewpoint. After *Insight*, Lonergan begins to prefer to work with the category of "horizon." "Horizon denotes the whole constituted by both the concrete subject and the
concrete totality of objects."[25] He was attracted to horizon because while the objects
are unrestricted, by now it is even clearer that the subject needs to be "practicing
transcendental method, the method that determines the ultimate and so basic
whole."[26]

In opting for horizon, Lonergan also shifts to method and to meaning. Now
metaphysics is only one of the fruits of transcendental method, rather than its primary fruit. "Transcendental horizons may be objectified in various ways: symboli-
cally, philosophically, theologically or methodologically."[27] And wisdom, too, is
now achieved by being faithful to method and to the total and basic horizon it opens
up. Horizon, meaning, and method are now all interconnected. By the late 1960s
and early 1970s, theology had become Lonergan's primary focus. He resisted doing
a theology of apologetics, however, because such theologies tended to neglect the
subject. Rather, he focused on the subject's capacity for moral, intellectual, and religious self-transcendence. These conversions, which take place in the interactions
between a subject and the objects encountered, including one's religious tradition,
can provide theology with its necessary foundations.

A few quotes from *Insight* enable us to return to Lonergan's treatment of notions
and what they strive to attain. Being is, of course, "the supreme heuristic notion;
prior to every content, it is the notion of the to-be-known."[28] It anticipates being
informed by "being," which can only take place concretely and cumulatively. "The
notion of being is not the notion of some essence. It becomes determined only as

correct judgments are made, and it reaches its full determination only when the totality of correct judgments are made," though there is "a still larger totality of possible judgments."[29] It is this matter of totality that has been the distinctive focus of this chapter.

"Being is the whole of what intelligence anticipates; . . . and so the notion of being is open to all the incomplete and partial moments from which cognitional process suffers without ever renouncing its all-inclusive goal."[30] This "whole" and this "all-inclusive goal" raise again for me the notion of catholicity, which is latent in the notion of being and complements it.

An appreciation of the heuristic notion of catholicity operating in all human beings could help us begin to see more clearly the point of all learning, but especially institutionalized learning. As in the move from arithmetic to algebra, we are always seeking higher syntheses. What is missing in educational theory is this notion of catholicity, a heuristic that pushes for a further whole, a connectedness between knowns that are also known to be partial. All cognitional endeavors, whether personal or collective, seek the good of order, the good of relating this particular thing to that. In brief, I contend that Lonergan's unnamed emergent is the notion of catholicity, without which he seemed unsettled as he moved from wisdom to the universal viewpoint, to general empirical method, to the totality of objects, to the larger totality of possible judgments, to horizon.

NOTES

1. Ong, "Yeast: A Parable for Catholic Higher Education," *America*, 349.
2. Lonergan, *A Second Collection*, 75.
3. Ibid., 80.
4. Ibid.
5. Aristotle, *A New Aristotle Reader*, 380.
6. Lonergan, "Cognitional Structure," in *Collection*, 207.
7. See appendix B for more on the notion of catholicity.
8. Lonergan, *Insight*, 384.
9. Ibid., 382.
10. Ibid., 384.
11. See, for example, Haughey, "The Driver in the Mind of Fethullah Gulen," 333–49.
12. Abbott, *Documents of Vatican II*, 718.
13. Leon-Joseph Cardinal Suenens, *Memories and Hopes*, 83.
14. Coelho, *Hermeneutics and Method*.
15. Here Coelho is quoting from chapter 14 of *Insight*; Coelho, *Hermeneutics and Method*, 60.
16. Ibid.
17. Ibid.
18. Ibid., 61.
19. Ibid., 61–62.
20. Ibid., 63
21. Ibid.
22. Lonergan, *Verbum*, 74.
23. Aquinas, *Summa Theologia* I, q.84, a.5c, quoted in Lonergan, *Verbum*, 85.

24. Lonergan, *Verbum,* 92. Lonergan gets this from Thomas Aquinas, *De Trinitate* q.1, a.3, ad 1m.

25. Coelho, *Hermeneutics and Method,* 125.

26. Ibid., 126.

27. Ibid., 129.

28. Lonergan, *Insight,* 380.

29. Ibid., 386.

30. Ibid., 396.

CHAPTER 5

◆

The Catholic Intellectual Tradition: Part I

ONE OF THE MAIN REASONS for the poverty of educational theory in our Catholic colleges and universities is the lack of clarity about the relationship between the Catholic intellectual tradition and "the Sacred Tradition." As long as these are lumped together, there will be a wariness in the Catholic university world about "the Church"; and more specifically, there will be a fear about ecclesiastical authority encroaching on academics' freedom.

Before going into any depth about the Catholic intellectual tradition, it is worthwhile to consider how any intellectual tradition comes to be. Such traditions usually are born from a unique matrix of ideas that capture and ground the tradition; they have someone or something original at their headwaters. Plato and, in a different way, of course, Plotinus were the originals who generated the intellectual tradition of Neoplatonism, for example. Following its initial spark, an intellectual tradition develops devotees and usually produces works that become classics in their tradition. The tradition's writings continue to speak with intelligence and value, far beyond the era of their first articulation. Jesus was the original who generated what became the Christian Sacred Tradition. From this one beginning, many traditions eventually evolved. Of these, the most capacious and continuous has been the compound tradition of the Catholic faith.

IS THERE SUCH A THING AS A CATHOLIC INTELLECTUAL TRADITION?

To answer this question we will first consider the Second Vatican Council's articulation of the foundational tradition: "In the supremely wise arrangement of God, sacred Tradition, sacred Scripture, and the Magisterium of the Church are so connected and associated that one of them cannot stand without the others. Working together, each in its own way, under the action of the one Holy Spirit, they all contribute effectively to the salvation of souls."[1] Yes, all three work together, "each in its own way, under the action of the Holy Spirit," but if the Council was an example of anything, it was that in addition to Sacred Tradition, scripture, and the magisterium, there has long been a fourth leg under the chair of Peter, that of the Catholic

61

intellectual tradition. Given the historical character and fragility of humanity and the fact that even the Church sees into the mysteries of the divine "through a glass darkly," both the magisterium and the Sacred Tradition for which it is ultimately responsible need the Catholic intellectual tradition. Each needs the other. The capacity of each to be critical of the other keeps both of them involved in a healthy dialectic. When the dialectic is not operative, either a "creeping infallibilism" or a creeping antinomianism can develop; either of these can generate a confusion about the truth of the faith.

Although the body of bishops has had the perennial responsibility of teaching authoritatively about matters of faith (*Lumen gentium*, 25), it is only since the nineteenth century that the hierarchy of the Church has come to refer to itself as the magisterium. The term *magisterium* derives from *magister*, someone who has attained a mastery of a body of knowledge. The mastery of the body of bishops is in matters of faith. But they, the magisterium, are not above the Word of God, which has been entrusted to the Church in the scriptures and its Sacred Tradition. "[T]his Magisterium is not superior to the Word of God, but is its servant. It teaches only what has been handed onto it. With the help of the Holy Spirit it guards the Word of God and expounds it faithfully" (*Dei verbum*, 10).

There are varying degrees of authority attached to the teachings of the magisterium. Some of these teachings are dogmas, and some are doctrines. Though every dogma is a doctrine, not every doctrine is a dogma, since a dogma must be explicitly proposed by the Church as a divinely revealed object of belief. Like dogmas, doctrines are teachings that have the status of being authoritative; that is, they are officially taught by the magisterium. Vatican II did not define any new dogmas, but its teachings were authoritative because of the authority of the body of bishops who approved them.

There is a dialectical relationship between the magisterium with its authority and the Catholic intellectual tradition, whose authority is located in the quality of the scholarship of each person seeking to connect the dots between his or her understandings and the doctrinal understandings of the magisterium. The relationship between the magisterium and the intellectual tradition has been largely beneficial to both, though they are not always on the same page.

The Catholic intellectual tradition grew out of the fact that the original message inevitably had to undergo development, and that development had to ferret out which of the plural meanings that were beginning to attach to the proclamation of the Gospel of Jesus Christ were right and which were wrong. So the Catholic intellectual tradition had its genesis in the difference between theology and religion. Faith sought understanding, and since various understandings developed— depending on the questions being posed and the categories available for answering them—different schools of theology arose. So since the beginning of the Church, there has been an interdependence between the reasoning about the faith done by theology and the determinations about these reasonings by the successors of the apostles, who have the pastoral authority to act as judges of what is an authentic or an inauthentic understanding of the faith of the Church. So there is an interdependence between the doctrinal tradition and the Catholic intellectual tradition.

But the Catholic intellectual tradition has become interested in so much more than theological questions. Its questions come from potentially every field of knowledge. In fact, there is no body of knowledge that is alien to it. But it has no magisterium to pronounce with authority on its understandings. There would be no Catholic intellectual tradition if the authority of the Church were to be indifferent to its understandings. Not only is it interested, the doctrinal tradition is continually fed by those who seek to connect the dots between their understandings and the faith of the Church. In rare cases, the magisterium rejects the way the dots have been connected.

The combination of these two traditions makes it more likely that there will be a "genuine, authentic, long accumulation of insights, adjustments, [and] reinterpretations that repeats the original message afresh for each age."[2] The original message was, of course, about the saving story of Jesus's life, death, and resurrection. This original message has generated many insights and undergone numerous reinterpretations and adjustments from that time forward. The intellectual tradition has been active in contributing to the doctrinal tradition. Of course, the Catholic intellectual tradition carries neither the same weight as the Holy Tradition, nor the same authority, nor the same burden. Nevertheless, this intellectual tradition derives its authority from its connection with the Sacred Tradition, as well as from right reasoning about those areas of knowledge that are germane to the faith and teachings of the Church. It is helpful, of course, when that reasoning is done by those who are enlightened by faith, and even more so if they identify with and understand the Sacred Tradition. But it must also be said that many non-Catholics have added greatly to the Catholic intellectual tradition.

One reason for differentiating between the Sacred Tradition and this intellectual tradition is that there is much that is taught by the Church that does not enjoy the same status as its dogmas and core beliefs, which include such teachings as the resurrection of Jesus and the assumption of the Blessed Virgin Mary into heaven. The Church speaks of "a hierarchy of truths," with some central to this Sacred Tradition and some that are less so. This is because, in the words of the Council, truths "vary in their relation to the foundation of the Christian faith."[3] There is considerable agreement among Christians about the truths that are constitutive of that faith, such as the incarnation of Jesus, or the Trinitarian character of God. Lower in this "hierarchy of truths" would be the social teachings of the Church, such as the principle of subsidiarity, the priority of labor over capital, and various teachings on economic and social matters. Though these are not insignificant teachings, they are not foundational to this "Sacred Tradition."

Though many teachings of the Church can be seen by the light of faith, they can also often be attained through judgments of right reason by people "of good will" without their being aware of the Church's teaching. The Church's moral teachings, for example, are usually in tune with the natural law written on human hearts universally (Rom. 2:15). Interestingly, John Henry Newman has called conscience "the aboriginal Vicar of Christ."[4] Aquinas described conscience as "nothing other than the light of intellect infused within us by God. Thanks to this we know what must be done and what must be avoided. This light or this law has been given by God to creation."[5] By acceding to this light, created beings participate in God's eternal law.

The Catholic intellectual tradition is primarily a learning tradition, with no discipline alien to it or irrelevant to its interests. Of all the disciplines, theology has been the most important, in every generation, for assisting in and critiquing the magisterium's understanding of the doctrinal tradition. Throughout the Church's history, theology has generated the most creative tension with the authoritative tradition. The magisterium has the last word in this dialectic, at least for the time being. Philosophy has also been a source of creative tension with the doctrinal tradition. Though the Church has not embraced one philosophy in the present era, it continues to be informed by philosophical insights. Both theology and philosophy have been invaluable sources for the development of the Church's own self-understandings.[6] Many cultures and academic disciplines have benefited from this compound tradition, and have in turn contributed to it.

THE VALUE OF THE DIFFERENTIATION

For whom is this differentiation between the Catholic intellectual tradition and the Sacred Tradition of value? I have in mind three constituencies who could benefit from such a distinction: the Church itself, the schools under the sponsorship of the Church, and administrators of these schools. This differentiation helps the school to be a school and not a Church, while at the same time connecting the school's offerings to a tradition that has a continuous history, longer than any other educational tradition operating in the world today.

Without the differentiation between the intellectual and doctrinal components within this compound Catholic tradition, a school's administration must constantly be on tenterhooks about whether it is too Catholic or not Catholic enough. Complaints multiply when the expectation remains undifferentiated, some coming from parents who think that the school is at fault because "it isn't making my kid a faithful Catholic," or some from students who believe that there is too much or not enough faith on their campus. Complaints also come from bishops who see the school as an instrument of the Church and judge it accordingly, or from faculty members who feel that their academic freedom will be encroached upon. In some cases, older faculty or alumni may protest that "This place used to be Catholic, but it has lost its identity." Any of these feelings can serve as evidence of the value of the differentiation I am suggesting in this chapter.

Second, from the point of view of the Church, the value of differentiation is that Church authorities could have a greater chance to relate to the school pastorally rather than juridically. A local bishop might then be a source of comfort to a campus, a sort of older brother in the faith, rather than the "bad cop" with the task of ensuring that orthodoxy is preserved. Respect for the religious authority of many bishops in the eyes of students, faculty, and administrators could be raised if both parties saw things this way.

There is a long history of tensions between Catholic higher education institutions in this country and the Church authorities. To cite just one incident: Several years after the Council, in 1967, Father Ted Hesburgh, CSC, convoked a meeting of twenty-six leaders in Catholic higher education in Land O'Lakes, Wisconsin. After this consultation, some feared that the beginning of the end had come for the relationship between the universities and the Church. The leaders who gathered in Land O'Lakes wrote a declaration stating that universities "must have a true autonomy and academic freedom in the face of authority of whatever kind, lay or clerical, external to the academic community itself."[7] This opening shot created a needless tension, since Rome and some members of the American hierarchy did not seem to notice that the convoked body also stated that "the Catholic university must be an institution, a community of learners or a community of scholars, in which Catholicism is perceptibly present and effectively operative."[8] The concerns on both sides might have been avoided, had the differentiation being emphasized here been adverted to.

The compound nature of the Catholic tradition is neither liberal nor conservative. It is simply factual. The faith and the faithful seek understanding, and in doing so have produced enormous fruit throughout the history of the Church. This connection between faith and reason is a thread of continuity that has not been cut, all the way back to the beginning of the Church. As long as these continue to be sufficiently coherent, it gives promise of assisting the magisterium into the very unclear future into which humanity is heading.

Sometimes those who stand on the outside of the whole enterprise of Catholic education looking in can see its distinctiveness more clearly than those who are on the inside. For example, in an address to the National Catholic Education Association in 1937, Robert Hutchins, who was then president of the University of Chicago, leveled the assembled administrators with his slightly scandalized observation that, in his opinion, Catholic universities "have imitated the worst features of secular education . . . Catholic education is not Catholic enough," despite the Catholic Church's possession of "the longest intellectual tradition of any institution in the contemporary world, the only uninterrupted tradition and the only explicit tradition."[9] I don't know exactly how Hutchins understood this tradition, but the point is that, for him, it was sufficiently distinct that he felt he had to chasten his listeners for their ignorance about the treasure it was.

The words inscribed on the base of Fr. Theodore Hesburgh's bronze likeness in front of the University of Notre Dame library capture the importance of this tradition's distinctiveness for the larger world:

A Catholic University should be a *beacon*, bringing to light, in modern focus, the wonderfully traditional and ancient adage, "'faith seeking understanding," it should be a *bridge* across all chasms that separate modern people from each another, and it should be a *crossroads* where all the intellectual and moral currents of our times meet and are thoughtfully considered. (Emphasis added.)

BOUNDARIES AND PLURALISM

It seems necessary to revisit the question about what, if anything, should set apart the education offered by Catholic colleges and universities. As Alasdair MacIntyre wrote, "to know what we are to become we must know the stories of which we are a part."[10] We are all formed by many disparate stories, but if educators only know or care to know their own discipline's stories, then amnesia will accompany what passes for education. A Catholic school that has no sense of this compound tradition does a disservice to students, leaving them ill equipped to deal with the confusions, ephemera, and biases of our contemporary culture.

The boundaries of the Catholic intellectual tradition are very wide. On one end there is faith, on the other there are understandings. Their conjunction gives the Catholic intellectual tradition its ever-developing contents. Now and throughout history, this tradition has both fed and been fed by many.

This compound tradition rests on the conviction that God made the quite dramatic commitment to have a constitutive member of the divine reality become a constitutive member of one of earth's created species, *homo sapiens sapiens.* The beliefs in God's self-communication in creation, and in the incarnation with Christ's birth, life, ministry, death, and resurrection, are the parameters within which this intellectual tradition understands itself. This compound tradition has passed on the classic picture of *exitus* and *reditus*—God coming forth from an infinity of love, followed by the human response, in myriad centuries-old forms—as human beings strive to return to the union from whence they came. There are, in other words, both a protology and an eschatology in the tradition in which Catholic schools are rooted; such schools share in the Church's memory and destiny.[11] For those who commit themselves to the Church's Sacred Tradition, it supplies a rule of faith.

Because of this compound tradition, the boundaries of Catholicism are widening. To see the Church's growing inclusiveness, one need only go back to a series of documents from Vatican II. I have in mind *Nostra aetate*; *Ad gentes* (especially section 7); *Lumen gentium* (16); and *Gaudium et spes* (22). To quote only from this last document:

> By his incarnation, the Son of God has united himself in some fashion with every person . . . For since Christ died for all and since the ultimate vocation of man is in fact one and divine we ought to believe that the Holy Spirit in a manner known only to God offers to everyone the possibility of being associated with this paschal mystery.

Karl Rahner, who was one of the masters of the Catholic intellectual tradition, spells out the implications of these conciliar texts in the light of all human history: "Because of God's universal salvific will, a Christian has no right to limit the actual event of salvation to the explicit history of salvation in the Old and New Testaments." More explicitly than the Council fathers, but consistently with their ever-widening boundaries, he observes that "a supernatural revelation of God to mankind must have been at work everywhere in the history of the human race . . . at work in such a way that it actually touches every person and effects salvation in each through faith."[12]

UNDERSTANDING SEEKS FAITH AND VICE VERSA

Wouldn't it be odd if God had initiated both creation and the incarnation, and then left the understanding of these events totally up for grabs? The compound Catholic tradition does not believe that God has been that cavalier. Rather, Catholicism has always claimed that there is an authoritative source—specifically, a teaching authority vested in the Catholic Church—that ensures some clarity about the inevitably plural responses of believers. But from the very beginning, there has been a dialectic working within this belief. In the Council of Jerusalem, which took place soon after Jesus's death and resurrection, "no little dissension broke out" in response to Paul's experience with the Gentiles who were converting to faith in Christ (Acts 15). The issue was as radical as whether Christianity was an extension of the faith of Israel, or a new, yet-to-be-named religion. The history of the Church has been marked by extreme views about its authority; the compound nature of the Church's tradition has helped the Church to find a mean between these extremes, between faith alone or reason alone.

The educational institutions that came into being because of this Church were founded by people who retained their belief in the Church's teaching authority, but these institutions were also influenced by this creative tension between the tradition's authoritative side and its intellectual side. This dialectic is still at work, thus making both the doctrinal tradition and the intellectual tradition the sharper for the difference. Faculty and administrators at Catholic institutions might ask themselves whether they are doing justice to their students if they do not make the time or effort to understand the tradition out of which the school was born.

For a number of reasons, it is understandable that many faculty members and administrators might be uninterested in the Catholic story, not the least of these being the Church's tardiness in clarifying its understanding of its relationship with the world, a topic not sufficiently addressed until the last Council. In many ways, Vatican II was a response to the Church's defensiveness toward the world during the previous four centuries. It was at this Council that the Church finally revised its needlessly narrow prior readings of the various ways that God has encountered human beings throughout history. The Church had expended much energy in these centuries defending itself against Protestantism, fighting modernism, and shoring up understanding of its authority, including the declaration of papal infallibility.

It may be helpful to recall some of this history here briefly. By the nineteenth century, modernism had become a more pervasive threat to the Church than Protestantism had been, because it spread throughout every arena of society: science, law, education, labor, politics, and economics, to name only a few. Each of these fields began to develop its own independence, logic, methods, and institutions; they all became increasingly disengaged from the moral and religious worldview that had preceded them. Religion became more a private than a public source of guidance. Eventually, people began to find meaning in ideologies such as communism, socialism, positivism, and scientism, after the master narrative of Christianity had lost some of its social standing. A combination of factors, including the need to counter both modernism and these ideologies, as well as positive developments, such as a newfound respect for history, empirical knowledge, progress, and freedom, began to move the Catholic intellectual tradition to depths it had not previously explored.

Again, the Church's intellectual tradition proved enormously beneficial as a catalyst for a new council, and as a source of food for the Council's deliberations. Vatican II eventually proved itself to be a meeting of the global Church. It laid the groundwork for the Church to become more hospitable, by trying to deal constructively with the ecclesiological developments within Protestantism that had begun in the sixteenth and seventeenth centuries. The Council was also able to acknowledge the world's religions for the first time, and to see in their adherents evidence of God's activity. The Council fathers were able to bring themselves up to date on some of the anthropological convictions springing from the Enlightenment, such as freedom of religion, the inviolability of human dignity, and reason's capacity to come to truth. They taught the need for all of created reality to be studied according to the autonomy of each aspect of it, rightfully enjoyed by reason of its distinctiveness: "[M]ethodical research in all branches of knowledge, provided it is carried out in a truly scientific manner and does not override moral laws, can never conflict with the faith, because the things of the world and the things of faith derive from the same God."[13] None of this would have been likely had the Catholic intellectual tradition not anticipated these lines of reflection.

After the Council, postmodernism began to flourish. It is as hard to describe postmodernism as it can be to date it, but regardless of its elusive tenets, it obviously implies a judgment that the promises of modernism have failed to materialize. Freedom led to pluralism, and pluralism often led to anomie. Empirical knowledge led to the near hegemony of science and technology, and science and technology sometimes led to the counterfeit whole of scientism. With postmodernism, each person was left with the task of constructing an identity that refused to be socially mediated. There was a growing market of options to choose from, any or all of them begging for adoption: a smorgasbord of horizons of meaning; an increasing variety in understandings of the true and the good, and of how these are attained; various contradictory worldviews; and a numbing number of possibilities for career paths.

The Catholic intellectual tradition currently finds itself both challenged and invigorated by this cultural context. It is, in a sense, always the first line of hospitality for breakthrough ideas, since the official Church is usually cautious about new developments. Several things stand out about the way that the Catholic intellectual tradition relates the world to the Church and the Church to the world, which is its Janus-like vocation. First, the tradition has developed a deeper appreciation of history, and of the emergences and fragilities human life faces. Second, it gives an increasing amount of attention to the sciences. Third, like the rest of the world it is beginning to see that the relation of the human species to its habitat is endangering both. Finally, there is new respect for the fecundity of human subjectivity, insofar as it is able to be self-transcending. Consequently, scholars are looking at methods more closely than ever before, largely due to the fact that content is so pluriform and bias so difficult to detect. The more we know of creation, the more we need to know about the identity of the self and of the self's Creator.

CLEAR BOUNDARIES MAKE GOOD NEIGHBORS

A university is an enterprise in understanding. A Catholic university is an enterprise in understanding that is linked to a faith tradition that has a history both of flights from understanding and deeper probes into understanding. Like all other universities, the Catholic university seeks knowledge, but it does so together with an intellectual tradition that is particularly open to the world in the light of faith. This tradition has also been the first court of appeal for the Church's discernment about knowledge of the world. So the question that surfaces for me at this point is: How is the Catholic intellectual tradition boundaried by the Sacred Tradition? In one sense it is not, since its fare is wherever faith and understanding are seeking each other. In another sense, it would seem that the best criterion for dealing with the question of boundaries is God's own (self-) communication in, with, and through the person of Jesus Christ.

The Catholic intellectual tradition's best insight into boundaries will come from Jesus through the Gospels. They depict a person who was able to see beyond the boundaries that Israel had set for itself, in order to consolidate its identity as a people. The boundaries for Jesus were the same as those for Israel, as recited in the *Shema*: "You shall love the Lord, your God, with all your heart, with all your being, with all your strength and with all your entire mind, and your neighbor as yourself" (Matt. 22:37–39). He taught his hearers to be reverent toward the Jewish tradition and those who communicated it: "practice and observe whatever they tell you, but not what they do" (Matt. 23:2). This is an interesting insight into Jesus's own discernment. But he also learned much from his association with those who were considered outside the pale of Israel's righteousness, so when people heard his teachings and prayers, it became clear that the boundaries he envisioned were nothing short of God's kingdom or reign. "His cause was the kingdom, God reigning now and forever, wherever the heart is willing to be reigned over by love."[14]

But the Jesus story does not end with the Gospels. The core doctrines of the Church are Christological. These mark boundaries that transcend eras, cultures, and even religions. The Church's faith shaped its doctrines; more accurately, the experience of the faithful, especially their choices and prayers, shaped these doctrines. Neither the Catholic intellectual tradition nor the doctrinal tradition of the Church springs from nowhere. Both came from the community of the faithful. The great value to the magisterium of the praying Church is its union with God and the ever in-breaking presence of mystery. The great value of the Sacred Tradition is that one does not need to start from zero for knowing the divine mystery. This tradition has to be appropriated personally, experienced appreciatively, understood critically, and judged prayerfully.

This brings us to the matter of the scriptural Word of God, which is the authoritative source for knowledge of the mystery of God. It is the source that must be appropriated by popes and the poor alike for knowledge of this mystery; it is the source of the Church's doctrines and an unparalleled source for discernment for those who would contribute to the Catholic intellectual tradition.

I return now to the issue of boundaries in relation to Catholic universities. For some, the boundaries of the university stretch to wherever "is" and "is not" are predicated correctly, wherever possible intelligibility is pursued with intelligence. But that is not enough. Again, one of Lonergan's insights may be helpful here: "Aristotle and Aquinas distinguish between the expert and the wise man; the expert orders everything within a restricted domain; the wise man orders everything! . . . The unrestricted viewpoint is ultimate and basic: it is wisdom and its domain is being."[15] The academy does not want for experts. What it lacks is wise men and women who are interested in bringing order to more than just the "restricted domain" of their own fields. An unrestricted viewpoint bumps into the questions of why, so what, what for? In a word, faith.

The central doctrine of the Christian faith, articulated in 451 at the Council of Chalcedon, was an incredibly capacious doctrine on boundaries. It claimed that the person of Christ was a union of two natures—a unique union called hypostatic. One of the peculiar things about this doctrine is that those who do not subscribe to it are not marginalized by it. Their nonacceptance of the doctrine cannot be judged negatively, since they may not have been in circumstances conducive to assenting to it. Grace is God's to give, not ours to judge. What adds to the peculiarity of this doctrine in terms of this reflection on boundaries is that it believes that Jesus's self-donation to God won the redemption of all people! The point of his ministry was reconciliation; thus the removal, not the setting, of boundaries. His followers were to go to the ends of the earth with this good news. The largesse of this doctrinal understanding of Jesus and God is at the core of the hospitality of these universities, and is a clue to the question of the university's boundaries.

WHY "CATHOLIC" AND WHY NOW?

A final question: Why is the adjective *Catholic* the right one for this intellectual tradition? For three reasons: one etymological, another ecumenical, the third doctrinal. I have already explained the etymological reason in chapter 4's discussion of the literal meaning of the term *catholic* ("throughout the whole"). This tradition should not find any portion of reality alien to it. The catholicity of the tradition has its origin in the universal drive people have to make sense, to make meaning, to make wholes that would not be unless they birth them. *Catholic* is the right adjective because the contents of this tradition derive from the notion of catholicity in human subjectivities, which is the drive that brings together what is intelligible into wholes.

This line of thinking is particularly relevant to those whose professional responsibility is to understand a particular body of knowledge. If educators are open to the further reaches of meaning that can be achieved through interiority and transcendence—the two realms of meaning that happen to be the least attended to by the present knowledge industry—this augurs well for their achievements being concordant with Catholicism and its Sacred Tradition.

The second reason I favor this adjective is ecumenical, in the sense that many people from many traditions, including some whose transcendental realm of meaning might not be Catholic, contribute to this tradition. It is not the Catholicism of the contributor that is salient (though this would be a plus), it is the value of the wholes attained.

There is a downside to using the descriptor Catholic for this reason, but other adjectives used by those with insights similar to mine do not appeal for several reasons. Each of these other potential descriptors for this tradition—the Wisdom tradition, the Great tradition, or the Christian tradition—conveys some sense of the tradition's essence, but each is also wanting in some way. The hesitation I have with calling it "the Wisdom tradition" is that other traditions also have wisdom. Besides, I am not sure that wisdom is ever a possession, either of a tradition or of a person. It seems more like an asymptote, an ideal, an aspiration. What about calling it "the Great tradition"? Again, this is appropriate to some extent, because of the tradition's duration and value, but it runs the risk of being a bit pretentious. Finally, "the Christian tradition" is very appealing, considering its accuracy and the fact that most Christians share a common belief in the Sacred Tradition; many also share common creeds, belief in the early councils, and reverence for the sacred scripture. Many Catholics have deep religious relationships with their Protestant, Evangelical, and Pentecostal brothers and sisters. Still, this term creates significant problems because of the fissures that have existed and continue to exist between Catholicism and the Eastern churches, and with some of the positions of the Western churches of the Reformation.

So, at the end of the day, "Catholic" seems the most appropriate descriptor for this intellectual tradition, because it includes both Catholicism and the quality of catholicity.[16] The downside of calling this tradition Catholic is that it seems to convey an exclusion of all who are not Catholics. The catholicity that this intellectual tradition seeks and is open to can be less than evident, since the differentiation being made in this volume is seldom articulated elsewhere. This chapter attempts to highlight that differentiation and seeks to exorcise the seeming exclusionary character of this tradition.

But the third and most important reason for sticking with the "Catholic" descriptor for this compound tradition is the Church's doctrine of the nature of Christ, a doctrine to which the majority of Christian churches also subscribe. This doctrine, as I have said earlier, articulates the ontological constitution of the one person of Christ Jesus as the union of two natures, one divine and one human. Again, this definition gives full play both to Jesus's humanity and through it also to the relative self-subsistence and autonomy of the whole created world in all its particularity, vis-à-vis God. That Jesus's humanity is at one and the same time other than God, and also united with his divine nature, is the key to understanding Christianity, and in turn Catholicism, and in turn Catholic schools. This is why Catholicism cannot accept a faith without reasoning or reasoning without faith. There is a direct link between the unique union of the two natures in Christ's person, and the Christian faith's insistence on reason. This is why the Church rejects any kind of integralism that would confuse or conflate divinity with humanity.

This dogma is also a bulwark against a division that would leave Christ's humanity, our humanity, the created world, and all the bodies of knowledge, developed and developing, nomadic. The incarnation of Jesus was, as von Balthasar so beautifully put it, "the gracious descent of God into multiplicity, into the realm of matter, in order to lead what is multiple back into unity . . . [It was] a gesture of the One towards the Many, beckoning it home into the One."[17] The Word's *exitus* from the eternal Trinity was to invite and make possible a *reditus*, the return of all created reality and its productivity to its Creator. The creation of Christ's humanity was to enable a return of all creation to its origin. His emptying of himself of his divinity (Phil. 2:5) is all the more remarkable because it makes possible the return of each of the autonomous particulars he has been given responsibility for bringing back to the One, including the autonomous disciplines.

Both the belief that the universe was created by a Creator and the belief in the incarnation respect the integrity of creation in all its multiplicity, particularity, and otherness with respect to God. On these two beliefs the Catholic intellectual tradition rests. These two beliefs also signal the direction of the fulfillment of creation in all its particularity. That fulfillment takes place through humanity, Christ's as well as our own. Our humanity is at its best when it is lived with and in him in the unity of the Holy Spirit. The return back "home into the One" is not a process of annihilation, but of sublation. This is why the adjective *Catholic* fits this tradition best; not necessarily because of its connection to the Church, but because it connotes the whole connection with human intentionality and with all that was and is and is to be known.

NOTES

1. *Dei verbum* (10), in Abbott, *Documents of Vatican II.*

2. Lonergan, *Method in Theology,* 162.

3. Decree on Ecumenism (11), in Abbott, *Documents of Vatican II.*

4. Newman, "Letter to the Duke of Norfolk" V, 248.

5. Thomas Aquinas, *Summa Theologia,* 1a, q.79, a.13.

6. On this point I recommend four new books: first, *How the Catholic Church Built Western Civilization,* by Woods; and second, Smith's *The Soul of Christianity.* Also, a new edition of what was already considered a classic has just been published: *The Rise of Western Christendom,* by Peter Brown, and finally, *What Is Truth?,* by John Rist.

7. Gleason, *Contending with Modernity,* 317.

8. Cf. Land O'Lakes Conference Statement, available at http://consortium.villanova.edu/excorde/landlake.htm.

9. Buckley, *The Catholic University as Promise and Project,* 5.

10. MacIntyre, *After Virtue,* 81.

11. See appendix B for a prehistory that can account for God's self-communication to primitive peoples.

12. Rahner, *Foundations of Christian Faith,* 147–48.

13. *Gaudium et spes* (36).

14. van Beeck, *Catholic Identity after Vatican II,* 58–59.

15. Lonergan, "Metaphysics as Horizon," in *Collection,* 198.

16. One of the ways this difference is sometimes described is big C and little c. This seems wrongheaded to me since the latter conveys the idea of Catholic "lite."

17. von Balthasar, *Cosmic Liturgy,* 44.

CHAPTER 6

◆

The Catholic Intellectual Tradition: Part II

ALL OF THIS PROMPTS A QUESTION: Who owns the Catholic intellectual tradition? Counterintuitive as it might seem, the Church does not. No one, in fact, owns this tradition. One might say that "God who conducts himself as One who labors" in human intentionality owns it.[1] Those who pursue truth and value, as these disclose themselves in innumerable and always particular ways, are participants in this tradition, albeit usually anonymous ones. This makes membership in this Catholic intellectual tradition very large. By the same token, it can be surprising who is not on the list of participants. This would be those who cannot transcend their prejudices or self-interests or biases. They would not be contributors to this tradition.

To put it another way, where one is seeking out truth and value, one is seeking "being," and if that pursuit is unrestricted and disinterested, one is contributing to this tradition whether one is aware of this or not. Such a person is also on the path to catholicity by reason of his or her openness to being, the good and meaning of which is never reached. It is helpful, of course, if one is able to find in one's journey certain paths that have already been trod in the pursuit of knowing what is or is not so, as well as what has been found by previous generations to be of worth. While some of these well-worn paths have enabled academic sojourners to be integrated and trustworthy in their beliefs, to worship, to express gratitude, and to live with a sense of communion with God, these are not essential prerequisites for availing oneself of or contributing to this intellectual tradition.

The difficulty in attaining an integration in academic pursuits is due in part to the fact that the vast sea of being contains a series of islands or bodies of knowledge, each with the ever-beckoning promise of further intelligibility. Any one of these islands can capture one's attention, leaving one with neither time for nor interest in anything beyond the one atoll on which one finds oneself perched. Any extreme form of specialization can greatly detract from one's other responsibilities and relationships. One of the major assets, therefore, of the Catholic intellectual tradition is that it beckons one to a more holistic anthropology. It has accessed and continues to access realms of meaning other than theory. It is not simply an intellectualist tradition, but one that has been enriched by cultural, philosophical, aesthetical, and

74

spiritual dimensions throughout the course of its long existence, and so has nurtured those who have accessed it in all its dimensions.

Hannah Arendt comes to mind at this point. In *Eichmann in Jerusalem*, Arendt saw something more than Adolf Eichmann's heinous criminality, something more universal: the banality of careerism.[2] The professional, as Eichmann considered himself to be, was so glued to succeeding in his own part of the larger operation that the rightness or wrongness of the ends for which it was operating became the furthest thing from his mind. Granted, this example might be too great a stretch, but anyone in the academic profession knows the pressure of productivity, of publish or perish, of competition for grants. Professors are continually tempted to be so narrow in their purview that there are some similarities here in terms of the professional being pressured to "forget the big picture" and "do your thing." Since education is a good in itself and its ends noble, any comparison to the evil of the Third Reich can seem preposterous. But education's presumptive goodness can keep one from examining and taking responsibility for the many uses to which education is put, some of which are good and some of which are not. The culture of increased specialization can be the mammon of modern academe. It can even bring one to despise faith (Matt. 6:24).

LOCATING THE CATHOLIC INTELLECTUAL TRADITION

It is not easy to locate the Catholic intellectual tradition because it is not in one place and it is not in one mind. Nor is there a list of its members. It cannot be found all wrapped up neatly in a tome, or even in the ecclesial instrumentality called the magisterium. Rather, this tradition consists in the totality of all those instances in which a higher viewpoint has been sought and achieved, either by those who identify themselves with the Sacred Tradition or by those who don't, but whose higher viewpoint has been appropriated by the Church. This tradition is formed by all those who have been prompted to seek an intelligible whole and have succeeded in doing so, who have connected dots that had not been connected.

Successive higher viewpoints have been accumulating in the course of the Church's history. The result is "the Christian tradition (which) makes explicit our implicit intending of God in all our intending."[3] In the classical period of Catholic thinking, these higher viewpoints were developed largely deductively from the Sacred Tradition, or were at least in some way directly beholden to this tradition. But especially since the Renaissance and up to the present, the growth of the Catholic intellectual tradition has paralleled and benefitted from the growth of secularity and subjectivity, in the positive sense of both these terms. This growth has been so characterized by pluralism that it is now difficult to imagine the Catholic intellectual tradition, since within its boundaries there are competing and legitimate positions on a number of questions. What gives this tradition a unity, then? More and more, it is the method by which one arrives at one's findings. Bernard Lonergan has been a big help in this development, in Catholic circles and beyond. Consequently, many can now subscribe to the idea that "the potential totality of all viewpoints lies in the dynamic structure of cognitional activity."[4] It is this focus that generates so much more energy in what I have called in chapter 4 "the heuristic notion of catholicity." The source of the energy is the dynamic structure of its cognitional activity. When inquiry is pursued through the invariant operations of consciousness, the future prospects of a trustworthy Catholic intellectual tradition are very promising. Ironically, it is insight into the potential catholicity of subjectivity that gives us a way of understanding and getting our bearings in the face of a pluralism that can otherwise be overwhelming. Conversely, specializations seem to be imitating the antigravity forces we are learning about in the cosmos, which push each planet and galaxy further and further away from each other in an ever-expanding universe.

What it has going for it is another topic. Each of us is responsible for this wealth of our subjectivity, but it can be dry-gulched. I repeat Aquinas's insight here: "The expert orders everything within a restricted domain; the wise man orders everything!"[5] This does not mean that the wise know everything, but that there is an order to what they know. This is in contrast to the experts who might have a well-ordered grasp of their field, but be unwhole or without order in other parts of their lives. One of the benefits of a religious perspective is that people's faith usually enables them to sublate other parts of their lives into the realm of transcendent meaning to which their religion draws them. Bodies of knowledge do not make a person whole. A disordered commitment to mastery of a body of knowledge can be a tragedy both to the one so committed and to those who depend on him or her.

To stay with Catholicism here, one can ask what societal results this compound tradition, with its sacred and its intellectual components, has produced. Where and insofar as authentic subjectivity is operating in those who subscribe to it, this tradition will have increased objectivity and knowledge, and, when this knowledge is acted on, greater goodness. Social progress depends on right judgments and meaningful human cooperation. But progress is unlikely without a tradition as a starting point. In the absence of traditions and of attention to the operations of one's own intentionality, social decline is inevitable; the goods of order and value either are not known or, if known, are not sought. Instances of inauthenticity and hence of decline are all too evident in society at present. St. Paul named the social consequences of inauthenticity, which he called the works of the flesh: "immorality, impurity, licentiousness, idolatry, sorcery, hatreds, rivalry, jealousy, outbursts of fury, acts of selfishness, [and] dissensions" (Gal. 5:19–20).

But a tradition is only as good as its continuous appropriation in the present of that which has been verified as authentic in the past. One has to admit also that authenticity, whether personal, collective, or ecclesial, is fragile. A tradition itself can be inauthentic in three ways. The first is reductionism, in which part of reality is factored out, while what is left purports to be a coherent whole. The second form of inauthenticity is similar: Having been satisfied with the moment of wholeness it has arrived at, the tradition disallows any further development. Stuck in a moment in time and incapable of self-correction or of expanding its horizon, it becomes a museum piece. The third kind of inauthenticity is an aggregation of discontinuities that merely poses as a cohering tradition.

There are many intellectual traditions, of course. Catholicism does not hold a monopoly on that genre by any means. What it does have is a founder whose life and message have attracted the allegiance of multitudes for centuries. It has a narrative that innumerable believers have adopted as the overarching narrative of their own lives. In this, the Catholic tradition is remarkable. What is also remarkable is the intellectual tradition that has developed alongside this narrative all through its history. This intellectual tradition is pluriform: It both informs and is informed by many bodies of knowledge. Think of law, politics, economics, the humanities, the sciences. Throughout its history, the Catholic intellectual tradition has also been a forum to which conflicting viewpoints have been brought, where ongoing arguments about different understandings of the true and the good have been heard and weighed, including arguments about the Church's own truth claims and understandings of its mission in the world. One does not easily or cheaply arrive at this synthesis of knowledge, especially because there is also a doctrinal tradition that must give its approval.

One has to approach this compound tradition, like any other tradition, with a hermeneutic of circumspection, since it has often been wrong about a given matter. Think of how blind this tradition has been and still is to sexism, to cite just one example. In fact, on many more occasions than we would like to admit, there has been an anti-intellectual element operative in the Church's use of this compound tradition. This is in part due to its being embedded in history. It is also due to the somewhat inevitable hubris of being in the image of a teacher without *pari passu* being a learner. All too often, there has been a denigration of the human dignity of, and even violence done to, those who did not conform to Catholicism's official teachings in their day.

The Catholic Church has had too many anti-intellectual moments when the truth was ignored, or those committed to it were run out of town, so to speak, or worse. It took four hundred years before Galileo was given his due. And, of course, some of the greatest figures of the Catholic intellectual tradition shared the biases of their day (think, for example, of Aquinas's views on women). In fact, all who contributed to this tradition in the past were naturally limited by their cultural and historical contexts, as all are. One thinks of Leo XIII, with his wonderful contribution to Catholic social thought and development of social questions on one hand, and, on the other hand, his slamming of the door on Catholic scriptural scholarship. It took fifty more years before Pius XII could pry this door back open.

But by that same token, we must also employ a hermeneutic of appreciation in regard to this compound tradition, given its singular antiquity, as well as the frequency with which it has been able to sort through the inadequacies of partial viewpoints, its own and others', and arrive at fuller ones. One thinks, for example, of Catholic relations with Judaism before Vatican II and subsequent to that seminal event. This is an example of a higher viewpoint being achieved through a group experiencing an intellectual conversion, beginning with John XXIII.[6] The Council fathers' openness allowed them to recognize their own biases and misreadings of the sacred texts and the Church's resultant anti-Semitism. The subsequent repentance by the official Church of the indignities to which Jews had been subjected for centuries was long overdue, but it did come.

What is also notable about Catholicism is its long engagement with questions about the true and the good. Because its compound tradition is itself a dialectic, Catholics have generally been open to its verifiable insights that come from its intellectual tradition. Throughout its centuries-long history, its responsibility has been to discern "whatever is true, whatever is honorable, whatever is just, whatever is pure, whatever is lovely, whatever is gracious . . . anything worthy of praise" (Phil. 4:8–9). Even the briefest overview of this history cannot overlook the tradition's successes in meeting this challenge. Think of the patristic era, when the tradition took on considerable theological depth. Add to that the scholastic period, in which Aristotle's work was revisited and its parameters widened, and the Enlightenment era, when the tradition's preferential option for conceptualism was exposed and superceded, to some extent at least. Think, too, of the Catholic Renaissance of the nineteenth and twentieth centuries, when the Church began to give modernity its due, and to articulate a social tradition with useful principles for making judgments on economics, labor, capital, and war. One could continue this appreciation with the conciliar event in the middle of the last century, when new voices from around the globe challenged the Church's Eurocentrism. With that Council, the Church entered into a period of rich interaction with other faiths and their intellectual traditions (or at least it started to, until a more consolidationist leadership felt the need to tighten things up).

Underlying both this and the previous chapter is the tension in this tradition between Catholicism and catholicity. The latter is the drive that seeks to make wholes; the former is the faith that seeks to tell and celebrate a continually updated story about the relation between God and human beings. This tension exists, in part, because of the Catholic Church's history of anti-intellectualism, which has made the Church at times wary of giving free rein to this drive for catholicity among its members. Thus it has sometimes failed to accept the wealth of subjectivity that its members could provide the Church. This failure is also due in part to the underdeveloped doctrine of the eschatological character of the mark of catholic, as has been said already.

But Catholics themselves need to locate their own failures of catholicity, not only those of Catholic institutions and Church authorities. By not bringing about the wholes to which our drive for catholicity leads us, we have been guilty of varying degrees of neglect. Members of the academic community who cannot seem to find the dots that connect their faith to their work would be counted in this number. Those who cannot make such connections fail to bear witness to their faith; they do not demonstrate how faith can help us to make wholes where they are needed, in academe. Objectivity in research is one ideal, but so is the integration of parts of one's life into a whole, so that others may see the value of faith. This approach puts a share of responsibility for the tradition on the shoulders of all who claim to have inherited it, in whatever degree. The gift of faith is also a challenge that falls on all who identify themselves with this Church. It is beautiful to find colleagues of other faiths bearing clear witness to their faiths. It can also be disconcerting to find an absence of clear witness where one would expect it, in institutions conducted in the name of Catholicism.

I have stayed at a level of abstraction from particular teachings and particular historical moments in the history of the Church in order to elaborate on my understanding of the Catholic intellectual tradition and the challenge of catholicity. The Sacred Tradition of Catholicism still supplies many with the transcendent horizon of meaning within which they live and trust in God and identify themselves as Catholic. A list of those who have also successfully and publicly lived the challenge of catholicity would be too long to make. In my own lifetime, some who have embodied catholicity for me have been Flannery O'Connor, Dorothy Day, Norris Clarke, Alasdair MacIntyre, Thomas Merton, Thomas Berry, Charles Taylor, Robert Shuman, Monika Hellwig, Abraham Joshua Heschel, Marc Tannenbaum, Said Nursi, and Fethullah Gulen. The last four are not Christians. These are a few of the more public names that spring to mind immediately, but there is a longer list of less well-known folk who have more intimately embodied the catholicity I have been trying to describe in this manuscript.

It can be difficult, however, to find this Catholic intellectual tradition operating explicitly on the ground in Catholic institutions of higher education. So why put in the effort at naming it? Because it is there and needs to be recognized in the understanding this volume has attempted to articulate. The dynamism of catholicity is what has fed and is still feeding this intellectual tradition, and given it its incomparability, its values, its age, its malleability, its potential, its authority, its singularity, its dynamism, its optimism, its rationality, its corrigibility.

THE SPIRITUALITY LATENT IN COGNITION

We can understand the intellectual component of this compound tradition more clearly if we can appreciate how knowledge itself comes about. Our consciousness is something that is untethered, always moving, constantly questioning, and usually finding answers to its always very particular questions. We spend our whole lives pursuing knowledge of reality, trying to determine what is so and what is worth pursuing and committing oneself to; so we are always moving to *become* rather than just *be*. That's the good news. But consciousness can also be scattered, inconsistent, impulsive, vacant, lazy, indecisive, a skimmer of much and a knower of little.

Lonergan's insights into the process of how knowledge comes about are helpful because, like it or not, the operations of our consciousness are always in play, so the more explicit we are about them, the better. Hence, experience differs from understanding, and understanding from judging, and judging from deliberating about one's subsequent actions and choices. Lonergan also differentiates between deliberations done from love and those done without love. He stresses the importance of attention to all of this, since we too easily ignore our subjectivity and interiority by focusing solely on objects.

By paying explicit attention to our interiority, we can come to appreciate the spirituality latent in human cognition. We can notice how insights emerge and, if verified, supply light to our understandings. This light is my soul in action. As I noted in chapter 4, the Catholic intellectual tradition would say it ultimately traces its power and efficacy to "the *prima lux*, which is God."[7] It is by understanding our own understandings that we should be able to see how they are representative of our "transcendence-in-immanence." We might even be able to understand this thing we call understanding as deeply as Aquinas did. He claimed that the intellectual light that we attain to is nothing less than a participation in the light that emanates from God. This can be a priceless insight into ourselves and our colleagues. Otherwise we can be blind to the spiritual character of thinking itself.[8] In the same vein, Pope John Paul II contended that every judgment that attains objectivity can be seen as having its origin in the Spirit. "All truth, from whatever voice it might derive, comes from the Holy Spirit" (*Omne verum, a quocumque dicatur a Spirito Sancto est*).[9] In this claim, John Paul was not original. The idea has a long history.[10]

If one were able to step back from each instance of one's mind trying to know this thing or that thing, one might be able to catch a glimpse of the intellect's penchant for infinity, its ability to become and know everything. The fact is that we are *capax infiniti*, capable of infinity, a Latin phrase that captures well our human dignity and human striving. We are hardwired to know being and to be in communion with being, the whole of being. But once we have a sense of the unlimited horizon of our minds, we should be able to appreciate the limitlessness of our capacities for knowing, while simultaneously realizing how little we know. We begin to see how easily, as classical thought put it, our knowing is always reaching out to be in communion with the Being whose being is to be. Here I am indebted to Ignatius's insight into the spirituality of cognition. Ignatius saw God "as conducting himself as one who labors" in our cognitional operations, and believed that this assistance could be discerned in the simple, everyday process of coming to knowledge.[11]

Lonergan's description of knowledge as a compound act is also relevant to the question of the spirituality latent in cognition. To minds confined to the more empirical, determinate categories of their fields, this line of thinking is sheer nonsense. It is this kind of confinement of their horizons that keeps many academics from seeing the dignity of their work of understanding, and its connection to the *prima lux* in which their thinking participates. I do not know if there ever was a university that was collectively made aware of the nexus between the endeavors of its personnel and the divine source of the light they indefatigably seek. For such a place to exist, its personnel would have to be able to recognize the transcendental character of the mind, even as it pours over the categorical data that can be all-consuming.

Every quest for the intelligible begins with questions—small questions, big questions, questions put to me by others, questions I put to myself. The mind is always moving from what is already known to the next unknown. It is also unlikely to be satisfied with disjoined knowledge; rather, the mind always seeks to integrate the disparate, to make meaning, to achieve a sense of the whole. It is the notion of catholicity that drives this dynamism in human consciousness. But it is not only the disparate pieces of information that one's consciousness tries to join into wholes; the different elements of one's life also need to be integrated. One can always settle for the partial, and try to make it satisfy for the whole. The movement, in this case, is towards idolatry.

One can, of course, disengage from the drive for fuller intelligibility by simply not pursuing further questions. The effects of not pursuing one's questions are multiple. Chief among them is ignorance, but cynicism, skepticism, relativism, and fundamentalism are also possible results. Within Catholicism, there are not a few who live with certainties that they have never bothered to examine critically. As a result of numbing their intelligence, such Catholics can have their own "isms," such as fideism, integralism, or magisterial fundamentalism, among others, all of which represent flights from understanding.

Obviously, minds can be open or shut. Less apparent but more ubiquitous are minds that are open, but only up to a certain point, and then shut to everything beyond there. In a university context, what would explain a mind that was totally open to "being" in one part of reality and completely closed to anything beyond that limited field? The most likely explanation is not ignorance but bias, with the partially closed mind habitually obeying whatever bias keeps him or her from exploring new questions. Without inference from bias, intelligence will be open to finding anything, without limits or conditions. The university, which is presumed to be an instrument of human progress, can be an instrument of social decline, if stunted, stymied, or numbed by biases. If "intelligence is a principle of universalization and of ultimate synthesis"—and this is one of Lonergan's central claims—then anything that impedes questions will be a source of fragmentation and incoherence for persons and communities.[12] While moral failures abound in our world, failures of understanding are much more ubiquitous and much less obvious. Like the biases that are so often their cause, these abdications of our responsibility to understand can be very hard to detect.

Since biases are so common and can have such a drastic negative impact on personal and social well-being, it is worthwhile to consider them in some detail here. Biases can be hard to detect because they are usually widespread and of long duration. They deeply affect one's insight, outlook, and desires. Lonergan finds evidence of four kinds of bias. Take dramatic bias, for example, in which one withdraws "from the outer drama of human living into the inner drama of fantasy."[13] This results in blind spots, not consciously chosen, but which radically affect one's reasoning, choices and immediate relationships. A second kind of bias can come from egoism: This bias is impetuously self-centered, leaving one's intelligence preoccupied with one's own small world. The bias of egoism prevents the mind from posing the further questions it would naturally pose if one were not mired in oneself. I think of Jesus's story about the man with the bumper crop of grain, which illustrates both of these biases. The man ends up a "fool" because he is so completely self-referential: What shall I do with my harvest? I shall put all my grain and my goods into my larger grain bins. "Then I will say to myself: You have blessings in reserve for years to come. Relax, enjoy yourself" (Luke 12:16–21). God asks him to whom the silos of grain will go, because on that very night "[his] life will be required of [him]."

A bias that occurs in the university setting more frequently than do the first two is the bias of the group, or group egoism. With group bias, the use of intelligence is yoked to the ethos and interests of the group with which one identifies. "Just as the individual egoist puts further questions up to a point but desists before reaching conclusions incompatible with his egoism, so also the group is prone to have a blind spot for the insight that would reveal its well-being to be excessive."[14] Finally, there is the subtlest of the four, the general bias of common sense, which we will examine shortly. Suffice it to say here that this bias is "a specialization of intelligence in the particular and concrete, but usually considers itself omnicompetent."[15] Competence in the categories of one's field will not produce the hubris of omnicompetence if one's mind is open to the classical transcendentals of truth, goodness, and beauty.

THE REALMS OF MEANING

If the Church is truly to be in the world and at the service of the world, in particular the university world, then their university's personnel must play the role of frontiers-people and mediators between their areas of competence and the Catholic intellectual tradition. Since they do not tend to see their work in relation to this tradition, a large part of the potential meaning of their work is lost on faculty. There seem to be three reasons for this ignorance of the tradition. The first is that this connection is seldom if ever made, so the faculties at such institutions remain distant from seeing their work in any relation to Catholicism and its intellectual tradition. The second reason is more historical. All too often, as we have seen, in the centuries leading up to the Second Vatican Council, Catholicism has been defensive, and hence not formally committed to being at the service of the world as such. So Catholic university personnel were largely indifferent to seeing their work in terms of the Church's relation to and commitment to the world as such. The third reason is the ethos of political correctness that typifies much of modern academe. Consequently, it is politically disadvantageous for the professor to have allegiances to anything that is not within the purview of the particular guild of which he or she is a part. Political correctness in a university is a subtle but pervasive matter.[16]

Insofar as the Church's leadership has been myopic, its members have been myopic, and it has prospered when its leaders have enlarged their horizons. One of the ways that individuals and institutions enlarge their horizons is by engaging with urgent human issues. Academics are uniquely equipped to be of service to the world by addressing these pressing needs. When they do, the world, the Church and they themselves benefit.

Just as the doctrinal and intellectual traditions of Catholicism need each other, so the Church's intellectual tradition needs the deep probes made continually by the research of academics. Bodies of knowledge are intrinsic to the universe of being and are thus inextricably linked to the Creator of being. But the bodies of knowledge that are themselves in a continuum with this intellectual tradition, which has been developing insight into the human condition for centuries, can add depth to that tradition. Faith and reason are not in competition with one another, since their respective approaches to the same reality have the same Source; hence, we should expect to find that their insights are complementary and that the world's needs are served by this complementarity.

Since so few academics know that there is such a thing as a Catholic intellectual tradition, there will not be any engagement between this tradition and the various disciplines as long as the differentiation being made in this text remains unknown. Maybe one way of interesting an academic to consider this tradition is to show how each discipline is a kind of a pilgrimage; the discipline goes wherever its data leads it. The Catholic intellectual tradition, too, has been journeying, but all too often on a path that is parallel to or at a distance from the disciplines. Both are pilgrims who, like Abraham, are called from where they have settled to seek "a city with foundations whose architect and maker is God" (Heb. 11:10).

If we take the time to notice, we might be able to see that it is our questioning that reveals our orientation to the divine. It would seem narrow-minded for those who work in the knowledge industry today to ignore the huge numbers of those who preceded them, who have formed and been guided by intellectual traditions that have also been on the same meaning-seeking journey.

All intellectual traditions have plenty of common sense and theory, but the Catholic intellectual tradition is, I believe, singular in the university world for its openness to and nurturing of two additional realms of meaning: interiority and transcendence. Interiority is the locus in which the self, with its judgments, decisions, and actions, is always in the process of becoming. The major enemy of any intellectual tradition has always been an inattention to interiority, or to be more specific, to the operations of consciousness, experience, understanding, and judgment of its adherents.

Since the advent of scientific rationality, objectivity has been prized, and rightly so, but subjectivity has all too often been taken for granted. The most important route to objectivity, besides the data being plumbed, is the operations of consciousness that bring subjectivity to objectivity. It is through attention to interiority that an inner word can be heard, that an answer can be attained, that the Spirit of truth can renew persons, and in turn the world. The ways in which interiority can be neglected are too numerous to count. It is easily sidetracked by anxiety, carelessness, or any of the biases that obstruct the path to objectivity. Interiority is ambushed by "the capital sins": pride, anger, gluttony, lust, envy, sloth, and covetousness. One who is inattentive to his or her interiority will always be a sucker for an apparent good rather than a real one.

Educating the whole person, the most frequent boast of the university world, would seem to require a systematic and programmatic attention to the four realms of meaning: common sense, theory, interiority, and transcendence. Common sense and theory are the bread and butter of any school, so they don't require any commentary. But understanding of the education of the whole person would require faculty and administrators to care for students' own unique interiorities, by teaching and modeling what it means to be attentive, intelligent, reasonable, and responsible. To perform these functions, a faculty member would have to be versed in plumbing his or her own interiority, with its insatiable desire for answers about the meaning of the true and the good. Secular universities tend to see their responsibility for the realm of interiority solely in terms of encouraging critical thinking, and stop there.

The contents of the realm of transcendent meaning, the fourth realm of meaning, differ with different individuals. One constant in the realm of transcendent meaning will be some account of the true and the good, from which the person's moral agency develops. This realm of meaning usually has its origin in the person's religious upbringing. Since there are many religions and ways of life, the content of the realm of transcendent meaning is pluriform. There was a time when the non-Christian religions were considered missionary territory for Christians. Many Christians assumed that the coming of Christ would either replace these or eventually prove to be their fulfillment.

With Catholicism's maturation, the Church has come to accept that there are other ways of understanding the transcendent realm of meaning. It has learned to be respectful of other faith narratives, since these supply the contents of transcendent meaning for their faithful adherents. This new openness is both an opportunity and a challenge to Catholic education. The challenge is to make a home for all faiths in its schools, while giving a priority to its own faith contents. The opportunity is to respect the transcendent realm of meaning of faiths other than its own.

There have been so many transmogrifications in the world's intellectual and religious cultural history in the past couple hundred years that it can be difficult to recognize the presence of a distinct intellectual tradition. In the case of the Catholic intellectual tradition, there are three cognitional moves made in the course of its admittedly jagged history that have enabled it to remain, to some degree, coherent. These are openness, sublation, and self-correction. I have discussed personal openness in the third chapter; what I would like to add here is openness collectively seen as a fact, an achievement, and a gift. Sublation has been central to this intellectual tradition's history because of its conviction that no dichotomy should be made between the knowledge attained by faith and the knowledge attained by right reasoning. Sublation leaves the latter in its own rightful order and autonomy, so that its appropriation by the tradition is not an expropriation of the knowledge in question. Hence, this tradition has a history of taking in and making room for the verifiable knowledge that continues to enlighten it. The tradition has grown with the growth of human consciousness; it has also had to be self-correcting, since its history has paralleled the ignorance and errors of human history.

THE MISSIOLOGY OF THIS INTELLECTUAL TRADITION

To repeat myself, I am talking about a compound tradition that needs to be differentiated in order to be effective in its service to the modern world, and to the disciplines in particular. There is a unity-in-difference between the Sacred Tradition and the Catholic intellectual tradition; though distinguished, they cannot be separated. And while they exist in a reciprocal and interdependent relationship, the Sacred Tradition does not have the same function or mission as the intellectual tradition.

The mission of the Sacred Tradition is to enable believers and would-be believers to inhabit the story of the faith. Conversely, the Catholic intellectual tradition's mission is to enable and encourage scholarship, especially the scholarship that would make the Sacred Tradition's outreach to contemporary people and cultures more intelligent and more credible. One way it can do this is to ensure that Catholic schools are open to giving attention to the four realms of meaning, particularly the realms of interiority and transcendence.

Another aspect of the intellectual tradition's mission is to ensure that the notion of catholicity be given full play, so that its concretizations keep producing higher viewpoints. One attains a higher viewpoint when one has an insight into an aggregate of insights, and with an organizing act of intelligence brings the aggregate together into a new unity and framework. In the process, dots are connected and a new whole is attained. The measure of success of the Catholic intellectual tradition will be a citizenry whose authentic subjectivity seeks out higher viewpoints and greater objectivity in service to the world.

Probably the most immediate threat to the integrity of contemporary Catholic higher education—or any higher education for that matter—is not secularism or anti-Catholicism, but the reduction of the purposes of learning to earning. Thus, universities need to teach their students about the full scope of learning, the expansiveness of its purpose and meaning. The tendency to reduce higher education to a preparation for employment springs from the bias of common sense, which has a tight grip on contemporary imaginations. Common sense as such, of course, is indispensable, as a source of both meaning and answers to practical questions. While we all use and benefit from the meanings that common sense brings to the practicalities of everyday life, common sense can also be accompanied by a bias toward practicality and utility, and an impatience for results. Such a bias doesn't have time for theory, wonder, or interest in the world of notions or of transcendence. Hence, it does not have time for knowledge for its own sake, or for relishing learning in and of itself. The crudest form of the bias of common sense is the saying that "Time is money."

Even academics can exhibit the bias of common sense, as when they have too great an interest in knowledge focused on publication, so that they are willing to settle for premature findings, just to have something to show for their research. Among the symptoms of this bias is a preoccupation with personal advancement, or with the need to impress one's readers, classes, administrators, or colleagues.

Common sense, though indispensable, is only one realm of meaning. If a university is to educate a whole person, it must promote the three other realms of meaning. The Catholic intellectual tradition encourages minds to forage in all realms of meaning—theory certainly, but also transcendence and interiority. The scope of this tradition facilitates the development of an ability to access all four of these. Otherwise, the bias of common sense can have a school and its students, howsoever unwittingly, settle for being consumers of knowledge who are satisfied by accessing, gathering, and commodifying information. Common sense of itself sees thinking pragmatically and knowledge in terms of power. The knowledge industry is reduced to a function of accruing more and more useful information. The antithesis of this reductionism of knowledge has been well articulated by the Council in *Gaudium et spes*: "The human spirit must be cultivated in such a way that there results a growth in its ability to wonder, to understand, to contemplate, to make personal judgments, and to develop a religious, moral and social sense" (59).

The Catholic intellectual tradition is voracious for adding to the body of knowledge that must grow in the world for the world's well-being. There are two groups who are unlikely to be contributing to this body of knowledge. First are those who are overly wedded to an already-defined past, one they want to retrieve and preserve. Second are the "neophiliacs," those who chase the ever-changing intellectual or social fads whose primary allure is that they are new. Lonergan wisely foresees a split of knowledge seekers into three different camps, the two largest I have just described. Members of the third camp, "a perhaps not numerous center[,] are at home in both the old and the new, painstaking enough to work out one by one the transitions to be made, strong enough to refuse half measures and insist on complete solutions even though it has to wait."[17] It is this third group, this not very numerous center, from which this body of knowledge will emerge. Its existence will be both formed by the Catholic intellectual tradition and, though usually unknowingly, informing it.

One of the tasks of this third "perhaps not numerous" population is to develop or appropriate insights born of authentic subjectivity and its resultant objectivities. These insights are to be used to break the vicious cycles of the illusions that hold the larger community hostage to common sense biases and the tyranny of the status quo.[18] The most knowledgeable members of this body take all four realms of meaning into account, and allow for plural forms of transcendent meaning. They model what it means to plumb one's own interiority as a realm of meaning. They know how to be attuned to the inner word that judgment can verify, that conscience can command, and that prayer can attain.

It must be admitted that all too often, the Church has seen its positions confronted by insights born of good scholarship, and yet remained unmoved. There is a peculiar kind of Catholic common sense bias that has been bred into this Church throughout its history. If it could speak explicitly, this bias would be ashamed to say something like: "Since we already possess the truth, we have nothing to learn that would change what we already know." This bias is particularly defensive about the realm of theory. The Catholic intellectual tradition, which opts to be open to all four realms, is continually learning from two orders of knowledge that are distinct, namely faith and reason. Since it is a learning tradition, it fully expects that the humanities and the sciences should use their own principles and their own proper methods to develop their bodies of knowledge, as it affirms the legitimate autonomy of human culture and the sciences.

Each of us can make our own tallies from our own experiences of people who were "painstaking enough to work out one by one the transitions to be made, strong enough to refuse half measures" and who insisted on "complete solutions even though [they have] to wait." One need not be dreaming about a golden past or a utopian future to see this body of knowledge, needed for the world's well-being, growing today. Where it is, and where those participating in the process identify with the Sacred Tradition, there the Catholic intellectual tradition is developing a trove of meanings invaluable for the world. Where authentic subjectivity is producing objective judgments and right reasoning and making them accessible to the world and the Church, the Catholic intellectual tradition grows by appropriating these judgments into the frame of reference that is faith. This process is going on with regularity even though most of those who are contributing to this intellectual tradition are unaware of doing so.

NOTES

1. Puhl, ed., *The Spiritual Exercises of St. Ignatius*, #233, 203.
2. Arendt, *Eichmann in Jerusalem*.
3. Morelli and Morelli, eds. *The Lonergan Reader*.
4. Lonergan, *Insight*, 591.
5. Lonergan, "Metaphysics as Horizon," in *Collection*, 198.
6. Alberigo and Komonchak, *History of Vatican II*, vol. 1, 395–97.
7. Lonergan, *Verbum*, 92.
8. Lonergan, *Insight*, 591.
9. Pope John Paul II, *Fides et ratio* (44), in *Origins*, October 22, 1998.
10. Pope Paul VI, Pope Leo XIII, Aquinas. All these references are in *Fides et ratio* (44), nn. 48–52.
11. See appendix A.
12. Lonergan, *Insight*, 245.
13. Ibid., 214.
14. Lonergan, *Method in Theology*, 133.
15. Ibid., 231.
16. Kronman, *Education's End*.
17. Lonergan, "Dimensions of Meaning," in *Collection*, 245.
18. Morelli and Morelli, eds., "Common Sense as Object," in *The Lonergan Reader*, 149.

CHAPTER 7

◆

An Invitation

GEORGETOWN WAS THE first institution of Catholic higher education in America. It was founded in 1789, so this year marks its 220th anniversary. This chapter is intended as a commemoration not primarily of Georgetown, but of Catholic higher education in this country. First, a generic description follows of the Catholic intellectual tradition, which is at the core of American Catholic higher education.

Dimensions of the Catholic Intellectual Tradition

(a) As a **faith** tradition, it is as strong as its adherents' exercise of the gifts of faith, hope, and love. Without these, there would be no intellectual tradition, in fact, no Church.

(b) As a **doctrinal** tradition, its texts are forged with the help of other intellectual traditions, initially and most notably those that grew out of the faith of the Jewish people.

(c) As a **theological** tradition, its contents are always developing. New understandings can deepen those already in place or misinterpret them. Theology can inform the magisterium or irritate it.

(d) As a **learning** tradition, it can learn from anyone, but especially from the academy. No discipline is alien or irrelevant to it. This tradition carries on an ongoing argument about the true and the good.

(e) As a **multicultural** tradition, its richness is in proportion to its appropriation of the distinctive gifts of many cultures—some literary, some liturgical, some artistic, some anthropological, etc.

(f) As a **self-correcting** tradition, it can revise its understandings in light of new evidence of their present limitations; however, it is also a continuous tradition, and is not blown off-course by the winds of change.

(g) As a **teleological** tradition, it knows that there is an end to which all its learning is tending. It anticipates a time when three "things" will last: faith, hope, and love, and the greatest of these is love.

(h) As a **moral tradition,** it is continually adding insights to its body of social thought on such topics as the economy, peace, labor, rights and responsibilities, the common good, and the family.

(i) As a tradition of **hospitality,** it seems to be unparalleled in its willingness and ability to host otherness. This quality means that its schools should be able to be a home for all faiths.

(j) As an **aesthetic** tradition, it seeks to convey the beauty of the realm of the divine, thus complementing its emphasis on truth and reason with an intuitive grasp of the whole.

(k) As **historical**, it grows as human knowledge grows, yet has a memory useful for people and communities that recalls its right choices, leading to the good of order and the good of values.

(l) As a **normative** tradition, it is anchored in faith's insight that Jesus can be a source of union between faith and reason because he is consubstantial with both God and our humanity.

The Catholic intellectual tradition at a university is nurtured by those who are committed, in both their research and teaching, to competence in their disciplines, right reasoning, objectivity, and the common good. What is it that makes this tradition Catholic, if it is being produced by so many, both Catholics and non-Catholics alike? It is Catholic in that the contributions of both inform and can be appropriated by the tradition, howsoever slowly. Furthermore, the party responsible for the transmission of this intellectual tradition into its own teachings is finally the Church, which becomes the patron, protector, and promoter of what it believes and learns. So, this tradition both feeds and is fed by the world of understanding. It owes to the next generation a more authentic version of the contents it has inherited, rather than an uncritical reception of the same. Though it is helpful when the academics contributing to this tradition are themselves followers of Christ, their intellectual self-transcendence is the *sine qua non* of the value of their contributions.

Given this description, the tone of this chapter will be invitational, not didactic. A college or university might use the material in this volume, maybe this chapter in particular, to examine whether such a thing as this intellectual tradition is operating on their campus. This chapter could be an invitation to create a symposium in which members of the faculty are asked: Does the way you go about conceiving your classes, syllabi, and research connect with the Catholic intellectual tradition's ways of linking reason to faith?

The context of the question should be obvious. As educational institutions, these colleges and universities must honor academic freedom. This means that Catholicism cannot predetermine the school's academic offerings. Further, it is no longer required that the professoriate on these campuses be Catholic. Consequently, there is a diffuse understanding of the relationship between Catholicism and its institutions of higher education.

This subject has been addressed authoritatively by Pope John Paul II in his 1990 Apostolic Constitution, *Ex corde ecclesiae*; this document will be commented on in chapter 10. But, rather than settling the question, the processes for the document's implementation only added to the tensions between these schools and the Church. These institutions are necessarily in competition both with their secular counterparts and with one another. Some have chosen to be competitive by stressing the Catholic side of the dialectic. Others have chosen to be competitive by stressing the academic side. It would be a happy institution that could maintain a creative tension between these two, but alas, that has not always proven easy.

What follows is a more detailed description of how this tradition might be understood operationally by faculty who ply their knowledge trade in Catholic colleges and universities.

TWO PICTURES

It is devilishly difficult to picture the Catholic intellectual tradition, and rightly so, since its scope takes in the intelligible universe. So, rather than attempt to define and therefore confine it, I will make use of two symbols taken from the scriptures to give a descriptive understanding of how one might see one's academic tasks in relation to it. The first symbol is one of Jesus's parables about the reign of God. The second symbol is Ezekiel's allegorical vision about the water that flows out from underneath the temple.

The parable that supplies a helpful image of how faculty might be able to see themselves and their work likens the reign of God to "the yeast that a woman took and mixed with three measures of dough until the whole batch was leavened" (Matt. 13:33). Jesus inherited the symbol of the coming reign of God from his Jewish faith, but he envisioned it as breaking in to the present. So for Jesus this reign was both present and awaited. The woman in the parable kneads yeast into three measures of dough, which exegetes tell us would produce a quantity big enough to feed one hundred people. What does this have to do with Catholic higher education? I imagine the dough as the different disciplines. The yeast is the methods the disciplines use on their data. The result is bread for those whom faculty members feed with their scholarship and teaching. Dough that is unleavened, by way of contrast, is flat, stale, and unprofitable for those hungry for meaning. If the horizon within which we do our work were seen in terms of the reign of God, it might be able to be enfolded within the transcendent heuristic of the final times. The reign of God was Jesus's horizon, and he proclaimed it as something that was both beyond and within, present and still to come, but human beings figure in the mediation of it, whether they know it or not!

Every discipline has a tradition of inquiry; some of these are of recent vintage, some of long duration. The various disciplines can connect to the Catholic intellectual tradition through the work of academics. So the first thing to examine is the nature of this yeast that makes the dough rise. In the course of this inquiry we will address the Catholic intellectual tradition's connection to the work of academics, and from there, the mission of the Catholic intellectual tradition in the knowledge industry at large.

What are the contents of the yeast that gets kneaded into the dough of a school's disciplines? For starters, the methods used by various disciplines. Second, the particular insights individuals take to the data of their disciplines. Academics knead their particular insights into their disciplines through their teaching and research, so that these might shape the discipline. It is insight that leavens the disciplines. "Inquiry through insight issues forth in thought that when scrutinized, becomes formulated in definitions, postulates, suppositions, hypotheses, theories."[1] Scholarship seeks to advance the discipline, to go beyond its current state, "but though it goes beyond, it does not leave behind (what is already known); it goes beyond to add, and when it has added, it unites."[2] This is how the dough rises, little by little. Successful scholarship is necessarily self-transcending. Citing Lonergan again, "the possibility of human knowing is an unrestricted intention that intends the transcendent, and a process of self-transcendence that reaches it."[3]

With regard to the Catholic intellectual tradition, the temptation that has to be stared down and avoided is to ignore method, and to look instead for contents that have already been established, on the assumption that to be faithful to this tradition, one's findings must somehow or other be isomorphic with or deduced from contents already arrived at by this tradition. But this tradition's interest is the horizon within which knowledge accrues. Yes, the Catholic intellectual tradition is a distinct tradition with distinct contents, but it is fed by those whose horizons are concerned with human dignity and the common good.

So there are other aspects, in addition to insight, that affect this yeast in the hands of the kneaders. There are the three attitudes of faith, hope, and love, which I discussed in terms of the virtues in chapter 2. Here I am looking at them only as they affect the horizons of academics. Academics must have faith that all their efforts to achieve competence and to contribute to their disciplines are worthwhile, that the long hours of studying, researching, teaching, and writing can amount to something good, something worthy of what is frequently a lifelong commitment. Closely connected to faith is hope, the hope that sooner or later what one thinks, writes, and teaches will make a difference in one's discipline and, in turn, to society. But the most energizing element in the kneaders' horizon is love—love of the subject matter, love of students, love of those unseen folks who will benefit from one's work, and finally, love of the light that comes on every so often in the search for intelligibility. What I want to claim here is that the horizon that the Catholic intellectual tradition has been interested in and developed throughout the centuries comes from verifiable insights: faith, hope, and love.

A university is necessarily a secular operation. It is secular in the sense that each discipline needs to be studied autonomously, without being encroached upon by any of the corruptions that can creep into the yeast, such as those from personal or group biases. Other threats to its necessary autonomy can come from ecclesiastical, ideological, political, or administrative sources. If the autonomy and overall integrity of academe are kept intact, then the imagined moat between the academic life and the Catholic intellectual tradition can shrink to the point of being crossable, virtually everywhere. While faith, hope, and love are treated as supernatural virtues by Catholicism, the same three elements are likely to be operating in academics across the board. While in the eyes of the Church, faith, hope, and love are raised to a new level of significance by their association with the sacrament of baptism, the Catholic intellectual tradition is also beholden to these ingredients in the anthropological sense I outlined above. Its intellectual tradition can be fed by all—particularly academics—whose work is energized by their faith, hope, and love, understood both naturally and supernaturally.

Since the reign of God is the horizon within which the parable of the yeast was articulated, one could try to imagine what leavened versus unleavened dough looks like "from the other side" of history. The eschatological scenario in Matthew 25:31–46 might give a hint of an answer to this question. "When the Son of Man comes in his glory," the "nations" will be separated into the sheep and the goats; the criterion by which they will be evaluated is whether or not they have taken action on behalf of the needy, and thus on behalf of Christ, who identified himself with them. The rewarded sheep are those who took action, though they had no idea that what they did to these, "the least," they were doing to Christ. Let us imagine him identifying himself with each of the bodies of knowledge that academics work in, since they can be and often are, *mutatis mutandis*, naked and needing to be clothed with relevant data, nomadic and needing hospitality, in conditions of imprisonment by biases and needing to be freed, with thirsts further questions like thirsts needing to be slaked, and hungers needing to be fed by those whose competencies and insights have the wherewithal to do any and all of this. Alongside each of these "nations," or disciplines, there are, of course, any number of people who benefit immeasurably from the justice that is done to bodies of knowledge.

What about the goats? There is a negative implication both in the parable and in the eschatological scenario that should not be overlooked. Regarding the parable, one can ask: What would keep the dough from rising? This can happen in any number of ways, such as: pursuing data to advance oneself, rather than the field or the common good; pursuing information in order to earn, rather than to learn; using one's position to curry favor or to gain attention or status; going through the motions of the hard work of scholarship, without any real care for the subject matter; distancing oneself from untidy data; carelessness in appropriating the available data; failure to keep up with the discipline; lack of preparation for classes, etc. Careerism in its many guises, culpable incompetence, or simple indifference—any of these can keep the dough of the disciplines from rising.

The reign of God parables are eschatological parables. The point of eschatology is to raise human activity to a higher viewpoint, and to try to see its fuller meaning in the light of the horizon of human dignity, the common good, and eternity. So the reader can judge whether this paralleling of the neediness of persons on the one hand, and to the disciplines as in a condition of continual need on the other, makes sense to him or her. Some confirmation of seeing things this way might come from another part of the Christian story. In John 6:39 Jesus describes his agenda not in terms of the reign of God, but as doing "the will of the one who sent me"; part of that will is "that I should not lose anything of what he gave me but that I should raise it up on the last day." Might that mean that there is some kind of role for bodies of knowledge in the final glorious condition of the reign of God? I don't know, but the scriptural imagery suggests a good outcome for those who have been industrious in making the dough of their disciplines rise to a greater abundance, notwithstanding their own ignorance of the religious significance of their efforts. One could also say that the work of academics is a major source of the bread of meaning in the life of the world (John 6:51).

Maybe a further confirmation for this line of thinking could be seen in the Second Vatican Council's statements on eschatology. The Council made a bold assertion about the eschatological dignity of all labor. "When we have spread on earth the fruits of our nature and our enterprise . . . we will find them once again cleansed this time from the stain of sin, illuminated and transfigured, when Christ presents to his Father an eternal and universal kingdom."[4] This connection to the new heavens and the new earth gives great dignity and value to what can otherwise seem like a slow and at times messy job with indiscernible progress, as one seeks to understand and contribute to one's field.

Jesus's horizon was God's reign. The Council's gloss on it can help one transcend what the adjective *Catholic* ordinarily connotes about this intellectual tradition: that it is an a priori construct into which one has to fit one's understandings to be legitimate. Both the parable and the Council's text are of great value for those who might wonder about the transcendent meaning of their academic labors. If believed, these help to answer the question about where one's own efforts, and indeed the overall human enterprise, are going. Without the heuristic of the new heavens and the new earth, one can be left wondering where, if anywhere, knowing is going. In brief, it would be helpful for professors to operate from a religious horizon, since that could help them to see the meaning of their work of teaching, researching, and publishing in a new light. But administrators of these universities cannot require the Catholic faith, or indeed any faith, of their faculty members. In a sense, it is none of their business.

How does this line of thinking end up describing a Catholic intellectual tradition? As I have already indicated, in my understanding of the "catholic" character of this tradition, I am indebted to the philological scholarship of Walter Ong, SJ. His understanding of the adjective *catholic*, to mean "throughout the whole" has ecclesial implications. What did the early Church's use of the descriptor *catholic* imply? That the yeast of the faith is to be kneaded throughout the whole. So, in the early centuries of Christianity, those who found their meaning in Jesus's life, death, and resurrection brought new yeast that was gradually kneaded throughout the whole of the then-known world. It was kneaded into the dough of each community or "nation" to which these Christians migrated or to which they went on mission.

Since then, the whole into which this yeast is to be kneaded has expanded profoundly, reaching not only new geographical territories but also new categories, so that it now includes what I am examining here, namely, the bodies of knowledge through which much of the world thinks and chooses.

The mission of the Catholic intellectual tradition is not confessional per se, but, like the Church itself, this tradition is meant to be a servant of the reign of God. Though beliefs have been foundational for Catholicism and its institutions, insights into values and their enactments extend its mission in the world. More particularly, the Church sees the world's increasing need for a longer perspective, for higher viewpoints, and for right thinking and valuing, in order that the conditions of personal, social, cultural, political, and religious well-being can be achieved and enjoyed. What makes the dough rise is growth in verifiable insight, as well as growth in accurate knowledge of what is so and not so, that is, knowledge of being in the classical and formal sense of that term.

As I have said, a differentiation between the doctrinal and the intellectual traditions is of value to both the world and the Church. Ironically, this differentiation helps both faith and reason develop a mature, mutual respect for one another, as well as a mutual dependence. It is also this interdependence that makes the Church effective in human affairs. It can bring a history of reasoning to such affairs that few other memories or traditions of reason are able to. The Catholic intellectual tradition serves both the Church and the world best by retaining a dialectical relationship to each of them. It is the cutting edge of further understanding in the Church; it is also dependent on the doctrinal tradition to be in a continuum with the Church.

Ong has a further insight into yeast that is helpful here. "Yeast is a plant, a fungus, something that grows with no particular limits to its borders. If the yeast is added to the mass of dough, it will grow into the added portion."[5] Notice, the yeast does not convert the dough into itself, but is able to leaven whatever it is kneaded into. The metaphor is pregnant because it indicates that the yeast's life has to be lost in the dough for the dough to come to its fullness and for the yeast to do what it was intended for. Furthermore, as I have argued, there is no body of knowledge that is alien to the Catholic intellectual tradition. If the professionals of a given discipline continue to predicate what is so, and to effect the good of knowledge, and in turn of order and of value, this is precisely what the Church is for. The Catholic intellectual tradition has something to contribute to each, and much to gain by learning from each.

What does this intellectual tradition have to contribute to a discipline? Without himself making the differentiation I have been proposing in this text, John Paul II gives a cogent answer to that question in his Apostolic Constitution *Ex corde ecclesiae*. He recalls Augustine's famous adage that one believes in order to understand and that one understands in order to believe (*Intellege ut credas; crede ut intellegas*). He explains how important it is "to evaluate the attainments of science and technology in the perspective of the totality of the human person" (7). John Paul is sure that this totality is more likely to be kept in view if "university research includes: (1) an integration of knowledge; (2) a dialogue between faith and reason; (3) and ethical concern; and (4) a theological perspective" (15). In a pithy high point of the document, the pope spells out the nexus between knowledge and value issues:

> It is essential that we be convinced of the priority of the ethical over the technical, of the primacy of the person over things, of the superiority of spirit over matter. The cause of the human person will only be served if knowledge is joined to conscience. Men and women of science will truly aid humanity only if they preserve the sense of transcendence of the human person over the world and of God over the human person. (18)

So far so good, but how should we imagine the whole that is being leavened, since there are so many academic fields, with new specializations emerging every year? Is each of these a part of a whole, or is each its own whole? The answer is both. First, a whole develops field by field, researcher by researcher, whether singly or in teams, incrementally by the insights that keep producing higher viewpoints within each of them, through questions that are asked and answered by them alone. Higher viewpoints are successful dot connections. Second, the Catholic intellectual tradition can help the dough of each discipline to rise and their relation to other disciplines to develop. And finally, the destiny of all these "batches" is somehow to be a part of the new heavens and the new earth. It would be ideal if the personnel of these Catholic universities understood themselves and their enterprise in relation to this notion of the whole.

The question that all Catholic institutions of higher learning must face is how to understand in what their Catholic identity consists. There is no quick and easy way to situate this Catholic identity matter, and there is no possibility of answering this question without the differentiation recommended here. Looked at only in terms of insights, this intellectual tradition can assist higher viewpoints and, in turn, assist in an interconnectedness between bodies of knowledge, so that a greater sense of coherence can develop throughout an institution that considers itself Catholic. But the ways of effecting a sense of coherence are particular, and they rely, of course, on the institution's history and the attitudes of its personnel, both toward the Church and toward its own administration and leaders.

The perennial rapport that faith and reason have had with one another throughout the history of the Christian faith gives us cause to be optimistic about the mutuality between academe and Catholicism. Think of the amount of critical, appreciative, and thorough attention each discipline gets from its own stable of scholars. Why not presume that the disciplines' contributions will be of value for faith's understanding of itself? What should add to our optimism about the future of sincere faith and professional reasoning is a belief articulated at Vatican II that "in the hearts of all people of good will grace works in an unseen way."[6] The virtual universality of this good will is operative in two of Catholicism's central beliefs. One is the belief that Jesus's redeeming act was for all peoples. The second is that there is only one ultimate vocation for all, and that the Holy Spirit, "in a manner known only to God," calls everyone to pursue this calling.[7]

Something more needs to be said here about the particulars of the yeast's leavening, and the mission of the Catholic intellectual tradition, which is to go "throughout the whole" batch of the disciplines. The Church's mission is and always has been to preach the Gospel to all the nations. The suggestion I am making here is that academe in and of itself lacks what the Catholic intellectual tradition could supply. While respecting the knowledge industry's proper secularity in all its parts, this tradition has grown in scope through the centuries, so that a given field of knowledge should be able to find in it a way to attain a higher viewpoint, one that allows it to take its place in a greater whole. In this way, this tradition could help the knowledge industry to be sensitive to the value issues, which it can easily overlook by concentrating on what is always only a part of a whole. Concretely, I think of four examples, all coming from academics working with or at the National Conference of Catholic Bishops. There are the Conference's recent letter on faithful citizenship, its 1991 letter on care of the earth, and its two well-known documents from the 1980s, one on the economy and one on peacemaking.[8] All of these are instances of the Catholic intellectual tradition generating an interconnectedness between academic fields and human values, each addressing a specific area of human well-being.

To take the darker side of the knowledge industry, disciplines can be permeated with yeast corrupted by biases. Such biases are not hard to find: empiricism, scientism, conceptualism, positivism, modernism, postmodernism, secularism, fundamentalism, and secular fundamentalism, to name a few. Such "isms" represent a closure to the desire to know, and a reduction of what could be known if the inquiry were not permeated by a bias. A discussion of each of these would take this chapter too far afield, so the reader has to fill in the blanks based on what is conveyed by these descriptors.

Here I will look at only one such bias, conceptualism, since it may be the least intelligible of the above set. Conceptualism is a lazy way of using the thinking of others; it is lazy in that it leaves the thinking to others, and simply takes for granted the judgments they have arrived at. Of course, we all have to rely on the judgments of others most of the time, but the bias of conceptualism is so stuck in the judgments made by others that there is no interest in determining how or why these have been arrived at, and hence takes no responsibility for their rightness or wrongness.

In terms of cognition, the biggest problem with conceptualism is its immobility; ignoring the nature of understanding, it disregards its own questions or fails to appropriate what has been learned. Each generation's experiences and understandings are different from the experiences, understandings, and judgments of those in the past, whose insights developed into concepts and judgments that were appropriate for their moment in time. Concepts themselves are immobile. They do not change of themselves; rather, they are changed by those who understand them and bring new insights and further judgments to them.

All of this can be applied to another "ism," Catholicism. Conceptualist Catholics are prone to take on the doctrinal concepts of the Church as if these concepts had all arrived from outside of time, and to employ them as if they are and always will be the last word. I do not say this to lodge a doubt about the doctrinal tradition of the Church, to which we who are Catholic are so beholden, but to underscore that there is no substitute for the doctrines' personal appropriation in the minds and hearts of believers. The Church's doctrines obviously have used concepts in order to try to do justice to the mysteries of God, but the concepts invite one to probe and rest in these mysteries, rather than to parrot them.

Along with intellectual laziness, there can also be an historical naiveté in a peculiarly Catholic kind of conceptualism. The "deposit of faith" metaphor often conveys a kind of stasis that assures the faithful that the money is already in the bank, so to speak, and it will be sufficient to meet all contingencies. Pope John XXIII's *aggiornamento* should have been seen as an invitation to internalize the deposit of faith as presently conceived, rather than be passive recipients or observers of it. The antidote to conceptualism is not to impugn the authority of the teaching Church, but to exercise one's interiority in letting the doctrinal tradition take the measure of one's life. And in relation to the professoriate, the antidote also involves assisting the Church with the duty and authority of scholarship, at least indirectly. Professors serve both the world and the Church best by tending to the business of their own competencies.

Again, St. Paul's insight into the difference between knowledge acquired to puff up the knower and knowledge used to build up both a body of knowledge and a community is germane. "All of us have knowledge," but when St. Paul speaks of the love that "builds up," he is talking about the knower's purity of intention, not about the contents of what is known (1 Cor. 8:1). A knower who is puffed up with his or her own importance might be competent, but be too filled with self-regard to be able to see the data objectively. Although purity of intention is precarious and no one is completely self-transcending, all other things being equal, good scholarship is more likely to happen when self-regard is severely curtailed. This is easier said than done. To put this in Christian terms, every act of self-transcendence is a kind of a death, and every attainment of verifiable insight is a kind of a resurrection. The death is to self-regard or self-interest, and the resurrection is to a higher viewpoint. Higher viewpoints expand the horizon of knowledge and interests of those who seek the true and the good and the meaning thereof.

Finally, the story Catholicism has been telling about itself from the beginning forms the key connection between the Catholic intellectual tradition and God's reign. This story has many chapters, and is always evolving, always accumulating more and more insight into truth as it learns from many sources, such as the disciplines, as well as from ambient cultures and traditions, religious or intellectual. This ongoing development makes the Catholic story more credible and capacious. The Church is a community of memories; it is a continual process of discerning what fits and what does not fit with its organic understanding of truth and values. What the Church learns from the hypotheses and theories, the verified results and theses of scholars in various disciplines become grist for its continuing narrative. Generation after generation of Catholics has relied on the interdependence between faith and right reason. The complementarity between the two helps each to grow.

THE RIVER

The second symbol that can help us to picture the depth and breadth of the Catholic intellectual tradition comes from the book of the prophet Ezekiel in the Hebrew scriptures (Ezek. 47). Like the symbol of the yeast kneaded through the dough, this one is valuable in that it captures a key insight about the Catholic tradition without having to go into its complex conceptual development. Again, I see this tradition as a compound of its two component parts, the doctrinal and the intellectual.

Ezekiel was the first prophet to receive a call to prophesy outside of Israel. He was among those deported by Nebuchadnezzar, the Babylonian king who was used by God to punish Israel's infidelities and call her to repentance. From Babylon, Ezekiel was given visions of the return of Israel to the new Jerusalem. One of these visions was of the temple in Jerusalem, which for Israel had been the epicenter of God's presence to her. In his vision, the prophet is transported by the angel of the Lord to the temple in Jerusalem, and is told to notice the water flowing out from beneath the threshold of the temple. The water flows out towards the east, and then it begins to trickle from the southern side, and then out the north gate. The prophet marvels at the growing depth of this water; he wades in it until he can no longer stand because of its depth. Then Ezekiel is brought to the bank of what by then had become a strong river, to sit and observe its effects. "Wherever the river flows, every sort of living creature that can multiply shall live" (v. 9). This vision foretells a new start for exiled Israel when God would restore her to her homeland.

There are similarities between the water coming out from under the temple and the yeast's permeating the dough. "Wherever this water comes, the sea will be made fresh" (v. 10). So there is fresh water pouring into the brackish water, which is not life-giving. Wherever it pours, the sea will come to teem with life and the trees on both sides of the river will become fruitful. The leaves of the trees, as Ezekiel is given to see, neither fade nor does their fruit become scarce, "for they shall be watered by the flow from the sanctuary. Their fruit shall serve for food and their leaves for medicine" (Ezek. 47:12). Water, of course, was a preoccupation for Israel, since its land was arid and its Dead Sea lifeless, unless God were to act and help the desert to bloom and the sea to become a source of abundant life (Isa. 35:1, Ezek. 47:9).

There are five angles from which this vision of Ezekiel's can help us to understand the origin and character of the compound Catholic tradition. First, this tradition traces its origins all the way back to the revelation of God to Israel, which began the Great Tradition. This Great Tradition is a record of God's self-communication to Israel. This record is central to the self-understanding not only of Jews, but of Christians and Muslims as well. Common to all three of these monotheistic religions has been their absolute dependence on God's initiative for their existence and well-being.

Second, water in the Old Testament often symbolized wisdom. The examples are numerous. In Proverbs, "the fountain of wisdom is a flowing brook" and "[t]he teaching of the wise is a fountain of life" (Prov. 18:4, 13:14). In the book of Sirach, the Torah fills humans with an abundance of wisdom, like a river overflowing its banks (Sir. 24:23–31). For Jeremiah, the "fountain of living water" was the Lord (Jer. 2:13, 17:13; Ps. 36:9). Living water was in sharp contrast to brackish water or salt water or enclosed cistern water. So the divine origin of the Great Tradition has enabled those who were able to quaff from it to come to wisdom. And, it is wisdom that gives one competence in keeping things in their proper order, as was already noted.

Third, this vision in the book of Ezekiel is preceded by one that is probably more familiar. It complements and fills out the implications of the water flowing from below the temple. The prophet's earlier vision is of a valley of dry bones that take on flesh and live (Ezek. 37:1–14). How does this happen? The Spirit plays a role in this vision that is more explicit than in the later one. "I will put my spirit in you [dry bones] that you may live and I will settle you upon your land; thus shall you know that I am the Lord" (v. 14). Though it is still only incipient in the Hebrew scriptures, one can see the beginnings of a Jewish theology of the Spirit in this and similar texts.[9] The new temple, and its new cult, and even the new Jerusalem will be breathed into and brought to life by the Spirit.

Fourth, the geography known by the human author of this book can help us to picture the point of the water which, as fresh, is flowing from under the temple, heading down the Jordan River, down into the Dead Sea, where otherwise nothing can live. By way of contrast, "wherever this river flows, every sort of living creature that can increase shall live . . . for wherever this water comes the sea shall be made fresh" (Ezek. 47:9). By the same token, anyplace that this fresh water does not reach, such as "the marshes and swamps," suffers the fate of being "left for salt" and not life-bearing (47:11). All of this imagery is redolent of the water that flows in the Garden of Eden, making it a garden (Gen. 2:10).

Fifth, and perhaps most important, this prophetic book launched a whole new direction for Israel, introducing the theme of taking personal responsibility for the tradition of Torah. Before the exile, Israel had understood this responsibility corporately; the new element added to this was the responsibility of the individual person for appropriating the law and the prophets. The Book of Ezekiel calls for individual Israelites to be in contact with the living water of the spirit and the wisdom of their tradition. That individual believers were called to become attentive, intelligent, reasonable, and responsible for the tradition each had access to was a major new development in the history of Israel, maybe even in the whole history of responsible consciousness. It continues to this day to be influential for all who derive their traditions from the Great Tradition of Torah.[10]

The value of metaphors is that they enable one to understand something more easily that is complex, through comparison with a simpler thing to which it bears a likeness. Ezekiel's vision of the temple and the river supplies a way of understanding the unwieldy, compound Catholic tradition. The Catholic tradition is a story that goes back to the beginnings of God's self-communication to Israel, which was the beginning of the Great Tradition. The Church appropriated that tradition and interpreted the life, death, and resurrection of Jesus in relation to it. This generated a strong current in this Great Tradition that is meant to freshen all it reaches, to flow

"throughout the whole," in other words. As it developed, this strong current generated the Church's doctrinal tradition and its derivative, the Catholic intellectual tradition. These enliven what they touch, or that is the hope, at least, of those who
follow Christ and are formed and informed by these traditions: that they would
generate life, abundance, and fruitfulness for both Church and world.

This river—this compound tradition in particular—has a story. One can swim
in its depths, or just be dimly aware of it. The story can be inhabited fully, or simply
known. Either way, what professors in Catholic institutions of higher education owe
to their schools and to their students is to be aware of this story of origins, either as
a simple, factual narrative, or, for some, as a normative story. If read as normative,
this story gives promise of supplying an account of the whole trajectory of a life:
work and productivity, family and love, children and flourishing, success and failure, health and sickness, diminishment and old age, birth and death.

The value of the story of the temple and the river is that it gives a sense of continuity with the past, from which one can gain an appreciation of the peculiarity of
the present enterprises, an appreciation of Catholicism's "peculiar" take on knowledge. The academic disciplines taught at Catholic institutions of higher learning
need to advert to this history, in order to know how they might contribute to healing, how they might help to grow "leaves for medicine" (Ezek. 47:12). What needs
healing? Within academe, there is fragmentation, not to mention amnesia, short-
sightedness, flights from understanding, one-sidedness, obscurantism, and bias.
Disciplines can get stuck in the swamps and marshes of what in effect is a tradition
of secular fundamentalism, which has no protology or eschatology. If not formally,
at least in effect, the disciplines can be closed off from any realm of meaning that is
external to them, and even function as gatekeepers that shut out any data or questions that are not rewarded by their particular areas of concentration. In this they
resemble cisterns.

Traditions have access to answers that questions without traditions may not
have. I like the way Huston Smith, the phenomenologist of religions, locates the
importance of questions:

> The ultimate questions human beings ask—what is the meaning of existence?
> Why is there pain and death? Why in the end is life worth living? What does real-
> ity consist of and what is its object?—are the defining essence of our humanity . . .
> it is the intrusion of these questions into our consciousness that tells us most pre-
> cisely what kind of creatures we are. Our humanness flourishes to the extent that
> we steep ourselves in these questions—ponder them, circle them, obsess over
> them, and in the end allow the obsession to consume us.[11]

While academic disciplines enjoy a rightful autonomy, they can misconstrue this
freedom if they disallow questions dealing with meanings that transcend them.
There is a similarity between a living discipline and living water. The characteristics
of a living discipline, as opposed to one that is encased within itself, are fruitfulness,
connection to people's basic questions, and further insight into reality. I count a

living discipline as among those things that "bear fresh fruit . . . [that] shall serve for food" (Ezek. 47:12). For whom does the discipline bear fruit? For those seeking understanding, insight, judgment, and meaning, personally and collectively, objectively and subjectively. When restrictions are imposed on the pure desire to know, the results are leaves that fade and fruit that is here today and gone tomorrow. If a discipline's purview is constricted a priori, or its efforts limited by disallowing some questions and rewarding only some answers, its contribution will be small in contrast to its potential.

The compound Catholic tradition, of course, is not the only current of water in this strong and mighty river. This river's volume has increased exponentially with the entry of every human being into history and with the exercise of each of their intentionalities. All created species have habits, but the habits of *homo sapiens* create traditions, some more authentic than others, some more polluted than others, some briefer than others. A key litmus test for the authenticity of traditions is whether they give human dignity its due; this is more likely to be the case in a tradition that can give an account of an Alpha and an Omega. In secular terms, this means the tradition knows where it has come from, in relation to the vast ocean of human intentionality and to the earlier fields of academe, and it seeks the common good as its end. In religious terms, the tradition can tap into its divine origins through its sacred texts, and can be open to an end of the same stature. Ad hoc traditions, on the other hand, inevitably suffer from narrowness of scope and shortness of memory, and are likely to be overly influenced by whatever is convenient or faddish.

Academics are entrusted with the legacy, such as it is, of their particular fields. Each discipline has a tradition, often more than one, and individual faculty members will likely understand their field's legacy quite differently. The issue here is the moral responsibility that these individuals have with regard to their field, and particularly its methods, history, data, heroes, and self-understandings. It is important that faculty members spend time discerning these various elements of their field, being attentive especially to what might be overlooked or neglected, and to what is being promoted (or not promoted) in relation to the common good. The responsibility we each have for our own moral development increases exponentially for those with responsibility for conveying a body of knowledge to neophytes, since the horizon being communicated by the educator, formally or indirectly, presumably has a formative influence on the horizons of the students. Whether the professoriate is intending it or not, students are learning more than the contents of the subject matter; they are learning what is important and unimportant to their professors. A key negative example here is careerism, in which one's own self can become the horizon of one's questioning; the self becomes that person's Alpha and Omega. Careerism is among the most subtle of the "isms" and the most imitated.

One of the implications of the approach taken here is that responsibility for the Catholic intellectual tradition no longer falls solely on the shoulders of the local bishop, or the school's administrators, campus ministers, or trustees; rather, a great portion of this responsibility is now on the shoulders of faculty members. Their responsibility is not that they be Catholic or even that they know the Catholic tradition, but that they be aware of the currents or intellectual traditions that are being implicitly or explicitly communicated in their discipline and its research. As any environmental scientist can attest, the water quality of a river differs along the course from its source to its end. Some parts can be polluted in varying degrees, other parts can be relatively clean.

It would be naive to imagine that the Catholic intellectual tradition is totally unaffected by the pollutants in the river of contemporary intellectual currents. On the other hand, if we apply here the idea of "catholic" as a permeation of the whole (as in the symbol of the yeast that leavens the dough), then the mission of a Catholic educational institution and its personnel is to the whole river, that is to say, to the intellectual, moral, and religious currents within which the disciplines operate, or their opposites. A discipline is part of a complex order of meanings. One discipline is not meaningful in itself, unless it is situated in a broader framework of meaning. For an academic to be wise, he or she must have clarity about where his or her work and discipline fit in this order of things. Such clarity is more likely when the faculty member's work is shaped by the four realms of meaning, in particular interiority and transcendence, elaborated on in a previous chapter.

It would be too facile to talk in terms of "the Catholic order of things," because we are not talking here primarily about the doctrinal tradition formed by scripture, nor the dogmas taught by the Church, but about the Catholic intellectual tradition. It is more extensive than the Church, and does not have evangelization as its purpose. Its ends are threefold: the good of order, or of intersubjective cooperation; the good of values, personal and social; and the good of helping individuals to be reflective about their insights, judgments, and choices of particular goods. The Catholic intellectual tradition reflects the expansiveness of the mission of Jesus, who in the last Gospel saw himself as having been sent so that human beings "might have life and have it more abundantly" (John 10:10). One strand within this intellectual tradition, Catholic social teaching, has been concretized by mediating principles such as the common good, the priority of labor over capital, subsidiarity, and solidarity. The Catholic intellectual tradition includes, but is broader than, its social teachings. It has a long memory, and a history of discernment of values not only in economics, politics, and culture, but in all the areas of human enterprise: the arts, the sciences, the humanities.

It is not essential, as I have argued, that academics be Catholic in order to do justice to the Catholic intellectual tradition. Rather, what is essential is for those teaching in such institutions to be attentive, intelligent, and responsible, since these are the ways they take account of the operations of their own consciousness. It is from these that one grasps the objective reality one is seeking to attain. It is also from being attentive to these operations that they can judge value. The key value that is central to both Catholicism and the university is to know what is true. Perhaps one could say that Catholicism's concern is with truth, including Truth (with a big T), and the university's concern is with truth (with a little t). The Catholic intellectual tradition is concerned with the plural latter, without separating it from the ideal, unitary former. Both the Catholic intellectual tradition and presumably the university would believe that the proximate criterion for truth is the sufficiency of the evidence for a particular judgment. The criterion for truth in the Catholic intellectual tradition, though not peculiar to it, is the proper unfolding of the pure—in the sense of unrestricted and detached—desire to know. When no further questions arise, the desire to know has been satisfied. Lonergan traces all incoherence to inauthenticity, and the attainment of unity to authenticity. Why? Because "the possibility of knowing is an unrestricted intention that intends the transcendent . . . and a process of self-transcendence that reaches it."[12]

Four things should become evident to the teaching profession. The first is that the variation in matters of personal meaning is as extensive as is the subjectivity of individuals. The second is that the operations of consciousness, including experience, understanding, judgment, and the movement from these operations into choices and actions, are universal when and if they are made explicit. The third is that all people seek the true, the good, and the beautiful, never abstractly but always concretely, and that all people need help discerning between true and false goods. And finally, that in the ocean of human intentionality, there are any number of currents, some polluted, some pure. The pollution is likely to come from thinkers who stop at the categorical, the conceptual, the determinate, the measurable, the useful; who neglect, scorn, or do not even guess at the transcendent realm of meaning.

Part of the mission of the Catholic intellectual tradition is to affect other intellectual traditions. Its mission is not to evangelize other traditions, but to complement them in their approach to interiority and transcendent meaning, assuming they value these, though in analogous ways. The Catholic intellectual tradition will accomplish its mission if it is attentive to the fact the "there are prior transcendental notions that constitute the very dynamism of our conscious intending."[13] These notions of being and the good intend the unknown that gradually becomes better known; they also seek to make meaning and a whole out of the known parts. The drive of the human spirit "is a conscious intending, ever going beyond what happens to be given or known, ever striving for a fuller and richer apprehension of the yet unknown or incompletely known totality, whole, universe."[14]

In brief, this chapter has made use of two images—that of the yeast in the dough, and that of the river—in order to stimulate an interested group at each Catholic college or university to explore at their school the issue of the condition of the Catholic intellectual tradition. These images may or may not help the potential organizers of such an inquiry. What is essential, however, is for Catholic institutions to take seriously their relation to this tradition. The contention of this volume is that if a Catholic institution of higher education is not moved along by this strong current and open to the horizon of the in-breaking reign of God, other ways of having a Catholic identity are likely to be superficial and extrinsic.

NOTES

1. Lonergan, "Cognitional Structure," in *Collection*, 211.

2. Ibid., 212.

3. Ibid., 213.

4. *Gaudium et spes* (39).

5. Ong, "Yeast: A Parable for Catholic Higher Education," 347–49.

6. *Gaudium et spes* (22).

7. Ibid.

8. The full titles of these documents are: *Faithful Citizenship: A Catholic Call to Political Responsibility* (November 2007); *Renewing the Earth: An Invitation to Reflection and Action on the Environment* (November 1991); *Economic Justice for All: A Pastoral Letter on Catholic Social Teaching and the U.S. Economy* (November 1986); and *The Challenge of Peace: God's Promise and Our Response* (November 1983).

9. Lodahl, *Shekhinah Spirit*, passim.

10. Whybray, *The Intellectual Tradition in the Old Testament*, 155–56.

11. Smith, *Why Religion Matters*, 274–75.

12. Lonergan, "Cognitional Structure," in *Collection*, 213.

13. Lonergan, *Method in Theology*, 12.

14. Ibid., 13.

CHAPTER 8

◆

Where Is Knowing Going?

THE QUESTION I WANT TO ADDRESS in this chapter, picking up from the last chapter, is: Where is our knowing going? The reason that academics put such an enormous amount of energy into knowing is that they believe that their knowing is going to benefit someone, be it themselves, their colleagues, their students, their discipline, contemporary society, or the common good. Research is nothing if not expectant and future-driven. Even historical research is aimed at knowing the past better for the sake of the future. There would not be much research done about anything if it were not driven by the engine of hope. This hope is largely of a secular character in the modern university. Again, there is the question of one's horizon, and whether one's research could be helped by giving more attention to one's horizon. Unless a scholar's horizon is formally secularist in the sense that it has closed off the transcendent realm of meaning as illusory, research that always has an immanent horizon can also be open to seeking a fuller explanation of where knowing is going. One of my basic claims in this chapter is that the question about one's horizon is worth asking, and could be beneficial to one's research.

I want to begin by considering three people's answers to the question about the destiny of our knowledge. Each of the three offers a distinct and concrete way of understanding his own horizon. One of these figures, Maximus the Confessor, comes from the patristic age; the second and third, the paleontologist Teilhard de Chardin and the theologian Karl Rahner, are from the modern age. They had three very creative ways of connecting the dots between the Catholic intellectual and doctrinal tradition, on the one hand, and the world on the other.

MAXIMUS THE CONFESSOR

Maximus the Confessor (580–662) lived in the period after the Council of Chalcedon (451), at which the Church had pronounced definitively that Christ was one person with two natures that were joined in a unique union called "hypostatic." But this definition did not put an end to the turmoil—political, ideological, religious—over the question of who he was. Maximus turned out to be the right person at the right time to deal with some of the post-conciliar confusion that arose from this understanding of Christ.

The Chalcedonian formula of Christ's two natures, one divine and one human, shaped Maximus's understanding, not just of Christ, but of everything. Instead of philosophical speculation about being and beings, Maximus saw the incarnation as an opportunity for construing a theological metaphysics. I see this construal as his notion of catholicity concretizing itself into a synthesis between classical metaphysics and Christology. Maximus believed that all that exists was in the process of being drawn up into a synthesis, and that Jesus was both the prototype of this synthesis and its causal agent.

Maximus's Christology saw Jesus, in his human mind and will, functioning as a human. He understood humanly and chose humanly. So what, then, explains his uniqueness? For Maximus, Jesus's life was an ontological synthesis of the two natures, without either of them being shortchanged by the other. In his earthly life he was led by the Spirit to understand that which he could not have understood were his human nature unassisted. By the same token, the Spirit also moved Jesus's will toward the good, without his human freedom being encroached upon.

Synthesis is not only Maximus's word for clarifying this creative tension of the two natures in Jesus; it is also his word for the role of human beings who are beneficiaries of the gifts of the Spirit. In fact, synthesis became so central to Maximus's outlook that it became a virtual metaphysics for him. He did not actually articulate a metaphysics, but had he done so, it would have been personalized around how God works in human intentionality, with the hypostatic union of the Son of God being the prototype of this co-laboring. Christ was a whole person, without his divinity being reduced to his humanity or his humanity absorbed into his divinity. In Trinitarian terms, the Son was not the Father and the Father was not the Son, yet the Father and Son are one. How can this be? It seems that the Spirit makes wholes where there would otherwise not be. Mary's "yes" in the annunciation story makes this connection more tangible and easier to understand.

As we have seen in the first two chapters, wholes are what faculty members seek to birth. Intuiting something incomplete in the body of knowledge for which they have responsibility, they seek to bring what is disparate together into a whole. Or, aware of the distance that separates need from privilege, they seek to bridge the divide between them with their projects. Maximus would see these aspirations, insights, and projects as tending toward syntheses. And for him, the original and originating synthesis behind all these initiatives is the whole person of Christ, human and divine.

But Maximus spent much of his life dealing with false syntheses. He suffered for his articulation and defense of what he understood to be true syntheses. The subject matter of his research was always Jesus Christ, and for him the criterion for distinguishing between true and false syntheses was whether or not they accorded with his understanding of the union of two natures in Christ's person. When this union of the two natures in the one person was correctly perceived through prayer and research, Maximus relished the judgment made by others or by himself. When that union was misunderstood, he said so and walked the gauntlet, derided by those who were in error, who unfortunately often happened to be those in power.

In Byzantium, religiosity was mixed with political power, and so was not taken lightly by anyone. The context was not one of academics politely exchanging ideas conjured up for the sake of discussion; rather, the participants in the debates were people who believed that truth was a matter of salvation and falsehood of damnation. So if one's ideas were deemed erroneous, he paid for it, sometimes even with his life. Maximus died of wounds inflicted by those whose ideas were discordant with his. So what we call "research" today was a matter of life or death for him and for his contemporaries.

For Maximus, the primary means God forged to bring the created world and the human species back from their exile was the union between Jesus's human and divine natures. The most valuable resources for his research were Origen, Denys the Areopagite, Evagrius, the two Gregories, and the Antiochene school of Christology. The false syntheses Maximus faced were Monophysitism and Monothelitism, the beliefs that Christ had only one nature or only one will, respectively. In both terms, the prefix "mono-" conveys the error. These belief systems were wrong in that they reduced or homogenized or confused divinity and humanity, in effect eradicating the autonomy of the created reality of Jesus's humanity. False understandings of Christ deeply troubled Maximus, because in one way or another they profoundly denigrated all human dignity, beginning with Jesus's own.

Hans Urs von Balthasar's monumental study on Maximus, *Cosmic Liturgy*, brought the Confessor out of the shadows, so that there is now a growing interest in his insights. He is the one to whom I am most indebted for knowledge of Maximus. He said of Maximus that "his role in the history of dogma was to a large extent that of stressing the full humanity of Christ . . . [Christ's was] not a passive human nature dependent on the activity of the personal divine Logos."[1] So, it seems to me that Maximus was a seventh-century forerunner of the twentieth century's low Christology.

Behind these theological *arcana* there is a whole worldview. It can be summed up as a search for syntheses of all that is intelligible. During his earthly life, Jesus developed his own synthesis, as the Gospels articulate. It was not ontologically static, but existentially chosen; one might even say, eked out moment by moment. After his passion, death, and resurrection, Christ Jesus "united earth to heaven through himself, connected sensible creation with the intellectual, and so revealed the unity of creation in the very polarity of its elements . . . and ultimately—in an ineffable way—he unites created and uncreated nature."[2] So Jesus can now be seen in his own totality, human and divine, gathering the universe into its totality and "revealing the unity of all things as that of a single person."[3]

He "stands before the Father" in possession of "a body with all its sensations, and a soul like ours, and an intellect, through all of which he binds together all the parts."[4] The Chalcedonian term that keeps this totality from becoming a homogeneity is *unconfused*; the two natures remain themselves. What Christ would generate in the course of history are syntheses at every level. The cost to him was the kenosis of the incarnation. "He did not grasp at equality with God but emptied himself" (Phil. 2:5). He stands before the Father now and for all eternity as one of us, yet consubstantial with God, so that the union between the created and the uncreated can be total, yet unconfused. Only Love could pull this off.

There is a parallel between Maximus's Christological approach and my understanding of how catholicity unfolds. That is, catholicity is eschatological, a gradual infilling of the created universe with the fullness that Christ's self-emptying made possible. And Maximus himself is an exemplary example of catholicity, in that he brought the wealth of Eastern Christianity out of Byzantium and into the whole Church. Von Balthasar, who sees Maximus as Byzantium's Aquinas, makes the trenchant comment that "he set each thing's integral completeness within an openness and a readiness for union that allows it to be elevated and brought to union."[5]

So where is knowing going? According to this genius, it is going toward a series of syntheses, all of them having the Creator God as their origin, the inspiriting God as their instigator, and the synthetic, hypostatic union of Christ as their model, and cause. For Maximus, the scene of the agony in the garden was the best place to see the struggle of the two natures and the two wills before their final synthesis in Jesus's self-sacrifice. "He was not subjected to nature or made a slave by becoming human; rather he has elevated nature to himself."[6]

Knowing does not inevitably lead to syntheses or wholes. But as we have seen in this volume, it seems to have an affinity for doing so. As Maximus intuited, for Christians the grand instance and paradigm for syntheses is the union of Jesus's two natures in his one person. This belief is foundational to the existence of Catholic schools. There is the reasoning that rational human nature can accomplish, and the complementary reasoning that the gift of faith can achieve. This belief is that it is through this complementarity that Christ came to be seen as the source of the recapitulation of reality in all its dimensions. Hence, all that can be known will be part of what Christ draws into himself (Eph. 1:10; Col. 1:15–20). It is not essential that those who teach in Catholic schools share this belief about Christ, but it is essential that they know this belief is part of their school's raison d'etre.

TEILHARD DE CHARDIN

Another person who asked the question about where knowing is going was the Jesuit paleontologist and geologist Pierre Teilhard de Chardin (1881–1955). He, of course, believed in knowledge being acquired for its own sake and for the common good, but he also saw more. His insight was that human intelligence was generating "the spiritualization of the universe."[7] Further, because of human consciousness, a "noosphere," or a sphere of thought, was developing around the planet. This makes humans agents in the spiritualization of matter. Research was his preferred term for the work of acquiring knowledge, although I think he would include a lowbrow dimension to this work as well—like keeping informed, finding out what's going on, by reading the newspaper or listening to the news; investing time in a book;

being attentive to a conversation; accessing one's memory; listening well—all of this simply in order to know. These ways of knowing complement the more formal research into the areas one has competence in, and responsibility for forming judgments about.

For Teilhard, "To think the world is not merely to register it but to confer on it a form of unity it would otherwise [not enjoy]."[8] Research is not just any old thing; it is "the solemn, prime and vital occupation of man, now [become] adult."[9] Without this cognitional effort, some of what could be known would not be known, and in this sense would be lost, at least for the time being for those who could have known but failed to do so. I don't know what he would say about the casualness about knowing in many of our contemporary practices, such as skimming rather than reading, selective hearing rather than listening, being satisfied with merely getting the gist of something, settling for sound bites, or judging and acting from impressions. I doubt he would see much of contemporary consciousness—already suffering from information overload—as spiritualizing the universe, insofar as we all too often allow the data we take in to bypass the natural operations of a reflective consciousness.

Teilhard recommended that we savor the import of knowledge itself. As he saw it, "every being has two existences": one the existence it has in itself, and the other the existence it has in the minds of those who know it.[10] He gave a priority to the latter. So, he would say, because of the primacy of mind, a given thing is constituted "more by its beyond-self than by its own center."[11] Of course, since many minds try to understand more and more about what is already partially known, any increase in knowledge of it would be an increase in "the spiritualization of the universe" that is taking place through the attainment of knowledge. So the creation of a noosphere encircling the globe is the first "place" where knowing is going.

But this is not the end of his savoring of knowledge. Teilhard began to understand physical reality or matter in a different way than his fellow scientists did. "My whole outlook is governed increasingly by the physical realness of thought, which is stronger than (or rather includes in itself) all the boundless properties that a century of research has attributed to matter."[12] For him, by being known, matter becomes spirit or mind or *esprit*. In his best-known work, *The Human Phenomenon*, Teilhard indicated that he operated under two assumptions. One of these was "the primacy accorded to the psychic and to thought of the stuff of the universe."[13] He viewed material evolution as on its way to becoming "ultimately psychic."[14] Since mind was more real than matter, he believed that the unique vocation of human beings is to spiritualize matter. If matter, when judged, becomes mind, it made sense for him to anticipate "the increasing domination of the world by Thought."[15] Furthermore, "everything in the universe is for *esprit*."[16] Not only that, but the second assumption that was operating in his work was that "everything in the cosmos is for Christ."[17] So, the processes whereby the world is being brought to its fullness depend on a humanity that thinks! And believes, to boot!

It gradually dawned on Teilhard that every acquaintance he had ever labored with or for (including the wounded he worked with as a medical assistant in the

First World War), whether believers or nonbelievers, were all seeking one thing, regardless of how or even whether they named it: union with the All or the Whole. He was convinced that "Man is not drawn to the Whole (*le Tout*), by his reason alone but by the full force of his whole being."[18] In the very first essay he wrote, he spoke of feeling called to join the great "All," as if he were a particle yearning to unite with the Whole.[19] Eventually he would see his entire life, and all other life, as tending towards what he would eventually call the Omega Point.

For Teilhard, research is best done with an explicit religious faith, since "in the nature that surrounds us . . . the creative power of God is hidden and operates most intensely. Through our research, new being, a further increase of consciousness emerges in the world"; he goes on to say, even more pointedly, that "every fruit of research is, by its nature, essentially, ontologically, Christifiable."[20] In other words, he was not satisfied with research understood in solely immanent terms.

He contrasts researchers who seek to understand the Ahead, because their horizon is immanent, with those whose eyes are fixed on the transcendent Above. There are, as he saw it, two different faiths operating in his fellow researchers. The one group has faith in humanity and the immanent, which is largely knowable; the other group has faith in God and the transcendent, which he would see as real but still largely unknowable. For Teilhard, both perspectives are needed; one without the other is too narrow. Why? "It is impossible to rise Above without moving Ahead or to progress Ahead without steering towards the Above."[21] This can sound rather abstract, but for Teilhard it was highly concrete. "Faith in man is not psychologically possible if the evolutionary future of the world does not meet in the transcendent some focal point of irreversible personalization."[22] Therefore, Teilhard personalized the Omega Point. So these two "faiths" need to converge because "If we are to love the universalized Christ, we must at all costs see to it that the universe and mankind push ahead, in us and in each of our co-elements—in particular in the other 'grains of thought,' our fellow-men."[23] Each subjectivity was and produced its own "grains of thought."

Teilhard thought that the hope-filled people he knew were beginning to share his way of looking at things. They were filled with "a sacred and impassioned hope of attaining *fuller-being*."[24] There were two new factors propelling this hope: the discovery of evolution and the realization that there can be a scientific control of this evolution. Hence, a new ambition takes hold of some hearts, namely "not simply to survive or live well but to *super-live*, by forcing our way into some higher domain of consciousness and action."[25] These intellectual seekers, as Teilhard calls them, believe in the Ahead. The challenge, then, was to get those who believed in the Ahead into alignment with those who believed in the Above.

Teilhard himself had discovered "the fire of a new faith" (faith in earth and its humanity) by his immersion in science.[26] It remained for him to integrate this new fire with that of his "old faith"; otherwise he would have had "an interior life torn in two ways."[27] Refusing to allow the disjunction in himself, he pressed on, and came to realize that there not only could be but must be "a fusion between two great loves, of God and of the World—a fusion without which I am convinced the Kingdom of God is not Possible."[28]

He saw himself and all researchers as mediators between God and the particular aspects of being that each of us is privy to know. For him, that meant offering to God, in thanksgiving and in petition, what we know. Predictably, these convictions brought the subject of his own priesthood front and center for him. Teilhard saw his own priesthood as formed by the discipline of the Gospel and the discipline of work. Consequently, he could write this synthetic vision that "everything in the universe ultimately proceeds towards Christ-Omega. Since the whole of *cosmogenesis* is ultimately through *anthropogenesis* expressed in a *Christogenesis,* it follows that, in the integral totality of its tangible strata, the real is charged with a divine Presence."[29] For Christians, this is as holistic an answer to the question, "where is knowing going?" as one is likely to find. But what about those who are not Christian?

One of the theses of this book is that Christians should be able to serve as hosts for the plural traditions of this world, so that they will be able to appreciate what these Christian traditions share in common with their own. It would be a poor host who did not give his or her guests the opportunity to explain their own understanding of the transcendent realm of meaning, to which they might see the whole human enterprise and creation tending. Besides, while Teilhard's vision is a cogent one for Christians, it is obviously not the only one, even for them. This vision stems from Teilhard's high Christology, that of the late New Testament and the Councils of Nicaea and Chalcedon.

Since Teilhard's death in 1955, the Church has come to see more clearly, in the Council and beyond, that God is reaching out to all of humanity, not only to those who can take comfort in Christ or in a Christological Omega Point. I believe in Teilhard's way of seeing these things, but I am aware of its potential for exclusion. It would be a misconstrual of both Teilhard's vision and of God's patience and generosity if "the Whole" in Teilhard's thinking became too conceptually tight. As we have seen in chapter 3, the Church should be like the Jesus of the Gospels, who played host to many horizons in his historical ministry. The only people for whom Jesus had no patience were those who were too sure that they knew about God, about what God wants and is pleased by.

In chapter 4 I examined Lonergan's insights into the difference between concepts and notions, and found the heuristic character of the latter very helpful. Knowing begins with the heuristic notions of being, value, and wholeness, and ends in symbols. Once we preempt or crowd emergent probability (which is Lonergan's hermeneutic for eschatology) with conceptual clarities, such as Christogenesis or Christ as the Omega Point, we could lose touch with the capaciousness and also the mystery of the kingdom of God that Jesus preached. The Omega Point is a good symbol unless it gets tribalized. The kingdom of God functioned in Jesus's mind as an eschatological heuristic, to put a modern description on it. It gave him hope and direction, and he refused to load it up with premature concretions that would try to put limits on God's freedom to be God.

There is good reason to believe that Teilhard himself was thinking in terms of a more capacious Omega Point. His notes from the period after he returned to France from China in 1945 give some hint of this. On the last day of his annual retreat that year, he wrote about what he called "pleromization," which he described as "the supreme constitution of totalizing Being."[30] Pleromization was for him the fourth divine mystery, in addition to creation, incarnation, and redemption. It is the fullness to which all of reality is vectored, and in which it will achieve its union with its Creator. "The human is not the center of the universe as we once naively believed, but something much finer, a rising arrow of the great biological synthesis."[31]

The last paper Teilhard wrote right before his death was titled "Research, Work and Worship." In it he recalls the number of times he was told by his religious superiors to go ahead with his scientific work, but to avoid "getting involved in philosophy and theology."[32] He complains that this counsel had been for him "psychologically inviable and directly opposed to the greater glory of God." He likens his superiors' advice to someone telling a mountain climber to climb but to stop short of the peak. For work to be human, it must "depend on a sufficiently powerful magnetic attraction exercised by the term of the work."[33] The term of his work was the "Above" as the reason for him journeying "Ahead." We are all richer for his posthumous disobedience.

This gallant man spent much of his lifetime not on peaks, but plodding along in very grungy, earthy work, digging up bones and rocks, and trying to learn with his colleagues what to make of these. He had the sense, however, to describe all these forays as an experience of "dark adoration"; dark because the unearthed material had not been subjected to the judgments that had to be made about its meaning. Nevertheless, Teilhard makes the captivating comment that "there is much less difference than people think between Research and Adoration."[34] What a connection! Even while the mind is still in the dark about the data, it has to assess the nature of the material, usually by forming hypotheses or weighing insights. And from there, one must verify these hypotheses or insights. In due time, the hypotheses leave the realm of "maybe," and enter into the sphere of an unconditional judgment, an "is so" or "is not so." The heart and mind can then come out of the tunnel of dark adoration into the clear, and into adoration itself! At least this is what happened for Teilhard. His whole experience of scientific research seemed to be that it was "haloed or irresistibly animated by a mystical hope."[35] This hope was what he needed for his knowing to keep going towards an Omega Point.[36]

He contrasts his own prayer life to that of others in this way: "The peculiarity of my sensitivity derives from the fact that things in the cosmos and in life have always presented themselves to me as objects to be pursued and studied—never just material for contemplation."[37] It seems that his prayer was the fruit of much empirical inquiry and pondering. So one would have to conclude that Teilhard found himself, for much of his adult life, in a stance of dark adoration. His was an empirical kind of mysticism, as compared to that of more typical mystics (such as they are), who can delight in God's presence with little or no empirical searching or discursive reasoning. As a scientist and an adorer, his prayer searched out and to some extent attained a unique kind of whole. He refused to deal with the material world and the divine, or with God and the cosmos, as separate. The paleontological materials led him to the anthropological, which led him to the noosphere, and to the world of thought. At the center of all of these was Christ, who was not in outer space. Teilhard accessed the Above through the Ahead. The Ahead kept him tethered to the material world, and the Above was an exercise in sublation; this was his mode of prayer. Or maybe it was simply the horizon within which he always forged Ahead.

KARL RAHNER

In the third part of this chapter, I want to begin by looking at where knowing—especially that being done in the sciences and technology—has taken us in this last century. Advances in this kind of knowledge have been coming quickly, with new discoveries, new hypotheses, and new instruments to communicate and to measure the world and even the universe. Just the following list of some of the twentieth century's more venturesome efforts is eye opening. All of these have been driven, I believe, by the notion of catholicity, moving human intentionality in so many ways to go from unknowns to knowns, from unintelligibility to meaning, from disconnections to making connections.

- Einstein's theory of special relativity (1905)
- Quantum mechanics (1900–30)
- Einstein's theory of general relativity (1915)
- Big Bang cosmology (1940s onward)
- Invention of electron microscope (1930)
- Discovery of microwave background in universe (1965)
- Discovery of black holes and quasars (1960s onward)
- Invention of transistor (1947)
- Discovery of DNA (1953)
- Quarks and fundamental particles (1964 onward)
- Invention of handheld calculator and microprocessor (1967–68)
- String theory (1968)
- World Wide Web (1989)
- Hubble Spacecraft (1990)
- Mapping of human genome (1990–2000)
- Neuroscience and the Decade of the Brain (1990–2000)
- Cloning and stem cell research (1997 onward)

The data coming to us from outer space, through all the devices devised in this last century for taking cosmological measurements, is becoming more and more astonishing. First of all, the magnitude. There are at least one hundred billion stars in our own galaxy, and easily a trillion such galaxies grouped in the form of clusters, each of these containing on the average one hundred million million stars.[38] But the theories and mathematical formulae that at one point satisfactorily explained how these measurements fit together are becoming uncertain. One reason for this is that with the realization of the existence of dark matter, dark energy, and massive black holes, there is a growing awareness about the finite character of our knowledge. The laws of physics begin to wobble. The more science gains knowledge about the whole that is the universe, the less sure it is of its hard-won knowledge.

Three issues in particular are making us more humble about whether we are getting it together. One of these is an awareness of the chaos and natural evil in nature. The poet Tennyson nailed it long ago: "Nature, red in tooth and claw."[39] More recently, Ernest Becker made it more concrete: "Creation is a nightmare spectacularly taking place on a planet that has been soaked for hundreds of millions of years in the blood of all its creatures."[40] I don't know if Becker knew about the meteorite that rendered extinct Earth's enormous dinosaur population in one hit, but he wouldn't have to know about this to paint the bleak picture he did. He would certainly have known about the Black Plague in Europe, which killed one-third of the population within three years, beginning in 1347. Recent tsunamis, earthquakes, hurricanes, tornadoes, wildfires, the unending extinction of species—how are we to account for all these, if there is an all-powerful goodness at the center of all this? This is not even to mention the violence at the galactic level, with massive black holes swallowing up all the ambient stars and matter, and galaxies crashing into other galaxies.

For the most part, this negative data was implicit in the second law of thermodynamics, which is that energy degrades, and that the material universe is heading toward greater entropy. But that was just a theory, and at first it was not taken seriously by most people. Besides, religion enabled most people to trust in their own specialness to God, and served to inure them against bad news. Furthermore, beliefs in an afterlife and heaven keep believers from needless perturbation about the material universe and planet earth. But the notion of catholicity has been driving many to connect the dots between these otherwise disconnected religious and scientific worldviews.

A second development that is making us all more humble is quantum thought, including quantum mechanics and quantum physics. Quantum thought developed in the 1920s because of a number of failures in classical physics in the realm of atomic data. It insists on "an intrinsically probabilistic component in the fundamental laws of physics."[41] Quantum theory's mathematical approach to knowing is much more abstract than even theoretical physics has been. So "seeing" is much less trustworthy, and scientists learn to work with the indeterminacy of dust, waves, particles, and quanta. Quantum thought is annoying to philosophers and theologians because of its indeterminism and the relative obscurity of the quanta and their interactions with one another. Classical understandings of causality become obscure. Though it has often been derided by descriptions such as "naive metaphysics" or "crude positivism," quantum thought has deeply affected both the sciences and philosophy. It has also generated a nagging question about the simpler bodies of knowledge that we presumed were relatively complete, but that we are not so certain about now.

A third thing that is making us more humble is time. We have assumed that "was" and "is" and "will be" are simple terms that indicate just what they seem to indicate: past and present and future. But the more we know, the more time gets complicated. So, for example, with the discovery of the universe's beginning as a Big Bang, time and space have become objects of intense interest to physicists, cosmologists, and astrophysicists. How can we be clear about "before" and "after" and "now," when our instruments have been able to detect the beginnings of the Big Bang in the red microwaves coming from outer space? If the very distant past comes into view in the present, time gets murky.

All of which is to say that we live in a world in need of connections; in this case, what is needed is a link between the developing worldviews of science, not to mention many of the other disciplines and theology. Questions are emerging in both science and theology that demonstrate the need for the two fields to work more closely together, for the sake of each and for the sake of the world, in which the two compete for allegiances and meaning. So theology has been moving beyond "the last things" of death, judgment, heaven, and hell for individual human beings, and slowly moving toward the question of the universe and its predicted "freeze or fry" future. If the deep story of faith cannot give an account of this scientific panorama, it will cease to be credible to those who are perforce growing up in the deepening mystery of the universe story. The challenge is to have a theology that can give an account of the virtual infinity of cosmology, and the natural evil of nature, and the indeterminacy of the *creata*. But this is where the drive to connect the dots kicks in.

The most impressive dot connectors that I am aware of are the scholars at the Center for Theology and the Natural Sciences at the Graduate Theological Union in Berkeley, California. It is a gathering place of theologians and scientists. Much of its work has been done in collaboration with the Vatican Observatory for the last twenty years. The Center's director is Robert John Russell, who is both a physicist and a theologian.

Russell has a beautiful image of the task the Center has set out for itself—linking theology and science—inspired by the construction of the Golden Gate Bridge. On one side of the river was San Francisco, on the other side, its neighbors to the north. Each side had to build from where it was, finding bedrock in its own field of inquiry. As each side towered over the waters, it needed bold adventurers from both sides who could troll cables across the divide between the two sides, and climb out on the slender cables hanging out in space to connect them.[42] So too with the Center's work to build a bridge between science and theology.

Here I will focus on just one of these bridge-building adventurers, who has also been one of the twentieth century's most prescient theologians: Karl Rahner. Rahner was able to anticipate some of the key questions that are now being asked in the dialogue between science and theology. He was also the most prolific dot-connector I have ever studied. His prowess will be evident in his following five insights regarding science and theology.

First, in dealing with the issue of time vis-a-vis eternity, Rahner was not content with the common sense understanding of time as linear, because he saw how an event within a linear, historical sequence can at the same time be an event outside of that sequence, and affect both the present and the future. For Rahner, eternity subsumes time as we experience it. It is not as though we live on a timeline until we die, and then proceed into unending time, as if death were only a change of horses. No, Rahner would say that the time we experience in the course of our lives is given "so that freedom and something of final and definitive validity can be achieved. Eternity is not an infinitely long mode of pure time but rather it is a mode of the spiritual freedom that has been exercised in time . . . [E]ternity comes to be in time as time's own mature fruit."[43]

These insights about time's relation to eternity are helpful for both theologians and scientists. Christians believe that the redeeming action of Jesus Christ in the past reaches into and affects the present. The presence of the act of redemption disrupts the linear timeline. So the idea that the beginning of the future is going on now is not as bizarre as it might have sounded before the microwaves coming from the beginning of the Big Bang were detected. Christian texts have been claiming for centuries that the historically past acts of the crucifixion and the resurrection are the beginning in time of the eternal future, or of God's untrammeled reign within creation, which has been awaited by all three monotheistic faiths, albeit with varying symbols to carry their beliefs.

Second, Rahner also carefully connected the dots between the human family's growing knowledge of the universe, on the one hand, and theology's growing insights into the meaning of Jesus of Nazareth, on the other. For example, on the question about the bodily resurrection of Jesus, he asserts: "Jesus' corporeal human-ity is a permanent part of the one world with its single dynamism . . . Consequently, Jesus' resurrection . . . objectively is the beginning of the transfiguration of the world as an ontologically interconnected occurrence. In this beginning, the destiny of the world is already begun. At all events, it would in reality be very different if Jesus were not risen."[44]

Rahner's Christology emphasizes Jesus's location in history and in the material evolution of the universe. He describes Jesus as developing over the course of his own earthly life, and gradually awakening to the nature of the divine self-bestowal. But his awakening is meant to be paradigmatic of the self-transcendence of all crea-tures into union with their source and Creator. Jesus's openness to God is the best evidence available that God had a plan all along to bring creation into union with God's own "self." He is "the way" to be taken if God's plan is to be fulfilled.

Third, the divine self-bestowal did not begin with Jesus. It began with the cre-ation of the universe, the immensity and duration of which is only now beginning to dawn on human beings. But salvation and creation have been in God's intentions all along, so they are co-extensive, one with the other. Creation itself is the addressee of the message that is offered in the person of Jesus Christ. The Christ event—his birth, life, death, and resurrection—is to be read as God's irreversible commitment to all peoples and to all of creation. There is only one divine self-offer, though in history this offer has been differentiated into different moments, such as creation, incarnation, and resurrection.[45] If "the Word became flesh" (John 1:14), then in a sense "God becomes world" and "expresses himself in his Logos which has become world and matter."[46] If this is so, then God has not created a world "as something different from 'himself' but rather he is the one who gives himself away to the world and who has his own fate in and with this world."[47]

Fourth, there is an observable pressure on created reality in every one of its instantiations "to become more than it is in itself," hence, the strivings of each creature for some kind of "more"; creatures are always emergent, not quiescent, inert passivities.[48] The apogee of this pressure of evolution to become more is the human being. In human beings, the cosmos can become conscious of itself. *Homo sapiens,* however, did not come forth randomly, "but at a definite point in this development, a point at which he himself can even direct this development at least partially by the fact that he now objectifies it and stands over against what has produced him and transforms the producer itself"; consequently, nature can "become conscious of itself *in him.*"[49]

So in personal consciousness there can take place a "recapitulating self-presence of the whole or of the cosmos."[50] Though this kind of consciousness is still in its infancy, it "can take place in an absolutely unique way in each individual," through the particular data the individual is inquiring into.[51] Insofar as this is going on in a person, inevitably he or she is seeking the meaning of his or her own life, and of humanity. Since consciousness is able to recapitulate itself, both against the whole cosmos and within it, a wonderful thing can happen. One's self-transcending conscious self can experience the self-bestowal of God within the medium of the whole that is both God and earth. Even though God has always been immanent in the creation, the Word was made flesh so that flesh could receive the Word.

Fifth and finally, a word on Rahner's treatment of the resurrection of Jesus. One of Rahner's disciples, Dennis Edwards, spells out some of the implications of the above insights. Eastern Christianity emphasizes the resurrection as the beginning of the transfiguration of all creation and the divinization of all humanity. Western Christianity has tended to shrink the meaning of the event by its focus on the juridical implications of the cross. But the resurrection needs to be seen as an event for the whole creation. It is an ontological event; it is the physical, biological "beginning of the glorification and divinization of the whole of reality."[52] The resurrection makes explicit and emphatic what was latent in the act of divine self-bestowal that began with creation itself, namely, that the whole universe is heading towards a transfiguration and that the risen Christ is the signal for all to behold or anticipate this. Love was present at the beginning of creation, and is the reason creation exists, but, as Gerard Manley Hopkins put it, "the beholder was wanting."

The above five insights demonstrate Rahner's particular genius for connecting dots. Concerning the last of these five points, instead of looking at the resurrection as God intervening to raise Jesus from the dead, it might be better understood as the most explicit instance we have of God's continuing faithfulness, in following through with the one act of divine self-bestowal that was the reason for creation in the first place. This is how both Rahner and Edwards interpret the resurrection. If their interpretation is correct, then we can come to a most useful insight into the natural evil in creation described by Tennyson and Becker at the beginning of this section. The insight would be that God was not intervening adventitiously and miraculously or overturning the natural world and its sufferings by raising his Son from the dead. Rather, the resurrection of Jesus is the occasion for the world to know what God has intended from the first moment of creation *ex nihilo*, namely that there will be new heavens and a new earth, and they are prefigured in his Son's death and resurrection. And furthermore, from the very beginning, the universe was made to be transfigured, and the resurrection is the signal that this transformation will take place: It has already begun in Jesus's resurrection.

"Where sin abounds grace doth more abound" now has a cosmic twist to it (Rom. 5:20). God's love, which has always been "the most immanent element in every creature," will transform the sufferings of creation in an eschatological con-summation.[53] Divine love is the reason for creation, and this Love has been living with and in creation's own processes, accompanying its acts of emergence and tran-scendence, and grieving its failures all along. With the resurrection, all of creation should now understand that death is not the last word, and that because the Word has become flesh, flesh is now part of God's eternity.

Faith contributes a further kind of knowing to scientific knowledge. Theology is a faith-knowing that seeks understanding about anything and everything, including scientific findings. The wholes arrived at by theology can satisfy the need for mean-ing or leave that need unsatisfied. The above understandings leave this author satis-fied. But they are not proffered with the intention of having the reader believe them, but only to inform the reader that this is how a theologian goes about trying to connect the dots between bits of data that cry out for connection.

In this chapter we have seen examples of three figures in the Catholic intellectual tradition who have tried to connect the dots by constructing a plausible account of the doctrinal tradition's relationship with data from other sources: scientific data in the case of Teilhard de Chardin and Karl Rahner, and theological data in the case of Maximus. Their contributions are not Catholic doctrine, but can become doc-trine or, more frequently, help us to see the old doctrines in a new light.

The predictions of ecologists about the perilous future of the planet due to human actions, or of scientists about the cosmological evidence of the planet's even-tual disappearance, prompt a pointed question: Will there be any faith left on earth, now that we know the magnitude of the universe and how infinitesimal and self-destructive the human species is within it? It would seem natural to expect that someone at a Catholic university might search the Catholic intellectual tradition—not necessarily expecting answers, but orientations—for how it has dealt with such questions. Johannes Metz's remark about the character of our eschatological knowl-edge is pertinent here: "What distinguishes the Christian and the secular ideologies of the future from one another is not that the Christians know more, but that they know less about the sought-after future of humanity and that they face up to the poverty of their knowledge."[54]

The three people studied in this chapter did not do their research because they saw the future. They, like all researchers, were energized by hope. The rationale for a Catholic institution of higher learning is built on hope, not sight. All scholars need models for their research, since research is a plodding process. The models here come from one faith, but all faiths inculcate hopes. Each has its distinctive symbols for shaping the hopes of their adherents. Israel's hopes were enlarged by Isaiah's prophetic word: "Lo, I am about to create new heavens and a new earth"(Isa. 65:17). Hopers do their research because of their hopes for what lies Ahead. People of faith do their research for the same reason, but within a horizon shaped by what is Above.

NOTES

1. von Balthasar, *Cosmic Liturgy*, 37.
2. Ibid., 273.
3. Ibid.
4. Ibid., 274.
5. Ibid., 71.
6. Ibid., 96.
7. Teilhard de Chardin, *Human Energy*, 163.
8. Teilhard de Chardin, *The Human Phenomenon*, 176.
9. Teilhard de Chardin, *Science and Christ*, 22.
10. Teilhard de Chardin, *The Human Phenomenon*, 156.
11. Thomas King, "Journal of Teilhard de Chardin," quoted in *Teilhard's Mass*, 71.
12. Teilhard de Chardin, *Letters from a Traveler*, 150.
13. Teilhard de Chardin, *The Human Phenomenon*, 30.
14. Ibid., 163.
15. Teilhard de Chardin, *Science and Christ*, 81.
16. Teilhard de Chardin, *The Heart of Matter*, 216.
17. Ibid.
18. Teilhard de Chardin, *Christianity and Evolution*, 102.
19. King, *Teilhard's Mass*, 90.
20. Teilhard de Chardin, *Science and Christ*, 201–2.
21. Ibid., 203.
22. Ibid.
23. Teilhard de Chardin, *Science and Christ*, 169.
24. Ibid., 215 (italics mine).
25. Ibid., 216.
26. Teilhard de Chardin, *Science and Christ*, 216.
27. Ibid., 217.
28. Teilhard de Chardin, *The Future of Man*, 322.
29. Teilhard de Chardin, *Science and Christ*, 168.
30. Teilhard de Chardin, Retreat Notes, 42.
31. Teilhard de Chardin, *The Human Phenomenon*, 156.
32. Teilhard de Chardin, *Science and Christ*, 214.
33. Ibid.
34. Teilhard de Chardin, *The Human Phenomenon*, 177.
35. Teilhard de Chardin, *Christianity and Evolution*, 22.
36. This insight is well covered in Thomas King, "Scientific Research as Adoration," *The Way*, 44, no. 3 (July 2005), 21–34.

37. Teilhard de Chardin, *The Making of a Mind*, 213–14.

38. Russell, *Cosmology*, 39.

39. Alfred Lord Tennyson's "In Memoriam."

40. Becker, *The Denial of Death*, 282.

41. Isham, "Creation of the Universe as a Quantum Process," in *Physics, Philosophy, and Theology*, 292.

42. Russell, Stoeger, and Coyne, eds., *Physics, Philosophy, and Theology*, 1–2.

43. Rahner, *Foundations of Christian Faith*, 437.

44. Rahner, "Resurrection," in *Sacramentum Mundi*, 333.

45. Rahner, *Foundations of Christian Faith*, 197.

46. Ibid.

47. Rahner, "The Specific Character of the Christian Concept of God," in *Theological Investigations*, 191.

48. Rahner, "Natural Science and Christian Faith," in *Theological Investigations*, 37.

49. Ibid., 188.

50. Ibid., 189.

51. Ibid.

52. Edwards, "Resurrection and the Costs of Evolution," 829. Edwards is quoting from Rahner, "Dogmatic Questions on Easter," 129.

53. Ibid., 823–24.

54. Metz, *Theology of the World*, 97.

CHAPTER 9

◆

Worship and the Catholic Identity of the Campus

I F ALL WHO WORKED on a Catholic campus were doing the work of the campus for the glory of God, then any questions about the identity of the college or university would be easily answered. Then the question wouldn't simply be about Catholic identity, but also about a Godly identity, or maybe a God-ward one. Would that things were that simple! First of all, not all of the personnel at a Catholic university would even understand what working for the glory of God means, or believe that it is possible. Second, there is the matter of the Catholic sponsorship of the university. Its preferred way of glorifying God has been through the celebration of the Eucharist. So, any change in the centrality of the celebration of the Eucharist at the school would be regarded as a change in how it sees its Catholic identity. One solution might be to soft-pedal the Catholic Eucharist, and press for some more inclusive way of campus worship. Another solution would be for Catholics to understand the specific implications of Eucharistic celebrations on campus in ways that they have not before.

I will explore this second possibility in this chapter, since I can imagine that one obvious push-back to this book's thesis about catholicity would be that regardless of the claimed capaciousness of the Catholic intellectual tradition, the bottom line is that the most significant act on these campuses is the Mass. "And to this rite, all are sincerely welcomed," I can imagine my responder arguing, "but they are not so welcome that they can receive the host and the cup, because if they are not Catholic, then they are misaligned in varying degrees from the Catholic faith. So, say what you will, at least at this place in the life of the campus, some belong and some do not."

I accept the discipline imposed by the Church about reserving participation in communion to baptized Catholics, and understand the reasoning behind it; namely, that the Eucharist is an expression of the Church's unity: It doesn't make a unity that is not there. But, of course, theologians, myself included, don't stop thinking at the door of praxis or discipline or doctrine. We are paid, so to speak, to think from the givens, but also through them, and, if possible, to see where they might be able to go. What I want to explore in this chapter is a way of interpreting the

Eucharist that will make the present discipline more understandable, less exclusionary, and more central to the rationale for Catholic institutions of higher learning.

Any university today is characterized by ever-increasing pluralisms—religious, ethnic, generational, philosophical, hermeneutical, anthropological. For Catholic universities, one would be right to presume that a deeper connection could develop about Eucharist in both the Catholic intellectual tradition and its doctrinal tradition. Each of these traditions is still evolving, and still producing new insights and theologies. While Christ is the same yesterday, today, and forever, this intellectual tradition never settles for a past understanding as the last word.

THE NEGOTIABLES AND NONNEGOTIABLES

When we consider the fact of religious pluralism, and even the number of faculty and students who come from no religious tradition, on Catholic campuses, we are faced with the question of how to accommodate this pluralism and still have worship be a central act on a campus. Germane to this issue is the theological category of worship-in-common (*communicatio in sacris*), which has naturally had a long history of doctrinal and canonical development in Roman Catholicism. The general principle that has governed this area of Church life is that the bread and the cup in the Eucharistic celebration may be received only by those who are in full communion with the Church and its teachings. By participating in these liturgies and partaking of the sacrament, one expresses and deepens this communion. Because communion with the Church is understood as the prerequisite for participation, the Church holds that the Eucharistic species, whether on campus or off, is not to be extended to those who are not Catholic.

But neither doctrine nor practice is static in the Church. The Second Vatican Council's Decree on Ecumenism hammered out several new positions with regard to prayer and Eucharist with others. First of all, "it is desirable that Catholics should join in prayer with their separated brethren."[1] This is a new and welcome recommendation. As far as formal "common worship," namely the celebration of the Eucharist with non-Catholic Christians, is concerned, the Council teaches that it should not be done "indiscriminately for the restoration of unity among Christians."[2] Presumably this leaves the possibility that such common worship can take place so long as it is done with prudence and does not generate a false irenicism. The Council goes on in the same section to outline the two principles that should guide such worship: The first is "that of the unity of the Church which ought to be expressed; the second, that of the sharing in the means of grace." The Council then explains that "the expression of unity very generally forbids common worship. Grace to be obtained commends it" (3).

Since the Council does not traffic in throwaway lines, one has to marvel at this masterful exercise in dialectic here. The most important term is *generally* (*plerumque*), obviously meaning "for the most part," therefore implying that exceptions are possible. The second sentence is equally beguiling. When grace is needed, the Council commends common worship (8). When is grace not needed? It seems to me that a university under the auspices of a diocese or religious order would clearly be an instance of a situation in which sharing in the means of grace is commendable, even conceivably called for on occasion, since the university is a work in common. But such a change in Eucharistic practice could only be effected by the local bishop or the regional bishops' conference.

It seems obvious that a business-as-usual conservatism in this matter of Eucharistic worship on campus hardly produces much fruit, in the sense of contributing something to the campus's common identity. One has to ask whether God is better worshipped or more glorified by retaining the restriction of the Eucharistic species to those who are Catholic on a university campus, or by generating a liturgical life on campus that would welcome common worship. Further reflection, therefore, seems called for in this area. There are multiple arguments for revisiting this issue. First of all, would it not be an empirical nightmare to try to answer the question of when the Roman Catholic communicants are in full communion with the institutional Church and its magisterium and hence worthy to be communicants? Second, are there not many fervent Christians who are not Catholic, but who give every indication of being faithful to Christ, of hearing and obeying the Gospel, and who believe that the elements distributed are sacred? Third, if Christ intended that "this bread is my flesh for the life of the world," should we begin to think of this "bread" as food for more than just Roman Catholics (John 6:51)? Finally, is the unity of the Church that the Eucharist expresses to be understood as its present unity? Perhaps, but does it not also include a promise of greater unity in the future, when every tear will be wiped away, and every dissonance will be superceded by the eternal banquet? If we celebrate the actuality of this unity with one another at Eucharist, is that really experienced? Or, since we live *in spe*, not *in re*, in hope rather than in sight, is it more the future eschatological unity with God and one another that we celebrate in the Eucharist? And if so, what does this say about the Eucharist as an expression of the unity of the Church? These marks of the Church—one, holy, and catholic—will be fully realized only in the eschatological hereafter.

THE INTELLECTUAL CONVERSION OF CATHOLICS

A Catholic university, of course, is not in a position to "go it alone" as far as Eucharistic practice is concerned. The diocesan disciplines must be observed and followed; the institution is led by its bishop with regard to the practices of the faith. So if there is to be any change in the way that campuses experience the Eucharist, it will have to come from another approach. The other approach I will propose here is for Catholics to be more theologically informed about the relation between the Eucharist and the purpose of the university. For their campuses to be affected, Catholic students and faculty need to have deeper insight about the Eucharist.

First of all, it is important to grasp the radical meaning of the Eucharist. One of the ways of doing this is by revisiting the prayer that ends the Canon of the Mass, which culminates with: "Through him, with him, and in him, in the unity of the Holy Spirit, all glory and honor is yours almighty Father, for ever and ever, Amen!" But this Trinitarian prayer is expressed by a congregation in a very particular locale. These particular people are praying this prayer, at this time, in this place, by glorifying God "in the unity of the Holy Spirit." This is quite a leap in the stature of the enterprise of the place, if one lets the doxology, as it is called, sink in. Could any other activity on campus be more efficacious than one done through, with, and in Christ, "in the unity of the Holy Spirit"? Would any other activity be more likely to bring about a wholeness than a school's celebrations of the Eucharist, which explicitly address the Trinity from the very particular clod of earth that is the campus? This prayer has an incredible degree of efficacy, second to nothing else, since it enters straight into the holy of holies, into the inner life of God, all the way to the throne of God, from this place at this time! The Eucharistic Prayer, therefore, is singular in contrast to any other act or the whole sum of acts done in the course of the day or in the life of the campus community. But this is of course a faith statement, not a description of what is experienced on campus.

The experience of those who celebrate the Eucharist on campus should be grounded in the belief that what is being offered in that event, through those particular people, is nothing less than the primordial sacrifice of Jesus's own self-donation to the Father on behalf of humanity. It is this concrete community that joins itself to the timeless and spaceless event of Jesus's passing over from this world into the life of God. It is this sacrifice of reconciliation that knits this people anew to God. So far, so good. Remember, the participants at a campus Eucharist are, presumably, all involved, each in his or her own way, in the other undertakings of the school, which are different from those of any other congregation. The Church is always local. When a congregation comes together to worship, it does not enact a generic act of homage, but one that is as particular as the people who are gathered there and the work that they do. It would make liturgical sense, therefore, if the participants in campus Masses were to understand and name their specific activities in service to the university's mission as part of what they offered to God's glory through, with, and in Christ. A Eucharist that isn't local in its ethos and enactment offers an odd, disembodied form of glory and honor to God!

A second way of grasping the import of the "Holy Sacrifice of the Mass" for the campus is by seeing it in terms of what we know of the agenda of the risen Christ as he is enacting that agenda in history. Paul's Corinthian passage (1 Cor. 15:22–28) clarifies this. Jesus's agenda, he says, is to hand over to God whatever has been entrusted to him and gathered into his care in the course of history. But what is entrusted to him is always particular, here the thing the university in its personnel does, especially in and through its disciplines. A campus's Eucharistic liturgy, therefore, should make explicit what it believes Christ is seeking to accomplish in that particular academy at that particular time. The fact that many on campus do not know, or if they know do not share, this belief or Jesus's agenda should not deter those who do believe, and who have come together to celebrate him and to commit themselves to active service of his agenda.

Thus, the belief at issue here is that "when everything is subjected to him (Christ), then the Son himself will also be subjected to the One who made everything subject to him, so that God may be all in all" (1 Cor. 15:28). God will be all in all. This image of, for example, the work of the disciplines coming under Christ's feet would be off-putting if it seemed to be redolent of an antiquated Christendom in which the Church controlled their meaning. But Christendom is embalmed history, and, in our time, the Church now formally embraces the rightful autonomy of the secular, as the Second Vatican Council indicated.[3]

The Church, of course, does not see this autonomy as the final meaning or destiny of any given thing. While the disciplines must be accorded their proper autonomy, and academic freedom accorded to those who work in them, theonomy is the final stage of the secularity of the world in all its parts. (Theonomy, a term used often by John Paul II, means that something is formally brought to God.) Between these two moments for the things of this world, autonomy and theonomy, the worshiping community exercises its priestly function of offering the particular things "our hands have made," thus rendering them *oblata* (offerings to God). Such an offering makes the work of our hands and minds pleasing to God. This interaction describes the completion effected through Christ in the Spirit of what his followers bring him, that is to say, the collective work of the campus. It is given a new status because Christ takes it up, without taking away its autonomy. In the absence of such an offering—if the school's labors are simply left at the stage of their autonomy, without this further act—Catholic schools are theologically no different from secular schools.

Several times in this volume, "Catholic" has been etymologically translated "throughout the whole." When will this be? When "God is all in all." How do we get from this moment to that ultimate denouement? Through worship, through offering to God ourselves and our work. The Church serves what remains God's sole prerogative, which is to permeate the whole of a given person or endeavor. The magisterium and the liturgical life of the Church play one role in this process, the Catholic intellectual tradition another. Their areas of mediation and discernment differ, as has already been explained in this volume.

Hence the importance of an oblation mentality on a Catholic campus. Of course, Catholicism does not have any exclusive title to the way of connecting God to the work of our hands and minds. I have before me a Service of Worship program from the Duke University Chapel for its upcoming Sunday worship. It reads:

This morning we give thanks for the Department of Mathematics, where students are challenged to use reason and imagination to understand the beauty and intricacies of abstract structure, and where they learn how to apply mathematics as an essential and integral tool of science and technology in areas as diverse as cosmology, finance, medicine, and environmental studies.

To symbolize the congregation's perception of the connection between God and the work of the university in math, a student brings a textbook and an icosahedron to lay on the altar. Over the course of a year, each of the disciplines is celebrated in this way.

Although it is not within the power of a Catholic university to change the rules for the reception of Eucharist on campus, the attitudes of those who frequent Eucharist on campus can change. So, to continue the alternative I am elaborating here, the specific work of the university can be brought front and center at Mass, rather than being left at the church doors. Or, to put it another way, we must take Martha, as well as Mary, to Mass (Luke 10:38–42). Further, we must bring not only our own work, but also that of our colleagues. To some extent this change can come through specific rituals, as in the Duke example; but more foundationally, it requires an intellectual conversion about what we think we are doing when we attend Mass. The Council in *Gaudium et spes* critiques the attitude of those "who think that religion consists of acts of worship alone and . . . imagine they can plunge themselves into earthly affairs in such a way as to imply that these are altogether divorced from their religious life." It goes on to say that "this split between the faith which many profess and their daily lives deserves to be counted among the more serious errors of our age." "Let there be no false opposition," the Council insists, "between professional and social activities on the one hand and religious life on the other."[4]

I am taking aim here at a compartmentalized mindset that thinks that the work of learning, research, and teaching of "secular" subjects are not part of the risen Christ's agenda or the Church's interest. This is too narrow a horizon to bring to the Eucharist; since nothing human is alien to God, neither should it be to God's Church. The new heavens and the new earth will be composed of all that has been transformed by Christ's redeeming act. "And, I, if I be lifted up, I will draw all things to myself" (John 12:32). Perhaps in this regard, the term *transubstantiation* could also be used of that "material" that Jesus's followers make available to him. What is this material? Themselves, what they do, what their colleagues do. Since there is nothing narrow about God's purposes and pervasive activity in the world, neither should there be any narrowness in the perspective of those who worship God through the Son in the Spirit. The breadth and depth of this divine scheme are breathtaking. So while the faithful remnant might be very small in number at a given campus liturgy, they should imagine themselves as being sent to haul in more fish or bigger game than their numbers represent or their own work indicates. They are not to huddle fearfully together, like the disciples in the upper room before the descent of the Spirit.

One of the perennial themes of Catholicism is the sacramentality of the created world. "All reality is potentially or in fact the bearer of God's presence and the instrument of God's activity."[5] This attitude toward the created world is rooted in scripture. Christ is the image of the invisible God. "In him were created all things . . . [they] were created through him and for him . . . in him all things hold together . . . through him all things are reconciled, making peace by the blood of his cross"

(Col. 1:16–20). If we believe this, then to separate our work and the things of time from the agenda of Christ is religiously ignorant.

The work being done in a university that claims a connection to this image of the invisible God is so much more than meets the eye. Those who see with eyes of faith, hope, and love should be able to see that there are many levels of Eucharistic meaning for a person and a congregation to plumb. Some are personal and intimate. But if these are the only meanings experienced, then the celebration of the Eucharist will be confined by a privatism or narrowness. The Eucharist is a tensive symbol with multiple meanings.[6]

Believers' personal and social needs should be met in the Eucharist, but it would be good to recall St. Paul's profound insight into the first Eucharistic assemblies in Corinth. He became alarmed about the parochialism of some of its members. He judged by their behavior that they were not in fact eating the Lord's Supper, as they presumed they were, but rather their own (1 Cor. 11:20). He so judged because there was an in-group that gathered before the latecomers—probably Christian slaves of wealthy Corinthians, who had first to feed their pagan masters—could arrive. The latecomers were left out or forgotten about, while the in-group ate, drank, and were satisfied that their religious needs were met. These early assemblies were celebrated in the context of an agape meal, which was something akin to a potluck supper. Paul warned the Corinthians about the religious import of their ignoring the other members of their community: "Anyone who eats and drinks without discerning the body eats and drinks judgment on himself" (11:29).

An application of Paul's insight to the question we are considering here might go something like this: While we accept that the Catholic Church is not changing its discipline about Eucharistic reception, this does not justify any insularity on the part of those who participate in the Mass. The challenge is to try to understand "the body" the way Paul did. The body he was asking the Corinthian faithful to discern was not simply the consecrated species (the bread and the wine), but the members of the body of believers. By emphasizing the vertical element of their piety at the expense of the horizontal (confining the sacredness of the Eucharist to the elements), they were ignoring their brothers and sisters in Christ. Vatican II extends even further the scope of the body we should be serving, so that it now includes "the body of a new human family . . ."[7] It would seem then that a worthy reception of the Eucharist on a university campus would include explicit reference to those involved in the work of the university.

There are at least five reasons why those attending Eucharistic liturgies on campus need to consider the meaning of such liturgies for the university. It is not just for themselves.

First, Catholics cannot expect that those who don't find meaning in Eucharist will find it there, but they must examine themselves about whether they have created a chasm between "us" and "them" by the attitudes they take to the Eucharist. What a difference it would make if Catholics attempted to bridge that chasm to the extent that they could! A common meaning that is shared and enacted benefits everyone. Individuals can become a community only to the extent that they share common meanings. And conversely, everyone loses when, despite working at the same enterprise, there is a poverty of shared meaning, hence an absence of community. A poverty of collective meaning is sure to produce disconnection from one another, and an ennui about the common mission of the institution.

Second, if common meaning energizes community, then a revisiting of the significance of the Eucharist for the whole of the university should be undertaken. Ideally, the Catholic members on a given campus might be able to generate new energy for the school's mission and purpose. Beginning with their Eucharistic assemblies, Paul and the first Christians seem to have developed a clarity about God's intention to make a relational whole of the physical whole of the human race. They came to see that no one was to be left outside of the pale of redemption by Christ's death and resurrection. The description in the Acts of the Apostles of the early communities is instructive. It describes a culture of "exultation and sincerity of heart" that outsiders saw in those who broke bread in Christ's name (2:46–47). While our world is still at a painfully incomplete stage of human and ecclesial unity, our Eucharistic celebrations should help to diminish this disunity, rather than prolonging obstacles to the experience of unity.

Third, if those who regularly repair to Mass with a sense that they are not to leave behind their own and others' endeavors at their common workbench, they will be more in synch with God's intentions for this world. This is a sacrament that should celebrate the act of the redemption of all, not just some. And as the Council puts it in *Gaudium et spes*, "the promotion of human unity belongs to the innermost nature of the Church" (42). Leaving the specific work of the university outside the chapel doors, or assuming that those who do not, for whatever reason, join in the liturgy therefore have nothing to do with it, will only serve to continue the divide between Catholics and non-Catholics on the campus. Consequently, "the body of a new human family" will not grow at such a place.

Fourth, and furthermore, the Eucharistic liturgy is also an occasion when the Church can acknowledge with thanksgiving the debt she owes to human intelligence and its developments that enrich the world. Think of every kind of progress in the arts and sciences, the intellectual and cultural treasures of the human race, past and present. There is and should continue to be an ongoing giving of thanks for all of these treasures. The university, it has been said, is the place where the Church does its thinking and learning. It should also be a place where, with the help of the Holy Spirit, gratitude permeates the culture: gratitude to those who contribute to the world's well-being and to God who supplies the material for this well-being.

Fifth, and finally, God's purposes are "to grow the body of a new human family."[8] Knowledge of these purposes is not new. They were evident in the Old Testament era, when it seemed only a matter of time before all peoples would go up to Mt. Zion to worship the Lord (Isa. 2:2–3, 56:6–8, 60:11–14; Mic. 4:1–3). Christians, too, proclaim the universality of God's offer of redemption, and praise and honor its source. Since their Eucharistic prayer is done "in the unity of the Holy Spirit," Catholics should try to be as inclusive and universal as the Spirit is. What is the Spirit seeking to unify? The Spirit is "the Go-Between God," who is "operating upon every element and process of the material universe, and is the immanent and anonymous presence of God . . . God works always through moments of recognition when mutual awareness is born. The Spirit's history is a history of facilitating encounters."[9] We think too narrowly if we imagine that the operations of the Spirit are confined to the Church. The Spirit blows where it will; its operations pervade the whole race. By their fruits they are known. Recall, these are "joy, love, peace, patience, kindness, generosity, faithfulness, gentleness and self control" (Gal. 5:22).

A PRIESTLY PEOPLE

There is an additional and perhaps even more salient reason than the five given above for the worshipper to consider the Eucharistic liturgy's meaning for their wider university community. Catholicism's understanding, as also that of most Christian denominations, is that to be baptized into Christ is to be baptized into a priestly role, one that mediates the things of earth to God and the things of God to the earth. So if baptism brings each of the baptized into the one priesthood of Christ, then Christ the priest, together with his priestly people, makes available to God the Father what they make and do, just as they also make themselves available.[10] The faithful are consecrated into Christ's holy priesthood! The community worshiping in the Spirit brings itself and its own work to God to be completed through his Son's self-offering. This act gives their work an efficacy and stature it would not have of itself, as far as we know.

"Everything that the Father gives me will come to me and I will not reject anyone who comes to me," Jesus said to the crowds. "I should not lose anything of what he gave me, but I should raise it on the last day . . . Everyone who sees the Son and believes in him may have eternal life and I shall raise him up on the last day" (John 6: 39–40). Notice the play between everything/anything and everyone/anyone. How will "these things" in effect "come to him" and also be raised up by him on "the last day?" Since things cannot believe, Christ has made of those who believe in him "a priestly people, a people set apart," so that they can offer these things as "sacrifices acceptable to God through Jesus Christ" (2 Pet. 5:9). And what if this consecrated, priestly people does not offer "these things," as well as themselves, as sacrifices acceptable to God? Only God can answer that question. But what we do know is that we who have been made mediators by the sacrament of baptism can make ourselves and "the work of our hands" part of what is offered in the Eucharist.

These texts from John's Gospel reinforce the go-between or mediating role of those who have come to believe in Jesus. It is up to believers to offer sacrifices acceptable to God, to make their own "things" part of what will be raised up on the last day. We do this by exercising our priestly role in the course of our lives, individually and communally. This brings Christ's work to completion, in the same way that he exercised his priesthood during his earthly sojourn.

So the most concrete and pervasive aspect of our priestly calling is being able to see the connection between the "things" that we touch, and work with, and are touched by, and the Christ in whom we have come to believe. What is the nature of this connection? A priestly people is a "go-between" people, called to mediate here-and-now things to Jesus, who in turn connects them to the One whom he called his Father. These "things" exist now in their autonomy or rightful secularity, but they are also capable of being brought from this condition into theonomy (that is, of being brought under the reign of God), through the mediation of a "go-between" people. God could have done otherwise, but apparently chose not to save the world independently of a people acting through, with, and in his Son. Their acts of mediating ensure that Jesus will not "lose anything of what he (the Father) gave me" (John 6:37).

In a simpler era, those Catholics who said the morning offering always offered their "prayers, works, joys and sufferings" to God; simply by saying this prayer, they caught the point I am making here, without needing any great degree of liturgical sophistication. Many still do this. The goodness of this prayer notwithstanding, the priestly act is exercised most formally when the people of faith (and hope and love, of course) come together for the most certain, social act of mediation available to them, "the sacrifice of reconciliation."[11] The risen Jesus is always interceding for humanity by working through, with, and in those whom God chooses to work with, through, and in. They extend his mediation to all that they bring to him. It would help if his priestly people were more knowledgeable and active participants in his work.

The passage from John being looked at here begins with Jesus's claim: "I am the bread of life" (John 6:35). But he also describes this bread as "my flesh for the life of the world." So while this bread is for the life of those who receive it, his flesh is for the life of the world. Therefore, those consuming the bread of life are instrumental not only in raising the "things" of earth up to Christ, and through him to his Father, but also in contributing the bread of meaning to the world in which they inhabit and operate.

One cannot but be impressed that only one priest was left standing by the end of the New Testament. In effect, as the Letter to the Hebrews indicates, Jesus abrogated the sacrificial function of priests by becoming the sacrifice himself. His action on behalf of the whole human race made the sacrifices offered by the Levitical priesthood passé. Christians believe that his self-offering became the sacrifice that God found acceptable once and for all:

> Come to him, the Lord, a living stone, rejected by human beings but chosen and precious in the sight of God, and like living stones let yourselves be built into a spiritual house, to be a holy priesthood, to offer spiritual sacrifices acceptable to God through Jesus Christ . . . You are a chosen race, a royal priesthood, a holy nation, a people set apart so that you may announce the praises of him who called you out of darkness into his wonderful light (1 Pet. 2:4–9).

It is the Christian community, first and foremost, that exercises Christ's priesthood now. Brought into this priesthood one by one through the sacrament of baptism, this community offers Christ's sacrifice of praise to God. This would all be preposterous if they had not been made participants in his priestly role by receiving the same gift of the Spirit who accompanied Jesus in his faith life on earth (Heb. 9:14). It is this gift of the same eternal Spirit who enabled him to offer himself to God. It is this same Spirit who empowers Jesus's followers, collectively and individually, to exercise their priestly responsibility of offering themselves to God as Jesus did.

The warrant for this line of thinking is found in Catholic doctrine. The Council's Dogmatic Constitution on the Church, *Lumen gentium*, speaks of the priesthood of Christ as a continuing act that gives the baptized a share in his "priestly function of offering spiritual worship for the glory of God and the salvation of human beings"(34). What does that mean? The Council's line of thinking becomes only slightly more concrete when the Constitution goes on to remark later in the same section that we the baptized are "marvelously called and equipped to produce ever more abundant fruits of the Spirit." The Council Fathers further specify that this "spiritual worship" consists of the "spiritual sacrifices" that we offer and that are made acceptable to God through Christ, the "supreme and eternal Priest." What are the contents of these sacrifices? "Our works, prayers, apostolic endeavors, ordinary married and family life, our daily labor, our mental and physical relaxation, the hardships of life if patiently borne." And all of these become one with Christ's continuing priestly act "if carried out in the Spirit." Where are these sacrifices offered and what is their effect in the world? "During the celebration of the Eucharist," section 34 concludes, "these sacrifices are most lovingly offered to the Father along with the Lord's Body. Thus as worshipers whose every deed is holy the laity consecrates the world itself to God."

These "sacrifices" are not meant to give the faithful something to do to while away their time while the priest is doing his thing on our behalf at Mass. The offerings of the faithful enter into Christ's continuing self-offer to the Father (Heb. 7:24). These offerings, which come forth from the wholly unique character of the person's life and work, become acceptable to God by being doubly "spiritual": They are spiritual first in the sense that they "were carried out in the Spirit," and second in that Jesus makes them part of his self-sacrifice to the Father.

There is an additional insight to be found in one of the connotations of the word "sacrifice," namely forfeiture or surrender. The offerings are left with the One to whom they are given. In some inchoate way, whatever is offered consecrates that part of the world from which it is offered, by those who have been sacramentally consecrated. It is "through baptism and strengthened by the power of the Holy Spirit through Confirmation . . . that we are consecrated into a royal priesthood and a holy priesthood."[12] Or to put it in even simpler terms, the faithful are consecrated "in order that they may offer spiritual sacrifices through everything they do and bear witness to Christ throughout the world."[13]

But the Council Fathers were not naive about the specific contents of this "everything they do," knowing that some work is not likely to be acceptable to God. So they add this qualifier: What is offered must be "work befitting" the Christian calling. This is an interesting note. It puts an ethical obligation on the offerer, to be sure that his or her work is worthy to be offered. One would have to examine one's conscience about whether some workplaces or industries or work cultures are acceptable to God, or whether the manner of the labor is careless or unfair to either employer or employees. Conceivably without this caveat of "befitting," a person could imagine that merely by offering his or her work to God, endeavors that had been offensive to God would become pleasing to God. It would be a misuse of the Mass to legitimize unjust structures or behaviors.

The question of the fittingness of one's work can easily get beyond the individual's capacity to analyze, of course. Take, for example, something as complex as the legitimacy of an economic system, or the implications of a particular practice or the policy of a given institution. A peaceful conscience or a troubled conscience is probably still the best signal of whether or not one's work befits the Christian calling and offering. We also need to be reminded of the overall context of the Eucharist, in which sinners approach the throne of God through the one who makes intercession for them and reparation for their sins. So the fittingness of the offerings we make will not be perfect, since we who offer them are sinners.

THE IDENTITY OF CATHOLIC SCHOOLS

The whole line of thinking taken in this chapter brings up further issues having to do with the Catholic identity of Catholic schools. Obviously, it surfaces the question about the relation between the work being done on campus and God. If we take these documents at their word, then the liturgical life of the campus is not peripheral but is central to campus life. And even for those who are Mass-goers, the further question is whether their purview is sufficiently holistic, whether they see that their own work, as well as the work of their department and of the school, is incomplete theologically if not offered to God. It would be religiously negligent if the enormous amount of labor that goes on in a school were to be left unoffered to the One for whom the school claims it is in existence. For a campus to take for granted a separation between these two worlds, the world of academia and the world of God, would seem to constitute a failure of religious and liturgical imaginations, at the very least.

Unfortunately, the way Catholic identity is usually conceived on campus seems to allow the separation of the work world and the worship world to go on without anyone seeming to mind. The point in this chapter is to say that there is a lacuna in the Eucharistic catechesis most Catholics have appropriated. Add to that the problem of the "for Catholics only" character of the Mass, which also invites and deepens the discontinuity between the work of the university and the worship of the university.

Catholic identity, which usually is connected with morals and doctrine, needs a liturgical foundation, one that is concerned with whether God is being acknowledged as the purpose and end of the work done on campuses founded in the name of God and Church. Can one think that God is pleased to be the One who equips the campus personnel with the wherewithal to come to knowledge, and also with the desire to discover it, and yet be ignored as the cause of all of it?

Yes, there are adherents of many faiths on Catholic campuses, and some of them have the opportunity, whether on or off the campus, to worship in the manner to which they are accustomed. This is all to the good. But would it not be even more to the honor and glory of God if there were some way that the common enterprise of knowing in a Catholic school could be connected to the enterprise of worship, notwithstanding the pluralism of faiths? The work is one, but the forms of worship are multiple, and the absence of common worship as a campus is taken to be inevitable, given the pluralism of our faiths and lack of faith. In effect, it seems to proclaim the sufficiency of secularity.

We do not all see God in the same light, but does that mean that the only way we can approach God is through the particular rituals and routines in which each of our faiths have approached the same mystery? In *Nostra aetate*, the Second Vatican Council exhorts the faithful to plumb the spiritual values found in the faiths (Buddhism, Hinduism, Islam, Judaism) (2). It does not say how. This open-ended exhortation would seem to be an invitation for creativity at a Catholic university. The benefit would hopefully be an appreciation of the religious import of the school's educational mission. A university might begin a process of gathering those who have competence in the theology of their respective faiths, their worship in particular, to see whether thanksgiving, for example, could be offered in common in ways that would credibly express and not infringe on anyone's understanding of God.

JEWISH WORSHIP AND MUSLIM WORSHIP

Christians have much to learn about how our Jewish ancestors understood the character of study, and how our Jewish brothers and sisters understand it today. In a tractate of the Mishnah, Pirqe Aboth, a number of wisdom sayings have been collected from rabbinic sages that regard the status of study of Torah as highly as a form of worship. The material studied by the Jewish believer was sacred in his or her eyes. The most intense presence of God accessible to rabbinic Judaism was via the Torah. So perhaps the Jewish believer's understanding of the process of bringing their intelligence to the text might be a model for us who are deeply indebted to that tradition in so many ways, leading us to reexamine the status of study. We might even find that our understanding of study, and the manner in which we undertake it, could be lifted out of its presumed secularity, and be seen as something closer to a religious undertaking than the mores of present scholarship are wont to allow.

The Mishnah tractates began to be assembled somewhere after the destruction of the Temple in AD 70, which was also the time of the later New Testament writings; their final redaction was between AD 200 and 220. But it is also clear that this rabbinic ideal of Torah study as a form of worship "was an ideal in Israel before the

Pharisees and especially before the Rabbis . . . and was in all branches of Jewry."[14] Thus it was known to be an ideal during the time of Jesus and the early Christians.

Does this ideal represent what Jesus thought? In Matthew 5:17–19, one finds Jesus reverencing Torah, which he claims he has not come to abolish but to fulfill, even in its smallest parts. Also, in Matthew 11:28–30, it is likely that the yoke that Jesus invites his followers to take upon themselves is the Torah, albeit lightened by his interpretation of it. "He is not setting up a second or even a new Torah against the old but inviting his listeners to approach the one and only Torah, once given by God on Sinai, through him and his teaching."[15] It is also likely that Jesus's main problem with some of the Pharisees was their elitist attitude towards those who were not students of Torah, and hence were not able to partake of this fount of sacredness. The exclusivism of these Pharisees was in stark contrast to Jesus's inclusivism.

Since these Old Testament texts have not lost their sacredness, the Vatican Council's Constitution on Divine Revelation teaches that "Christians should accept them with veneration; these writings give expression to a lively sense of God, are a storehouse of sublime teachings on God and of sound wisdom on human life, as well as a wonderful treasury of prayers; in them, too, the mystery of our salvation is present in a hidden way."[16] Does it seem too great a leap to believe that we should approach these texts with the awe recommended by both the Aboth tradition, described above, and the Council, and to approach texts of a more secular nature with a proportionate respect, when such respect is warranted by their status as classics?

Though the materials studied by most scholars would seldom have the aura of sacredness that the presumptively inspired texts have, there are derivative implications of viewing study if not as worship, at least as of great worth in God's eyes. One of these implications is that serious scholarship can be looked upon as continuing the task asked of Adam, who was "created in God's image": that is, to name the reality set before him (Gen. 2:19–20).

It seems that a Catholic university should be in the forefront of developments in matters of religious practice, and not be content to simply be an extension of the practices of the parishes in the diocese. Such a university should be a place where there is a prudent experimental attitude; if for no other reason than because it is teaching the next generation of Catholics, whose lives will be intertwined with peoples of other faiths, as they already are at their schools. It is one thing to teach the beliefs of another faith and the differences between faiths. It is another to host events that enable participants to experience and celebrate the similarities shared with other faiths, while retaining the integrity of our respective faiths. Practices affect beliefs. No change in practices, no change in beliefs.

Catholicism has rightly been concerned that its worship practices mirror its beliefs. But what if the beliefs of Catholicism about another faith are developing, and its practices do not yet reflect these developments? Then it would seem that a Catholic college or university should be a place that could try to see in what ways it is possible for faiths, while retaining their own integrity, to celebrate what they have in common, which is faith in God, hope in God, and love of God. On November 7, 2008, 58 religious authorities and experts from 28 countries representing each of the two faiths signed a formal declaration of common agreements between Catholicism and Islam. This forum, convoked by the Vatican's Pontifical Council for Interreligious Dialogue, represents a recent development in understanding about the Muslim faith.[17] The full text of the declaration can be found in appendix C. Here I will highlight those statements that seem to call for more than words of agreement.

Catholics and Muslims are called to be "instruments of love and harmony." That certainly is a consummation to be fervently wished for in this world. "Christian love is forgiving and excludes no one, including one's enemies. It should be not just words but deeds. This is a sign of its genuineness." Could those deeds include some common prayer services on occasions like Thanksgiving, for instance? The declaration does not say. The Muslim part of the declaration, which waxes eloquent about the compassion of God, quotes from its tradition that for "those who believe and do good works, the Merciful shall engender love among them." Love engendered for one another by good works! Again, the question arises of whether these works might include common expressions of piety that elicit a greater love of God, while ensuring the integrity of each faith's understanding of God. Both of these faiths experience the same "summons and imperative to bear witness to the transcendent dimension of life through a spirituality nourished by prayer in a world that is becoming more and more secularized and materialistic."

"Young people are the future of religious communities and of societies as a whole . . . It is essential that they be well formed in their own religious traditions and well informed about other cultures and religions." Would they be less well formed in their own religious traditions without any experience of prayer with those of another religious tradition? Or is it possible that they could be both more informed and better formed in their own tradition by such experiences? The present practice of always separating the worship of the different faiths needs to be examined for its formative consequences.

In its 1965 Declaration on the Relation of the Church to Non-Christians, the Second Vatican Council itself exhorted the faithful to "acknowledge, preserve and encourage the spiritual and moral truths found among non-Christians."[18] It is merely speculation, but what if that exhortation had been implemented with deeds between 1965 and 2001? Would we have the same context of terrorism we have today?

WWJD

It seems natural for Christians to wonder what Jesus would think and do about the separation of faiths on a campus. Granted, the Eucharist remains the best way to praise God for those who understand the importance of Christ's passion, death, and resurrection for all humanity throughout history, but does it have to be the sole way of celebrating the God who is the Alpha and Omega of knowledge? That would seem to be a failure to understand Jesus's own ministry.

When we ask the question about how Jesus dealt with the issue of authentic worship, we know several things. First, he always seemed to annoy those with tight religious boundaries and a tidy religiosity. His norms, by contrast, might be seen as porous. He frequently practiced table fellowship with the wrong people. He seemed much more concerned about the sheep who were strays or alienated or shunned or made marginal than with the sheep already gathered. He acted where he saw need. He had intended to pass through the town until he saw Zacchaeus, who was marginalized by the townspeople (Luke 19:2). He saw God already at work and the fields already ripe for the harvest (John 4:35). What made them ripe? God was already active in the people, even before Jesus arrived and could see it. He only gradually learned the breadth of his mission, that it was so much wider than "the house of Israel." I suggest he would be delighted if his followers came to understand that their mission was nothing smaller than human unity.

I can foresee a reasonable objection to my suggestion of liturgical enactments of the relationship between worship and work on campus: "Why not just forget about it lest humanists or non-theists feel excluded?" I like the answer that the avowed atheist Salman Rushdie gave to Bill Moyers, when the latter admitted to being puzzled about how often Rushdie spoke of God in his answers to Moyers's probing questions. "You would be surprised, Bill, to know that we atheists think more about God than you theists do."[19] The rare atheist on a Catholic campus already knows about the religious affiliation of the campus, and could hardly be surprised or bothered by yet another expression of it. Besides, such a demonstration could give the campus Rushdies something more to ponder. They might even be made more comfortable by the effort to widen Catholic identity issues to a more inclusive category of godly identity. Catholicism has feared relativism and indifferentism, and if inclusivity became normless, that fear would be warranted. But a university whose secularism grows to the degree that the faiths of its personnel are treated as a private matter should be a greater concern than keeping non-theists on the campus comfortable.

It seems to me that each academic's relationship to his or her discipline could benefit from a longer look at this matter of worship. It might be instructive to contrast what seems like a nonworshiping attitude on the part of most academics with something like early Israel's attitude toward work. Take, for example, this injunction from the book of Leviticus: "When you come into the land which I am giving you and reap your harvest, you shall bring a sheaf of the first fruits of your harvest to the priest who shall wave the sheaf before the Lord that it may be acceptable for you" (23:10–11). This ritual of waving the sheaf of grain before the Lord is the perfect image for the formation of the Eucharistic oblation spirituality I am recommending in this chapter. For the Israelites, worship meant that you take what you do with you, and in a sense forfeit its first fruits in acknowledgment of your indebtedness to the One who has given you the land and the means to make it fruitful. There is also an ethics implied in the gesture of oblation, since one is not likely to offer ill-gotten goods to God. A work lacking in integrity is not a fitting offering to God.

Ironically, Catholic worship has so totally identified the oblation with the Christological meaning of the offering of bread and wine that it has largely lost its Jewish meaning. Our forebears were saying in effect, in the gesture described in Leviticus: "I have been plowing your fields, planting your seeds, and harvesting your crops, and doing this with an awareness of being in your debt as your servant. So I hand these first fruits over to You, God, as my way of expressing my view of myself and my productivity, and of You."

But oblation was only one component of Jewish liturgical understanding. The second component was the formation of the participants' minds and hearts, so that they could return to the fields and to the tilling of the soil more attuned to the mind of the Lord of the fields. Their owner is the Lord of all the earth, and the worshipers knew themselves as his or her stewards, whose task was to sow and till and reap, but now more conscious that "the earth is the Lord's and the fullness thereof." Their identity was that of stewards, because oblation deepened the offerers' self-understanding and consciousness about the need to make the piece of earth at their disposal productive, and to forfeit its first fruits as an oblation.

The English term *steward* comes from two Greek words: *oikos* (house/household) and *nomos* (law, norm, order). The steward, therefore, is to manage the owner's household according to the mind of its owner. The steward's mind is to be informed by the owner's mind; in this case, that of the owner who is Lord of the earth and the fullness thereof. If one takes the act of creation not as a singular, completed, past event, but as an ongoing process, then the connection between God and the recipients of God's largesse grows even stronger. The point is that there should not be a separation in our perceptions about the source of the resources needed to produce, and the oblation of what is produced from these resources.

The parable of the man who wholly lacked a sense of stewardship (Luke 12:16–21) reveals the great cost of ignorance of our primordial identity as stewards. He had a bumper crop of grain, and in deciding how to dispose of it, thought only of himself. His horizon included neither worship and thanksgiving, nor charity and others' needs. His ignorance about himself, others, and his indebtedness to God for the good harvest elicits a harsh response: "You fool! This very night your life shall be required of you. To whom will all this piled-up wealth of yours go?" (v. 30) Both academics and nonacademics could mull the import of the lesson Jesus draws from this parable. "That is the way it works with the man who grows rich for himself instead of growing rich in the sight of God" (v. 31).

How does one grow rich in the sight of God? In Paul's first letter to the Corinthians there is a further dimension of stewardship, namely, being "stewards of the mysteries of God" (4:1). This complements the reflections offered above about being aware of the mind of the Owner, whose resources one uses and whose property one manages. Plumbing the mysteries of God enables one to be more knowledgeable about the mind of the Owner. Or, maybe better, it makes one sensitive to the horizon within which one's work needs to be done; thus, a whole new level of meaning is acquired.

NOTES

1. Decree on Ecumenism (8).
2. Ibid.
3. *Gaudium et spes* (36).
4. *Gaudium et spes* (43).
5. Irwin, *Models of the Eucharist*, 44.
6. Irwin lists these various models as follows: Cosmic Mass, the Church's Eucharist, the Effective Word of God, the Memorial of the Paschal Mystery, Covenant Renewal, The Lord's Supper, Food for the Journey, Sacramental Sacrifice, Active Presence, and The Work of the Holy Spirit.
7. *Gaudium et spes* (39).
8. Ibid.
9. Taylor, *The Go-Between God*, 64.
10. *Lumen gentium* (10, 1).
11. Eucharistic Prayer II for Masses of Reconciliation, in *The Sacramentary*, 1131. This is the Roman missal revised by decree of the Second Vatican Council and published by authority of Pope Paul VI. See Lectionary for Mass in bibliography.
12. Decree on the Laity (3), in Abbott, *Documents of Vatican II*.
13. Ibid.
14. Viviano, *Study as Worship*, 194.
15. Ibid., 191.
16. *Dei verbum* (15).
17. Catholic-Muslim Forum Final Declaration, Nov. 7, 2008, available at http://www .zenit.org/article-24175?l = english.
18. *Nostra aetate* (2), in Abbott, Documents of Vatican II.
19. Interview between Bill Moyers and Salman Rushdie, "Bill Moyers on Faith and Reason," PBS, June 23, 2006.

CHAPTER 10

◆

Ex corde ecclesiae,
Its Strengths and Limitations

ANY INQUIRY INTO the rationale for a Catholic university would be incomplete if it did not take into account *Ex corde ecclesiae*, the Apostolic Constitution published in 1990 by Pope John Paul II. This vision for Catholic colleges and universities is not the first formal papal document produced on the nature and role of the Catholic university, but it is the most recent and most complete. It was thirty years in preparation, so it reflects the work of many minds. The initial impetus for the document came long before John Paul was pope, and it both benefited and suffered from many exchanges between the ecclesiastical authorities and academic representatives during its long period of gestation. The initial need for the document came from Catholic institutions in the Communist bloc, who needed support for their argument that they should be allowed to function without political interference from governmental ideology. In those circumstances, the patronage of the Vatican was considered essential for the immunity that was needed to exist and function freely as a Catholic institution. As the years went on, the nemesis of communism was superseded in the eyes of the Vatican by a new enemy, the secularization of universities under Catholic auspices, especially in the United States. Not much notice was taken of this document after publication until the American bishops, at Rome's behest, proceeded to implement the *mandatum*, which was an attempt to create a juridical link between those teaching Catholic theology in their institutions and the local bishop. The point of this move was to safeguard orthodoxy by allowing the bishop to cite any failures in the matter of orthodoxy in Catholic colleges or universities in his diocese.

THE ISSUES

There are several salient factual issues and questions surrounding this document, including some about the Latin title itself. Does the Catholic university of today come from the heart of the Church, as the title of the document itself asserts? Only in part. Historically, the Church was the patron of these educational institutions, but the university as a research institution—the target of the document—had its beginning not in the Church but at the University of Berlin in 1810, and later in that century at Johns Hopkins and the University of Chicago. From these beginnings, research universities have sprung up across the globe in various forms. Since the Church did not give birth to the form of these research institutions, they are not exactly *ex corde ecclesiae*, but *ex corde universitatis*. A second issue about *Ex corde ecclesiae* is that it was conceived transculturally, almost platonically, which is reflected in its approach to the nature of Catholic universities. Universities are treated as if they are the same in all cultures, which is not the case.

A third issue is that to date, no bishop has actually utilized the *mandatum* to ensure orthodoxy. The bishops have been busy with more important matters, including dealing with the sexual abuse of children by some of their priests. Also the ecclesiastical authorities seem to have overlooked, perhaps understandably, the question of how the civil courts in the United States would decide if a faculty member were to sue a bishop for his or her expulsion for alleged heterodoxy. To my knowledge, the bishops have not even published the names of those teachers of theology or religious studies who have sought and been given this mandate. One of the reasons for this silence is that the bond between the bishop and the faculty member, though juridical, is a personal one, in contrast the relationship between the institution and the diocese, which is an institutional one. Finally, it would be rare that a Catholic theologian would teach something as part of the Catholic faith that is not taught by the magisterium. This would only happen either if the theologian did not know what the Church taught on the subject, or failed to differentiate between his or her own views of what constituted a theologically defensible position, on the one hand, and what the magisterium teaches, on the other. It should also be noted that the bishops in this country have handled this issue of requiring a mandate from Catholic theologians in their dioceses very unevenly. Some have been quite deliberate about it, while others have ignored it. Behind the scenes, a few have even scorned the whole idea as having been ill-conceived from the start.

My interest does not lie with the juridical side of this papal initiative, but with the reasoning of *Ex corde ecclesiae* about the subject matter of this volume: namely, the Catholicism issue at a Catholic university. The document seeks to define the relationship between the Church and the Catholic university in terms that can raise hackles, because they seem to threaten the academic freedom of faculty, which was not the intent of the author(s). The document's main concern is with theologians. Theology as a discipline is seldom inert. That is the value of good theology—it is *fides quaerens intellectum*, faith inquisitive, seeking understanding. Thus, a professor of theology will ordinarily have more time and liberty to be up to date with developments in his or her area of specialization than will a bishop or his staff. Both theology and the tradition can continually develop in light of new information. "Theology," Lonergan wrote, "has become an empirical science in the sense that Scripture and Tradition now supply not premises, but data."[1]

Bishops do have a responsibility to protect the integrity of the faith, but this *mandatum* has proven to be an unenlightened means of going about it. The pope, of course, could not have avoided taking the juridical route to ensure the purity of doctrine in *Ex corde*, since he had to take into account canon 812 of the 1983 Code of Canon Law, which requires that an explicit mandate be given by the local bishop to teachers of theology in his diocese. The unworkability of that canon is evidenced by the near universal inaction on the part of bishops the world over for seven years after its articulation. The canon was a product of perfect logic—who could deny that bishops must protect the integrity of the faith in their dioceses?—but it was a logic disconnected from the character of theology done in these universities.

Ex corde ecclesiae has some valuable insights into the nature of a Catholic university. Its hopes are that these universities will assist the members of the university community "to achieve wholeness as human persons," each of them helping to "[promote] unity according to his or her role and capacity" (21).

Some of the high points of this Apostolic Constitution are as follows:

"The privileged task of a Catholic university is to unite existentially by intellectual effort two orders of reality . . . the search for truth and the certainty of already knowing the fount of truth" (1).

"A Catholic university is called . . . to evaluate the attainments of science and technology in the perspective of the totality of the human person . . . By its Catholic character a university is made more capable of conducting an impartial search for truth, a search that is neither subordinated to nor conditioned by particular interests of any kind" (7). (Hence, the Catholic university offers a disinterested service of impartial knowledge, sought "for the sake of the whole truth about nature, man and God") (4).

"A Catholic university has to be a living union of individual organisms dedicated to the search for truth . . . It is necessary to work toward a higher synthesis of knowledge" (16).

"While each academic discipline retains its own integrity and has its own methods . . . methodical research within every branch of learning . . . can never truly conflict with faith" (17).

"It is essential that we be convinced of the priority of the ethical over the technical, of the primacy of the person over things, of the superiority of the spirit over matter. The cause of the human person will only be served if knowledge is joined to conscience" (18).

"The Church, accepting the legitimate autonomy of human culture and especially of the sciences, recognizes the academic freedom of scholars in each discipline in accordance with its own principles and proper methods, and within the confines of the truth and the common good" (29).

These assertions constitute a wonderful and freeing horizon for the work of the Catholic university.

ECCLESIOCENTRISM AND DISAPPOINTMENT

But *Ex corde ecclesiae* is often problematic. For example, it lays out the rights of the hierarchy in safeguarding orthodoxy, without indicating any limits on the exercise of episcopal authority to prevent it from encroaching on the rights of faculty members when there is a dispute. Granted, the authority of the bishops with respect to the deposit of faith is the primary concern of the document, but there are also the authority of scholarship and the rights of those who produce it to be considered. Horizons are bounded by knowledge and interests; the interests and knowledge of the horizon of the author(s) of *Ex corde* can be summed up in one phrase: the integrity of the faith. Meanwhile, the interests and horizons of those who labor in the Catholic colleges and universities especially in this country are more complex, inasmuch as they cull from and forage in the whole realm of being with minds that are filled with nearly an infinity of data. There is a disparity between the horizons of the bishops and those of the faculty.

Because the document lacks a perspective on catholicity and the kingdom of God, an ecclesiocentrism diminishes the breadth of its insights. It would have been possible for the document to include such a perspective, since another papal document published the very same year, one that carried the greater weight of an encyclical, *Redemptoris missio*, beautifully articulated this catholicity/kingdom dimension. The absence of the eschatological category of the kingdom of God in *Ex corde ecclesiae* makes it almost inevitable that the document would view a Catholic university as an instrument of the institutional Church. In order to show how valuable the eschatology of *Redemptoris missio* would have been to the university, I will touch on what John Paul says about the kingdom in this text, which, as was noted, came out in the same year as *Ex corde ecclesiae*.

Redemptoris missio celebrates the twenty-fifth anniversary of *Ad gentes*, and represents a leap forward from the eschatology that that document of the Second Vatican Council had articulated. It teaches that "the Kingdom's nature is one of communion among all human beings—with one another and with God" (15). (This is the horizon all in the university should be working towards!) Some of its insights are as follows:

- "Working for the Kingdom means acknowledging and promoting God's activity, which is present in human history and transforms it. Building the Kingdom means working for liberation from evil in all its forms" (15). (The faculty's efforts to come to knowledge not yet attained are liberating people from at least the evil of ignorance; might this be seen as related to "God's activity" in them?)
- "The Kingdom cannot be detached either from Christ or from the Church . . . If the Kingdom is separated from Jesus, it is no longer the Kingdom of God which he revealed. The result is a distortion of the Kingdom" (18). (Yes, these are not to be separated, but by the same token, it is essential that they be distinguished from one another. Jesus neither identified himself with the kingdom, nor did he proclaim a Church!)
- "One may not separate the Kingdom from the Church . . . The Church is not an end in herself since she is ordered toward the Kingdom of God of which she is the seed, sign and instrument" (18). (The Church, at present, is somewhere between seeing itself as the kingdom's sole seed, sign, and instrument and the possibility of other such seeds, signs, and instruments.)

- "The Church is effectively and concretely at the service of the Kingdom" (20). (This commends a continual self-emptying of any accrual of power. A university can be at the service of the kingdom through its pursuit of truth and with a sense of humility about how much ignorance accompanies its pursuit.)
- "The inchoate reality of the Kingdom can be found beyond the confines of the Church among peoples everywhere, to the extent that they live 'gospel values' and are open to the working of the Spirit who breathes when and where he wills" (20). (Where human values are being pursued and human dignity promoted, the Spirit is the explanation of these enactments.)
- "The Church serves the Kingdom by her intercession, since the Kingdom is by its very nature God's gift and work . . . We must ask for it, welcome it, and make it grow within us; but we must also work together so that it will be welcomed and grow among all people until the time when Christ delivers the Kingdom to God the Father and God will be everything to everyone" (20). (The kingdom is the operative symbol of the whole both for Jesus and here for the pope.)

John Paul complains about the loose use of the category of the kingdom of God by theologians. He notes that their stress on that aspect of the mystery of God in the world's present and its future led them to accuse the Vatican of being too ecclesiocentric, and "the Church of being only a sign, for that matter a sign not without ambiguity" (17). But is it a sign without ambiguity? However we answer that question, it remains true that when eschatology is left out of ecclesiology (as in *Ex corde*), ecclesiocentrism seems to be the inevitable result. If the Holy Father's own theology of the kingdom in this encyclical had been given greater play in the Apostolic Constitution on Catholic universities, the value of the document would have been considerably enhanced.

Those who responsibly bring academic disciplines one by one, study by study, year by year to a greater intelligibility and wholeness are serving God's agenda in the world, whether they are cognizant of that horizon or not. The fact that the contributions of most faculty members and their disciplines are cognitional in character, rather than formally religious, does not justify their being seen either by the faculty themselves or by the leaders of the Church as peripheral to God's agenda.

HELP FROM THE PARABLES

Both bishops and faculty members can examine their knowledge of what already is, and wonder how well this knowledge equips them to know what is not yet. The Gospel suggests that we are to become like the scribe "instructed in the kingdom of God," who continually brings forth from his storehouse not only the old, time-tested truths of the faith, but new things as well (Matt. 13:52).

Being "instructed in the kingdom of God" also entails learning how to wait! The Gospel of Luke contrasts "the man who had a fig tree planted in his orchard," only to order the gardener to cut it down when it seemed fruitless, with the wise gardener who had the forbearance and hope that the first man did not (Luke 13:8–9). The wise man protected the tree, realizing that it had great potential to "bear fruit in the future."

It seems that Matthew had that same theme in mind at the end of his long section of parables. There is the scribe who is being "trained for the kingdom of heaven," who, again, is "like the head of a household who brings from his storeroom both the new and the old" (Matt. 13:52). So in Luke and Matthew at least, Jesus would not think highly of those who only bring forth the old things from the storeroom. Rather, he would look favorably on those who are also open to instruction, surprised by new findings, and patient about matters that are not yet clear, and that perhaps will not become clear before the final harvest.

Both the bishop and the theologian have to be aware that in the storeroom of Gospel wisdom, there are ancient treasures about which much remains to be known. The scribe who brings forth only the old from his storeroom will have less to do than the scribe who has been instructed in the kingdom of heaven, because the latter will have the additional work of discerning the relationship between the old, the tried and true, and the new, whether the new consists of experiences that others bring, or of knowledge of matters beyond their scope, like scientific findings. The scribe who is comfortable passing on the same old teachings in the same formulations in which he received them is not being trained to discern the in-breaking future. The wise will be faithful not only to tradition, but also to the new data that is only now coming into view. The scribe must not determine that something is "good" or "bad," before he or she is able to give an account of his or her judgment that can persuade others of its objectivity. A resolution of the old and the new will come from the interiority of a discerning scribe and a discerning church.

Two other parables shed light on this same matter: the one about the tares and the wheat, and the one about the net that catches fish of every kind. In both cases, there is the question of having to sort out the good from the bad, to separate that which is worthy from that which is worthless. In both cases, there is the question of the timing of the judgment. Furthermore, what is at stake in both cases is discernment.

In the first parable, the householder's servants are upset because weeds have encircled the good seed they have planted, and they are passionate about uprooting them, sure that some enemy has sown them (Matt. 13:28). The master teaches his servants that they are not to attempt to anticipate a final judgment that is not theirs to make, by excluding what does not give evidence at present of being worthy of inclusion. There will be a harvest time for the great separation, when the master of the harvest will gather the wheat into his barn and do the threshing himself. So, for now, let there be forbearance!

The second parable likens the kingdom of heaven both to a net that is thrown into the sea and to the sorting of the fish caught in it. This is enlightening for anyone who is prone to what one might call premature separationism. First, there is the question of the competence of those who would sort the good from the bad. Have they not (like all of us) been hauled ashore because of the mercy of God? At the final judgment scene in the Gospel of Matthew, the sheep and the goats don't sort themselves out, the eschatological Judge does. So also in this parable, it is "at the end of the age" that "the angels will go out and separate the wicked from the righteous" (Matt. 13:49). Part of the issue here is the ubiquity of sinners, whose hearts only God can judge. There is also the matter of timing. A *kairos* sense of time, which may be more in line with the chronology of God's thoughts and God's ways, is mercifully more patient and lenient than the *chronos* sense of time, which we tend to live by. *Chronos* time is inexorable: minutes, hours, days, years, decades. *Kairos* time is time when God's work is perceived to be operating.

CANON LAW

Something should be added here about the canon (812) that has thrown this papal effort about Catholic higher education into turmoil. There are two values in conflict here: The first is the value of keeping the saving story of the faith intact, and free of what would compromise it or confuse its adherents. The only way to ensure this is to have a wise authority that oversees communication of the contents of this faith. This role of oversight (*episcope*) lies with the bishop, as the canon in question states. The second value is that a university is only as credible (as a learning institution) as its scholars are free to pursue and teach their findings. If a university either is or is seen to be under an authority extrinsic to its scholarship, it would lose its credibility within academic circles. Ordinarily, the alleged violations of the institutional arrangements between a Catholic university and the local bishop occur in the theology communicated by the faculty within such universities, although decisions by campus ministers and administrators can also cause tensions at times.

One of the things that makes episcopal and papal authority especially difficult is the untidy way the Spirit enlivens the Church, which is through the charisms given by the Spirit for the community's upbuilding (1 Cor. 12:7). The Council affirmed the presence and ubiquity of the charisms, "even the most ordinary ones," and claimed that "for each of the faithful [there is] the right and duty to exercise them in the Church and in the world for the good of people and the building up of the Church, in the freedom of the Holy Spirit who 'blows where he will'" (*Lumen gentium*, 3). Overseeing the exercise of the charisms is the responsibility of the hierarchy, but they are not generated by the hierarchy. The exercise of the charisms is one of the primary ways the Church serves the world: "The laity derive the right and duty with respect to the apostolate from their union with Christ their Head . . . they are assigned to the apostolate by the Lord himself. They are consecrated into a royal priesthood and a holy people in order that they may offer spiritual sacrifices through everything they do and may witness to Christ throughout the world."[2]

Charisms can freshen and renew and lead, but they can also upset the order of a community. Hence the Decree on the Laity emphasizes the need for good "judgment about the true nature and proper use of these gifts," and about rights and duties, "not in order to extinguish the Spirit but to test all things and hold fast to what is good" (3). What keeps all of this from disorder is "communion with one's brothers and sisters in Christ, especially with their pastors" (3).

Into this mix of charisms and, yes, their counterfeits comes canon 812, which speaks of the *mandatum docendi* (the mandate for teaching), in which the local bishop accords the teacher of theology a mandate to teach. But even the Congregation of the Doctrine of the Faith, in its Instruction on the Ecclesial Vocation of the Theologian, locates the calling of theologians within the charisms.[3] It considers "theology indispensable for the Church" (1).

There has always been this tension between keeping the message pure and keeping the message fresh. When authority goes overboard, it juridicizes the purity side; when scholars go overboard, they bristle at any critique of their freshening efforts. Cardinal Ratzinger, before he was raised to status of pope, made an interesting remark on the first imbalance: "Theology is not simply and exclusively an auxiliary function of the magisterium. . . . Tensions between the magisterium and theology can be fruitful if they are faced by both sides with a recognition of the inner correlation of their roles. . . . The Church needs a healthy theology. Theology needs the living voice of the magisterium."[4]

Theology's job is to exercise a critical function with regard to the magisterium. It has to take responsibility for what the magisterium teaches, both respectfully and critically, and it plays a key role in the process of the whole Church's discernment. For the teachings of the magisterium to be received by the whole Church, those competent in theology must be allowed to use their scholarship to advance, refine, or at times question the assertions made by Church authority. If the authoritative statement issued by the leadership does not pass muster in the community, it will not be received. *Humanae vitae* (1968) and *Humani generis* (1950) have been two of the twentieth century's examples of the people of God giving the magisterium a failing grade.[5] In the absence of theological scholarship, the teaching role of the Church can become narrow. It is equally true that without the magisterium, theology can become fissiparous and rationalistic.

"A PERHAPS NOT NUMEROUS CENTER"

The tension that sometimes exists between the magisterium and the academic community of theologians has much less to do with faith, and much more to do with cultural conflicts, than I think has been appreciated by both sides. The lay academic community is rarely peopled by professionals who have matriculated in a classical culture. And the hierarchy is rarely peopled by professionals who have been formed in a modern academic culture. This is not to say that members of the hierarchy are ignorant, or unsophisticated, or lacking intelligence, or out of touch. Rather, it is to say that most members of the hierarchy have not done their studies in a secular university, and most often their degrees are in canon law or in theology of a more classical character. The lay theologians in their schools have seldom been trained where and how their bishops have been. Both populations are, of course, on the same search for meaning. Although they labor in different institutional cultures, both bishops and academic theologians face the same broader mass culture where values and meanings are so conflicted that it is difficult for them to make the judgments they each have to make to fulfill their respective professional responsibilities.

If I am correct in my judgment that the crisis is more often one of theologians and their bishops coming from different cultures, while being besieged by the same mass culture, then a further insight seems germane. The insight is that they have the same extremes to avoid and the same center to inhabit. One inhabits the center by making oneself "at home in the old and the new and [being] painstaking enough to work out one by one the transitions to be made and strong enough to refuse half measures," and by being open "to complete solutions even though [one] has to wait."[6] In any interaction between bishops and theologians, logic and content would not be insignificant, but an understanding of their respective cultures would also have to come into play. And it is most unlikely that "complete solutions" would be arrived at if love were not the principle that guided their interaction—love of one another, love of the truth, love of the Church, and love of Christ.

If this "perhaps not numerous center" described here is the mean, what would the extremes be? A solid right forms "that is determined to live in a world that no longer exists," and on the other side, there forms "a scattered left, captivated by now this, now that new development, exploring now this and now that new possibility."[7] Notice, the left is scattered, whereas the right finds itself uniform in its efforts to hold back the dawn. All three are seeking to make wholes, but the middle is patient enough to work out solutions.

NOTES

1. Lonergan, *A Second Collection*, 58.

2. Decree on the Apostolate of the Laity (3).

3. Congregation for the Doctrine of the Faith, "Instruction on the Ecclesial Vocation of the Theologian" (5, 6), May 24, 1990. Available at http://vatican.va/roman_curia/congrega tions/cfaith/doc_doc_ index.htm.

4. Comments made by Joseph Ratzinger at a press conference on the occasion of the publication of the "Instruction on the Ecclesial Vocation of the Theologian," available at http://catholicism.org/theology-not-private-ratzinger.html.

5. In his encyclical *Humanae vitae*, Paul VI took a negative view of the use of contraceptives in marriage. Pius XII, in *Humani generis*, deplored theological innovation and saw the role of theology as reinforcing the teachings of the magisterium.

6. Lonergan, "Dimensions of Meaning," in *The Lonergan Reader*, ed. Mark and Elizabeth Morelli (Toronto: University of Toronto Press, 1997), 401.

7. Ibid.

Afterword

AFTER ALL THESE WORDS, an afterword. In this volume I have been esteeming and extolling the value of dot-connectors. The line of demarcation in this regard is not between Catholic and non-Catholic faculty members, but between those who ask questions and those who do not, between those who strive to make the connections their particular areas of competence have prepared them to make, and those who do not. The strivers are contributing to the upbuilding of the "noosphere," as Teilhard de Chardin liked to describe the sphere of mind and spirit that surrounds the earth.

This volume claims that the energy for dot-connecting comes from subjectivity as it is moved to know being and pursue value. But these two classically named transcendental notions, while necessary, are not sufficient to explain the intellectual activity going on in modern academe, which is increasingly experiencing the fragmentation that accompanies specialization. This is why I have suggested another drive working in human intentionality, a drive that seeks to make further meaning by connecting dots or making wholes. Academics are usually well equipped for birthing these wholes, because their daily work involves putting together data that is in some way disconnected.

This book has been an argument about the identity issue in Catholic educational institutions, but it doesn't go the usual way of such arguments. It grounds its argument in the universal character of cognition and its operations, used in ways that can both account for and transcend subjectivity. But being a Catholic theologian, I have also looked at the relation between this activity of making wholes or connecting dots, and the Church to which I belong. Catholicism has a long history of connecting these dots in a continuum, in a Godward continuum at that. It also has a history of disconnecting dots, but it has learned much in the course of the centuries and corrected errors about its previous construals. It is still doing so. While most of the Church's best teachers have come from within its own ranks, some have not. Either way, the Church has been trudging along developing the story it wants all to be able at least to hear. It is still adding new chapters to this story, as new questions arise and further meanings develop. The story is credible as the drive of catholicity develops and appropriates its further meanings. An intriguing aspect of this study is that an emergent catholicity is also the passion of most educational institutions worth their salt.

In looking back over this whole manuscript now, I recall my first book, *The Conspiracy of God, the Holy Spirit in Us*, which I wrote in 1972. I wondered whether there was any connection between that book and what I have been writing here. Happily, I found that there is, since I still believe what I wrote then about the theology of the Spirit. But in this present volume, there is an appreciation I didn't have then for the nobility of a life dedicated to searching for knowledge, meaning, and value. It seems to me that a number of the ideas in this present volume are connected to my first book. First is the insight that the Spirit is a searcher, the Searcher *par excellence*. "The Spirit searches everything, even the depths of God" (1 Cor. 2:10). And when the Spirit is at work in someone who is also searching, connections get made in that person. One needs no more evidence of this than the connecting of the human and the divine in the womb of Mary. Or of the world and God at the creation. Or of the Church and the world at Pentecost. Or of faith and reason at the moment of insight when the connected dots can be verified. And as this volume has been implying, the Searcher and the researchers are much more likely to be working together than the academy has noticed up till now.

Another scriptural passage from another of Paul's letters suggests something the present volume does not address. Romans 8:26–27 speaks of the Spirit as the one who "comes to the aid of our weakness," and although the passage refers to the weakness of our prayer, why not expand our understanding of this weakness to include other things we seek to know and are also weak in attaining? The Spirit can aid "true" intentionality in the sense that it can assist people in making judgments of fact, value, and meaning. The Spirit, therefore, could assist us not only in our praying but in our entire pattern of choosing and acting. And "the One who searches hearts" knows where the interceding, intervening, coaxing, assisting (but not determining) Spirit would move us; that is, beyond our "groanings" and further in the direction of understanding. Three important instrumentalities used by the Spirit to help us align ourselves with the true and the good are the family, the church (or mosque or temple, etc.), and the school. Both this passage from Romans and the previous Corinthian text would have one believe that there are two intenders at work in human consciousness: the human being and the Spirit.

Still another scripture text connects my first book with this one. In Luke 13:10–13, Jesus heals the woman who has been bent over for 18 years—all her adult life, let's say. Jesus straightened her so that her horizon could now take in what she would not have been able to see before. For the rest of her life she would be able to give attention to what is, to what is of value, to what its meaning is, and to act on it. I see Lonergan as an important voice in this kind of healing. The human vocation is to know the real, and not from the stooped over, narrow perspective from which we all too often look out at the world. The vocation of the educator is the same, to free students from a narrowness and enable them to be beholders of what is worthy of their attention. There is no end of objects that can keep one's consciousness mired in too small a terrain. A good education helps one learn to pay attention to that which is of worth, and to be discriminating enough to find pearls of great price instead of expending one's life on pearls of great nonsense.

What I was trying to say in the first book is beautifully encapsulated in a brief essay of Lonergan's, titled "Existenz & Aggiornamento."[1] He describes the move from being in Christ as "the being of substance" to "the being of the subject" in Christ. In the former state one is "in love with God without awareness of being in love." This distinction must be a lot more autobiographical than he admits. Remaining at the "being of substance" level of experiencing Christ has its merit, since "quietly, imperceptibly, there goes forward the transformation operated by the *Kurios*, but the delicacy, the gentleness, the deftness of his continual operation in us hides the operation from us." By contrast, "inasmuch as being in Christ Jesus is the being of the subject, the hand of the Lord ceases to be hidden." As a result, "the substance in Christ Jesus becomes the subject in Christ Jesus." He likens the latter experience to being in love with another mortal with all the concreteness, immediacy, and meaning of such an experience. Being a subject in Christ Jesus becomes the constitutive meaning of the person.

The consequence of this movement from substance to subject is that a person's everyday concerns, interests, hopes, and plans, together with the emotions that accompany these, "are thought out in Christ Jesus" with whom one abides in love. I had not read Lonergan at the time of my first book, but what he is describing in this article is the experience I was trying to describe there. This kind of conversion released in him the love for God, the other, and himself that had previously touched his will and had enabled him to be antecedently effective in seeking the true and doing the good. But God loving him had been hidden from him. There is much behind the differentiation Lonergan is making here. Interiority takes center stage and scholastic metaphysics takes a walk. The meaning of being in Christ becomes constitutive of his meaning. It is both a conscious state and yet an experience of mystery: "to it one belongs; by it one is possessed."[2]

NOTES

1. Lonergan, *Collection*.
2. Lonergan, *Method in Theology*, 106.

APPENDIX A

◆

An Autobiographical Note on Prayer

I HAVE PERSONALLY been helped by the prayer that asks God for "an intimate knowledge" of the blessings that consciousness, intelligence, and understanding are for me and for all of us. This prayer was recommended by St. Ignatius Loyola, the founder of the Jesuits, in his *Spiritual Exercises*.

Ignatius's suggestion was not just that we ask for the gift of intimate knowledge; it was more specific.[1] He supplied two images of God to help us acquire this knowledge. One image is of God the Creator; the other of God the Co-Laborer. With the first of these, Ignatius recommends that we reflect on how God indwells all creation, and how this indwelling differs depending on the species—whether the elements, the plants, the animals, or humans. God's indwelling with humans operates by God "bestowing understanding on them."[2] The Creator indwells our understanding and intelligence! The sheer wonder of this horizon puts the learn-to-earn purpose of education in its rightful, lower place in the order of educational ends. A school would be a very different enterprise if this belief were to be accepted, its practice were to be honored, and the experience of God at work in one's efforts at learning savored.

The second image is even more compelling. Ignatius suggests that we imagine God not just as indwelling all of creation, but as laboring in all creatures "He has made," laboring in them according to their particular nature. But of all of these, there is only one created "in the likeness and image of the Divine Majesty."[3] "He conducts himself as one who labors" in human intelligence, seeking to help it to come to understanding and right judgment, while leaving the person free, and usually totally unaware of this presence. It would be a shame if this Co-Laborer were to go unnoticed over the course of a whole lifetime. But how many of us truly have this "intimate knowledge" of our Co-Laborer's assistance in trying to come to know what is so and not so, true and not true, good and only seeming good? Hence the prayer for the grace to come to an awareness of this assistance.

Ignatius adds still another image to help our imaginations. It is suggested that we imagine this assistance to our intelligence, understanding, consciousness, and insights as if it were descending from above—from an unlimited, supreme, infinite intelligence. So, "as the rays of light descend from the sun and as the waters flow from their fountains," we seek to recognize that our consciousness, our intelligence,

151

our understandings, and our insights are linked to a transcendent Source.[4] Meditation on these images can help to sacralize the work of attaining knowledge; we can come to see this work as accompanied, even companioned, by the Divine Intelligence assisting our knowing. This prayer, called "The Contemplation to Attain the Love of God," is done with a view to receiving a more intimate knowledge of ourselves and greater insight into our insights.

This line of thought is not so naive as to believe that all human knowledge and understandings are fashioned with the help of the divine mind; it does assume that there is a nexus between the Source and the products of human intelligence, when the latter are authentic. By authentic, I mean sufficiently thorough so as to get beyond a self-interested refraction of the data, so as to be able to weigh the data objectively. It is unlikely that most of us have ever even thought of this nexus, hence the value of the exercise. If this "intimate knowledge" accompanies our desire and labors at coming to know, then insofar as it is attained, it will be deepened by a response of gratitude. And on a good day, perhaps our efforts will even be characterized by love of and service to the God who "makes a temple" of us for this lifelong enterprise of coming to knowledge and acting upon it.[5]

The fingerprints, if I may call them that, of the Co-Laborer on the minds of human beings are evident from the good that people are able to do with their intelligence, and even more so from the wholes they seek to confect in their (academic) careers. The recommendation here is that all who labor as professors, administrators, students, or staff in the knowledge industry importune God (however we understand that transcendent Being) for an intimate knowledge of our indebtedness to the Co-Laborer, who generates and accompanies our desire to know the true and do the good. This intimate knowledge would enable us to appreciate the intelligence operating in ourselves, in our colleagues, and in those working in other fields, and to trace all of this work to its Source. Insofar as we can make such connections, a sense of disconnection from one another and from the mission of the school can begin to be reduced, at least to some degree.

NOTES

1. Puhl, *The Spiritual Exercises of St. Ignatius*, #233.
2. Ibid., 102, #235.
3. Ibid., 103, #236.
4. Ibid., 103, #237.
5. Ibid., 102, #235.

${\mathcal A}$PPENDIX B

◆

The Categorical and the Transcendental

H AVING LISTENED EXTENSIVELY to many groups of faculty over the last few years, I have been impressed with how invested each one is in his or her endeavors. But I have also imagined how much greater their contributions would be if they were aggregated in some way, and assembled into a greater whole. There seem to be three constituencies that are disfavored by these efforts remaining separate: the faculty themselves, who perforce have to be more loners than colleagues; the students, whose education would be enhanced by being able to have a sense of an integration of the good to which each of their mentors is contributing; and the larger community, which is deprived of examples of human solidarity to aspire to and replicate.

The Catholic intellectual tradition can seem like something foreign, like something that would have to be dropped into these schools by magisterial savants from a far-off headquarters. What I have been suggesting is that this tradition is in many ways already present in Catholic academe, but its presence remains largely unnoticed.

How could it be better noticed? One way would be for faculty members to open their eyes to the commonalities in the collective undertakings of themselves and their colleagues. Among those commonalities is the fact that all are moved by questions that need to be answered to attain their next level of competence. Where do these questions come from and where do they lead? One answer: "The question of God, then, lies within their horizons. Their transcendental subjectivity is mutilated or abolished, unless they are stretching forth towards the intelligible, the unconditioned, the good of value."[1]

Why is this kind of stretching beyond immediate questions to this deeper reflection infrequent? One reason is that faculty members are usually so immersed in the determinate, determinable matters of their own areas of competence, without adverting to the fact that there are deeper realms of meaning that can be accessed. The principal division among sources of meaning is between the categorical and the transcendental. Transcendental sources of meaning are at the foundations of categorical sources. They can be glimpsed if one becomes cognizant of "the very dynamism of [one's] intentional consciousness, a capacity that consciously and unceasingly both heads for and recognizes data, [and seeks] intelligibility, truth, reality, and value."[2] But these sought-for things, like truth, reality, and value, are the transcendentals, so called because they go beyond the data of sense and of determinate, determinable matters. Aristotle called these "the categories" or qualities that can be classified of known reality. Unless invited, productivity-intent faculty members do not usually reach beyond the categorical data of their specializations to reflect on these transcendent aspects. They could if they were able to attend to their own intending and its horizon. The transcendent is not opposed to the categorical, but includes it and goes beyond it. One way to become good at noticing this is to plumb another's intending and horizons so as to experience the differences within which they and their colleagues work.

Categorical thinking is obviously the bread and butter of academe, so this is not a disparagement of it. It is usually productive and valuable, but it can also produce researchers who lack any advertence to the transcendent. These deeper reaches can also be accessed through the notions, as I have described them in this book. If these are noticed, one can see that one's intentionality is only partly explained by the categories. In earlier centuries, scholars had a greater sense of ease and familiarity with the transcendentals, because the empirical world of science, including the social sciences, was relatively undiscovered. Now the complete opposite is true. But one does not have to become a metaphysician or a theologian or a contemplative to come to the realization that one's mind is operating with more than categorical specificities and classifications.

Reflection on one's own horizon, with its many interests, values, and ends, can enlarge this horizon. Without such an exercise, one's work on the terrain of the categorical can be all-consuming. One of the fruits of this distinction between the categorical and the transcendental is that it can make clear that in order to be contributing to the Catholic intellectual tradition, one does not have to be a Catholic, or to teach literature written by Catholic authors, or to think like Catholics are presumed to think, or any combination of these. The Catholic intellectual tradition is at its best when the classical transcendentals, like truth, goodness, beauty, are operating in its contributors.

Because Catholic institutions have tended to overlook the difference between the categorical and the transcendental, they have often responded to the perceived identity crisis of the schools by developing Catholic studies programs, including majors, minors, and even graduate degrees. Valuable as these are, the Catholic intellectual tradition is more capacious than the categories of Catholic materials, Catholic issues, or Catholic history. It reverences the transcendentals of goodness, truth, and beauty, irrespective of their being connected to Catholicism.

It is not that the Catholic intellectual tradition is without categories; on the contrary, it is full of them. I think, for example, of the category, consubstantial. The Church had a difficult time trying to name the uniqueness of Jesus and at the same time to express his relation to God. It found an ingenious concept from Greek thought: consubstantial, or in Greek, *homoousios*. The Council of Nicaea (321) picked up this language, so now one can say and believe that Jesus Christ was consubstantial with God. Or take the example of the number of sacraments. Opinions about the number of sacraments slid up and down until the twelfth century, when Peter Lombard supplied the Church with a category for defining a sacrament. A sacrament is an efficacious sign of grace; it signifies grace and it gives grace.

NOTES

1. Lonergan, "Religion," in *The Lonergan Reader*, 474.
2. Lonergan, *Method in Theology*, 73.

$\mathcal{A}$ PPENDIX C

◆

First Seminar of the Catholic-Muslim Forum (Rome, November 4–6, 2008), Final Declaration

THE CATHOLIC-MUSLIM FORUM was formed by the Pontifical Council for Interreligious Dialogue and a delegation of the 138 Muslim signatories of the open letter called "A Common Word," in the light of the same document and the response of His Holiness Benedict XVI through his Secretary of State, Cardinal Tarcisio Bertone. Its first seminar was held in Rome from November 4–6, 2008. Twenty-four participants and five advisors from each religion took part in the meeting. The theme of the Seminar was "Love of God, Love of Neighbor."

The discussion, conducted in a warm and convivial spirit, focused on two great themes: "Theological and Spiritual Foundations" and "Human Dignity and Mutual Respect." Points of similarity and of diversity emerged, reflecting the distinctive specific genius of the two religions.

1. For Christians the source and example of love of God and neighbor is the love of Christ for his Father, for humanity, and for each person. "God is Love" (1 John 4:16) and "God so loved the world that He gave his only Son so that whoever believes in him shall not perish but have eternal life" (John 3, 16). God's love is placed in the human heart through the Holy Spirit. It is God who first loves us thereby enabling us to love Him in return. Love does not harm one's neighbor but rather seeks to do to the other what one would want done to oneself (Cf. 1 Cor. 13:4–7). Love is the foundation and sum of all the commandments (Cf. Gal. 5:14). Love of neighbor cannot be separated from love of God, because it is an expression of our love for God. This is the new commandment, "Love one another as I have loved you" (John 15:12). Grounded in Christ's sacrificial love, Christian love is forgiving and excludes no one; it therefore also includes one's enemies. It should be not just words but deeds (Cf. 1 John 4:18). This is the sign of its genuineness.

For Muslims, as set out in "A Common Word," love is a timeless transcendent power which guides and transforms human mutual regard. This love, as indicated by the Holy and Beloved Prophet Muhammad, is prior to the human love for the One True God. A Hadith indicates that God's loving compassion for humanity is even greater than that of a mother for her child (Muslim, Bab al-Tawba: 21); it therefore exists before and independently of the human response to the One who is "The Loving." So immense is this love and compassion that God has intervened to guide and save humanity in a perfect way many times and in many places, by sending prophets and scriptures. The last of these books, the Qur'an, portrays a world of signs, a marvelous cosmos of Divine artistry, which calls forth our utter love and devotion, so that "those who have faith, have most love of God" (2:165), and "those that believe, and do good works, the Merciful shall engender love among them" (19:96). In a Hadith we read that "Not one of you has faith until he loves for his neighbor what he loves for himself" (Bukhari, Bab al-Iman: 13).

2. Human life is a most precious gift of God to each person. It should therefore be preserved and honored in all its stages.

3. Human dignity is derived from the fact that every human person is created by a loving God, and has been endowed with the gifts of reason and free will, and therefore enabled to love God and others. On the firm basis of these principles, the person requires the respect of his or her original dignity and his or her human vocation. Therefore, he or she is entitled to full recognition of his or her identity and freedom by individuals, communities, and governments, supported by civil legislation that assures equal rights and full citizenship.

4. We affirm that God's creation of humanity has two great aspects: the male and the female human person, and we commit ourselves jointly to ensuring that human dignity and respect are extended on an equal basis to both men and women.

5. Genuine love of neighbor implies respect of the person and her or his choices in matters of conscience and religion. It includes the right of individuals and communities to practice their religion in private and public.

6. Religious minorities are entitled to be respected in their own religious convictions and practices. They are also entitled to their own places of worship, and their founding figures and symbols they consider sacred should not be subject to any form of mockery or ridicule.

7. As Catholic and Muslim believers, we are aware of the summons and imperative to bear witness to the transcendent dimension of life, through a spirituality nourished by prayer, in a world which is becoming more and more secularized and materialistic.

8. We affirm that no religion and its followers should be excluded from society. Each should be able to make its indispensable contribution to the good of society, especially in service to the most needy.

9. We recognize that God's creation in its plurality of cultures, civilizations, languages, and peoples is a source of richness and should therefore never become a cause of tension and conflict.

10. We are convinced that Catholics and Muslims have the duty to provide a sound education in human, civic, religious, and moral values for their respective members and to promote accurate information about each other's religions.

11. We profess that Catholics and Muslims are called to be instruments of love and harmony among believers, and for humanity as a whole, renouncing any

oppression, aggressive violence and terrorism, especially that committed in the name of religion, and upholding the principle of justice for all.

12. We call upon believers to work for an ethical financial system in which the regulatory mechanisms consider the situation of the poor and disadvantaged, both as individuals, and as indebted nations. We call upon the privileged of the world to consider the plight of those afflicted most severely by the current crisis in food production and distribution, and ask religious believers of all denominations and all people of good will to work together to alleviate the suffering of the hungry, and to eliminate its causes.

13. Young people are the future of religious communities and of societies as a whole. Increasingly, they will be living in multicultural and multireligious societies. It is essential that they be well formed in their own religious traditions and well informed about other cultures and religions.

14. We have agreed to explore the possibility of establishing a permanent Catholic-Muslim committee to coordinate responses to conflicts and other emergency situations.

15. We look forward to the second Seminar of the Catholic-Muslim Forum to be convened in approximately two years in a Muslim-majority country yet to be determined.

All participants felt gratitude to God for the gift of their time together and for an enriching exchange.

At the end of the seminar, His Holiness Pope Benedict XVI received the participants and, following addresses by Professor Dr. Seyyed Hossein Nasr and H. E. Grand Mufti, Dr. Mustafa Ceric spoke to the group. All present expressed satisfaction with the results of the seminar and their expectation for further productive dialogue.

APPENDIX D

◆

A Contrasting Optic

Aᴏᴛᴇʀ ꜰɪɴɪꜱʜɪɴɢ ᴛʜɪꜱ ᴠᴏʟᴜᴍᴇ, I had a chance to read *Catholic Higher Education: A Culture in Crisis* by John Piderit, SJ, and Melanie Morey. I had known Fr. Piderit at Loyola University Chicago, where I was a faculty member during his tenure as president. As then, so also in this volume, I found his view of the work of Catholic higher education different from mine on a number of key issues. It should not be surprising to readers that two Jesuits who respect one another see things differently. Where he sees a crisis, I do not. His data (and that of his coauthor, Melanie Morey) comes from administrators; mine comes from listening to the faculty in some of the same institutions.

For the reader interested in the subject of what these Catholic schools should strive to be, I will note some of the differences between the Piderit/Morey book and the ideas developed in this one. First of all, their perception of a crisis comes, I believe, from a more traditional ecclesiology than mine. For example, they have a different understanding of what the mark "catholic" implies, so the horizons related to this term differ considerably. The horizon of the reign of God is more Christological and eschatological than the horizon of Catholicism, though we believe in both.

Another difference is my embrace of the Donald Rumsfeld metaphysical principle about "going to war with the army you've got." Because of the authors' a priori assumption that personnel at Catholic universities should be more Catholic, Piderit and Morey's promotion of the Catholic tradition seems more interested in hires who are not in these institutions. One gets the feeling that they want a train that has already left the station to back up into it, so they can fill seats that are actually already taken. My own method is to interview faculty already on the train, to find out where they are intending to go with their values and knowledge. The more I listened to these faculty members, the more positively I felt about the theological import of their work, whatever their faith or lack of it. Though the Catholic intellectual tradition is a matter of interest to both the Piderit/Morey book and this one, mine looks at it more fully.

Undoubtedly, the cultures of our Catholic colleges and universities could be improved, as can any culture, but the judgment that these cultures are in "crisis" could be tempered by paying more attention both to the value of intelligence and to its exercise, in order for God's agenda to succeed in this world, whether the scholar has such a horizon or not. Perhaps a difference between Piderit and Morey's approach and mine is that a theologian always expects more understandings from a faith that is potentially infinite in its possibilities than do non-theologians, who are more satisfied with the understandings this faith has already arrived at. Their volume, for example, sees "the faith" as having a content so discernible that students applying for entrance into a Catholic school should be tested about their knowledge of Catholicism. Further, they suggest assessing a graduating senior's "basic knowledge of the Catholic tradition," and recommend acknowledging students' acquisition of such basic knowledge at graduation "in some appropriate fashion." They also suggest awarding those with "more extensive knowledge with some institutional accolade" (358). The wisdom of this way of understanding Catholicism and insuring its continuance in these institutions seems to me to be wanting.

Piderit and Morey see the Catholic intellectual tradition as having "a baseline from which to measure" the success of these institutions, one that needs to be learned by those who don't know it, and to be communicated to them by those who do. This seems to me to generate a cleavage that cuts into the faculty, implicitly marking off the worthies, the *sophoi*, from the less knowledgeable unworthies, in the hope that enough of the former are in place to keep the institution Catholic. This might be a worthy pastoral aspiration, but it intrudes into a university setting as if a parish census were being taken.

My volume gives more attention to the methods for getting to the unknown from the known, and to the values being pursued and embodied by the would-be knowers. The history of a contents-already-known kind of Catholicism has too often generated an intellectual laziness and too readily linked power and knowledge. Piderit and Morey's book seeks to have faculty integrate faith with their teaching and, while that is an important goal, it depends on the horizon of what counts as integration.

The data compiled for *Catholic Higher Education: A Culture in Crisis* helpfully finds four different kinds of Catholic colleges and universities operating at the present time, and divides them as follows: the immersion model (vast majority of students and faculty Catholic, many Catholic courses, strong nonacademic culture); the persuasion model (a lesser majority of students and faculty Catholic, fewer courses given that involve a knowledge of Catholicism, strong nonacademic Catholic culture); the diaspora model (minority of students and faculty Catholic, minimal number of Catholic courses, consistent Catholic culture in nonacademic areas); and the cohort model (a small cohort of well-trained and committed Catholic students and faculty, and "a much larger group of students educated [by the cohort] to be sensitive to religious issues with a view to influencing policy," presumably that of the campus) (89).

Their volume is also useful in addressing what it calls the "inheritability" issue. A culture has to be sufficiently distinctive to be handed on to the next generation; if the latter receives what is distinctive, there can be an inheritance. Piderit and Morey see this hoped-for inheritance being shaped by three components of Catholic higher education: the general culture of university life, the Catholic culture in higher education, and the particularities of the institution's own culture. A Catholic university's administration, therefore, must be sensitive to these components, and seek to promote the best practices of Catholic culture in higher education by its policies and strategies.

But there is a more subtle side to this inheritability question. Generation after generation have fed the faith, but their contributions have only been as fresh as their questions and the thoroughness with which they have sought to answer them, both from their own experiences and from their understandings of Catholicism. Hence, the sense of the faithful that emerges from each generation is not likely to be the same as that which it inherited, since the personal appropriation of faith has to be true not only to the Church's understandings, but also to the experience, understandings, insights, and judgments of believers. "The faith" isn't an abstraction; its life depends on believers' fidelity to it, and to their own conscious operations and consciences.

There seems to be a kind of nostalgia running through Piderit and Morey's book; the more concrete its suggestions get, the more it seems to imagine a past that is irretrievable. For example, one suggestion is "to bring faculty and pastoral people back into the dormitories to help create living environments where students can be mentored in the Catholic tradition" (362). In addition, "to enhance the character formation and moral education of students," residence assistants should be schooled in "the Catholic approach" to issues such as drugs, sex, and alcohol (363). Along the same lines is the idea of creating honor codes that set a high behavioral standard rooted in the Catholic tradition and its moral and social teachings, and to ask students to sign statements signifying their intention to abide by them (365). Finally, Piderit and Morey propose to "enfranchise" some trustees so that in their "normal oversight activities they would be able to monitor religious performance and evaluate which programs had the greatest promise for enhancing that performance for the future" (370). They admit that some of these ideas might be rejected by students as too controlling. I believe that such ideas are not usually workable in practice.

Piderit and Morey see the Catholic intellectual tradition as having a conceptually deliverable content. This is largely true of the doctrinal tradition, but largely false of the intellectual tradition. My volume goes a different route, by suggesting that both the reality and the dynamism of the Catholic intellectual tradition are connected to the notions of being, of value, and the whole of meaning. From these known unknowns can come understandings and concepts that keep the doctrinal inheritance credible and fresh. Depending on how one understands the role of the Catholic faith in higher education, administrators, bishops, devout faculty, and staff can be in a position of great challenge and opportunity or in an awkward position.

Bibliography

Abbott, Walter, ed. *The Documents of Vatican II*. New York: Herder & Herder, 1966.

Alberigo, Giuseppe, and Joseph Komonchak, eds. *History of Vatican II*, vol. 1. Maryknoll, NY: Orbis Books, 1995.

Aquinas, Thomas. *Summa Theologia*.

Arendt, Hannah. *Eichmann in Jerusalem: A Report on the Banality of Evil*. New York: Viking Press, 1963.

Aristotle. *A New Aristotle Reader*. Edited by J. L. Ackrill. Princeton, NJ: Princeton University Press, 1987.

Becker, Ernest. *The Denial of Death*. New York: Free Press, 1973.

Bissoli, Cesare. *Decree on the Apostolate of the Laity: Adult Catechesis in the Christian Community—Some Principles and Guidelines*. St. Paul, MN: Libreria Editrice Vaticana/St. Paul Publications, 1990.

Boeve, Lieven. *Interrupting Traditions: An Essay on Christian Faith in a Postmodern Context*. Louvain, Belgium: Peeters Press, 2003.

Braaten, Carl, and Robert Jensens, eds. *The Last Things: Biblical and Theological Perspectives on Eschatology*. Grand Rapids, MI: William B. Eerdmans, 2002.

Brann, Eva. *Paradoxes of Education in a Republic*. Chicago: University of Chicago Press, 1979.

Bretherton, Luke. *Hospitality as Holiness*. Burlington, VT: Ashgate Publishing, 2006.

Brown, Peter. *The Rise of Western Christendom: Triumph and Diversity, A.D. 200–1000*. 2nd ed. Malden, MA: Blackwell Publishers, 2003.

Buckley, Michael. *The Catholic University as Promise and Project*. Washington, D.C.: Georgetown University Press, 1999.

Bulliet, Richard W. *The Case for Islamo-Christian Civilization*. New York: Columbia University Press, 2004.

Burtchaell, James. *The Dying of the Light: The Disengagement of Colleges and Universities from Their Christian Churches*. Grand Rapids, MI: William B. Eerdmans, 1998.

Buttiglione, Rocco. *Karol Wojtyla: The Thought of the Man Who Became Pope John Paul II*. Grand Rapids, MI: William B. Eerdmans, 1997.

Catechism of the Catholic Church. Liguori, MO: Liguori Publications, 1994.

Cernera, Anthony, and Oliver Morgan, eds. *Examining the Catholic Intellectual Tradition*. 2 vols. Fairfield, CT: Sacred Heart University Press, 2000 and 2002.

Clarke, W. Norris. *The One and the Many: A Contemporary Thomist Metaphysics*. Notre Dame, IN: University of Notre Dame Press, 2001.

Clooney, Francis X., ed. *Jesuit Postmodern: Scholarship, Vocation and Identity in the 21st Century*. Lanham, MD: Rowman & Littlefield, 2006.

Coelho, Ivo. *Hermeneutics and Method: The Universal Viewpoint in Bernard Lonergan*. Toronto: University of Toronto Press, 2001.

Cohen, Patricia. "On Campus: The 60s Begin to Fade and the Liberal Professors Retire," *New York Times*, July 3, 2008.

Congar, Yves. *I Believe in the Holy Spirit*. New York: Seabury Press, 1983.

Connor, James L., ed. *The Dynamism of Desire: Lonergan and the Spiritual Exercises*. St. Louis: The Institute of Jesuit Sources, 2006.

Costigan, Richard. *The Consensus of the Church and Papal Infallibility: The Background of Vatican I*. Washington, D.C.: The Catholic University of America Press, 2005.

Decree on the Apostolate of the Laity, *Apostolicam Actuositatem*. November 18, 1965. Vatican: The Holy See. www.vatican.va/archive/hist_councils//ii_vatican_council/documents/vat-ii_dec.

Decree on Ecumenism, *Unitatis Redintegratio*. November 21, 1964. Vatican: The Holy See. www.vatican.va/archive/hist_councils//ii_vatican_council/documents/vat-ii_dec.

Dolan, Jay P. *The American Catholic Experience: A History from Colonial Times to the Present*. Notre Dame, IN: Notre Dame University Press, 1992.

Dulles, Avery. *The Catholicity of the Church*. New York: Oxford University Press, 1985.

Edwards, Dennis. "Resurrection and the Costs of Evolution," in *Theological Studies* 2006.

Friedman, Thomas L. "The Taxi Driver," *New York Times*, November 1, 2006.

Gaillardetz, Richard. *Teaching with Authority: A Theology of the Magisterium*. Collegeville, MN: Liturgical Press, 1997.

Gallin, Alice. *Negotiating Identity: Catholic Higher Education since 1960*. Notre Dame, IN: Notre Dame University Press, 2000.

Gleason, Philip. *Contending with Modernity: Catholic Higher Education in the Twentieth Century*. New York: Oxford University Press, 1995.

Haughey, John C. "Catholic Higher Education: A Strategy for Its Identity," *Current Issues in Catholic Higher Education* 16, no. 2 (1996).

———. "The Driver in the Mind of Fethullah Gulen," in *Islam in the Age of Global Challenge*. Washington, D.C.: Rumi Forum Publication, 2008.

———. *Revisiting the Idea of Vocation*.Washington, D.C.: The Catholic University of America Press, 2004.

Heft, James L., ed. *Believing Scholars: Ten Catholic Intellectuals*. Bronx, NY: Fordham University Press, 2005.

Hellwig, Monika K. *Public Dimensions of a Believer's Life: Rediscovering the Cardinal Virtues*. Lanham, MD: Rowman & Littlefield, 2005.

Henry, Douglas, and Michael Beaty, eds. *Christianity and the Soul of the University*. Grand Rapids, MI: Baker Academic, 2006.

Himes, Kenneth R., Lisa Sowle Cahill, Charles E. Curran, David Hollenbach, and Thomas A. Shannon, eds. *Modern Catholic Social Teaching: Commentaries & Interpretations*. Washington, D.C.: Georgetown University Press, 2005.

Hopkins, Gerard Manley, "Hurrahing in Harvest," in *The Penguin Book of English Christian Verse*. Edited by Peter Levi. London: Penguin, 1984.

Irwin, Kevin. *Models of the Eucharist*. Mahwah, NJ: Paulist Press, 2005.

John Paul II. *Fides et ratio: Encyclical of Pope John Paul II on the Relationship between Faith and Reason*. Origins: CNS Documentary Service, October 22, 1998.

King, Thomas, and James Salmon, eds. *Teilhard and the Unity of Knowledge*. Mahwah, NJ: Paulist Press, 1983.

King, Thomas M. *Teilhard's Mass: Approaches to "The Mass on the World."* Mahwah, NJ: Paulist Press, 2005.

Kronman, Anthony. *Education's End: Why Our Colleges and Universities Have Given Up on the Meaning of Life*. New Haven, CT: Yale University Press, 2007.

Langan, John, and Leo O'Donovan, eds. *Catholic Universities in Church and Society: A Dialogue on Ex corde ecclesiae*. Washington, D.C.: Georgetown University Press, 1993.

Lectionary for Mass. English translation approved by the National Conference of Catholic Bishops and confirmed by the Apostolic See. Revised version, Catholic edition. Collegeville, MN.: Liturgical Press, 1970.

Lewis, Harry. *Excellence without a Soul*. New York: Perseus Books, 2006.

Lodahl, Michael. *Shekhinah Spirit: Divine Presence in Jewish and Christian Religion*. Mahwah, NJ: Paulist Press, 1992.

Lonergan, Bernard. *Collection*. Edited by Frederick E. Crowe and Robert M. Doran. Toronto: University of Toronto Press, 1988.

———. *Insight: A Study of Human Understanding*. Edited by Frederick E. Crowe and Robert M. Doran. Toronto: University of Toronto Press, 1992.

———. *Method in Theology*. Toronto: University of Toronto Press, 1971.

———. *Method in Theology*. New York: Herder & Herder, 1972.

———. *A Second Collection*. Edited by William Ryan and Bernard Tyrrell. Toronto: University of Toronto Press, 1996.

———. *A Second Collection*. Toronto: University of Toronto Press, 1996 [original edition 1974].

———. *A Third Collection: Papers by Bernard Lonergan*. Edited by Frederick E. Crowe. Mahwah, NJ: Paulist Press, 1985.

———. *Verbum: Word and Idea in Aquinas*. Edited by Frederick E. Crowe and Robert M. Doran. Toronto: University of Toronto Press, 1997.

Lowell, James Russell. *The Complete Poetical Works of James Russell Lowell*. Boston: Houghton Mifflin, 1968, Part 13/21.

MacIntyre, Alasdair. *After Virtue*. Notre Dame, IN: Notre Dame University Press, 1981.

Mahoney, Kathleen. *Catholic Higher Education in Protestant America*. Baltimore: Johns Hopkins University Press, 2003.

Marsden, George. *The Soul of the American University: From Protestant Establishment to Established Nonbelief*. New York: Oxford University Press, 1994.

Messbarger, Paul. *Fiction with a Parochial Purpose: Social Uses of American Catholic Literature, 1884–1900*. Boston: Boston University Press, 1971.

Metz, Johannes B. *Theology of the World*. Translated by William Glen-Doepel. New York: Herder & Herder, 1969.

Metz, Johannes B., and Jurgen Moltmann. *Faith and the Future*. Maryknoll, NY: Orbis Books, 1995.

Morelli, Mark D., and Elizabeth A. Morelli, eds. *The Lonergan Reader*. Toronto: University of Toronto Press, 1997.

Newman, Elizabeth. *Untamed Hospitality: Welcoming God and Other Strangers*. Grand Rapids, MI: Brazos Press, 2007.

Newman, John Henry. *The Idea of a University*. Notre Dame, IN: The University of Notre Dame Press, 1982.

———. "Letter to the Duke of Norfolk" V, in *Certain Difficulties Felt by Anglicans in Catholic Teaching*, vol. 2. London: Longmans Green, 1885.

Nichols, Aidan. *Divine Fruitfulness: A Guide through Balthasar's Theology beyond the Trilogy*. New York: T&T Clark, 2007.

O'Brien, George Dennis. *The Idea of a Catholic University*. Chicago: University of Chicago Press, 2002.

O'Connor, Flannery. *A Good Man Is Hard to Find and Other Stories*. New York: Harcourt Brace, 1955.

Ong, Walter J. "Yeast: A Parable for Catholic Higher Education," *America*, April 7, 1990.

Paul VI. *Humanae Vitae: Encyclical of Pope Paul VI on the Regulation of Birth*. July 25, 1968.

Piderit, John, and Melanie Morey. *Catholic Higher Education: A Culture in Crisis*. New York: Oxford University Press, 2006.

Pius XII. *Humani Generis: Encyclical of Pope Pius XII Concerning Some False Opinions Threatening to Undermine the Foundations of Catholic Doctrine*. August 12, 1950.

Prusak, Bernard. *The Church Unfinished: Ecclesiology through the Centuries*. New York: Paulist Press, 1989.

Puhl, Louis, ed. *The Spiritual Exercises of St. Ignatius.* Chicago: Loyola University Press, 1951.
Rahner, Karl. "Dogmatic Questions on Easter," in *Theological Investigations*, vol. 4.
———. *Foundations of Christian Faith.* Edited by William Dych. New York: Seabury Press, 1978.
———. *Sacramentum Mundi*, vol. III. New York: Herder & Herder, 1972.
———. "The Specific Character of the Christian Concept of God," in *Theological Investigations*, vol. 21.
Reubin, Julie. *The Making of the Modern University.* Chicago: University of Chicago Press, 1996.
Rist, John. *What Is Truth? From the Academy to the Vatican.* Toronto: University of Toronto Press, 2008.
Russell, Robert John. *Cosmology: From Alpha to Omega.* Minneapolis: Fortress Press, 2008.
Russell, Robert, William Stoeger, and George Coyne, eds. *Physics, Philosophy, and Theology: A Common Quest for Understanding.* Notre Dame, IN: University of Notre Dame Press, 1988.
The Sacramentary. Totowa, NJ: Catholic Book Corporation, 1985.
Schwehn, Mark R. *Exiles from Eden: Religion and the Academic Vocation in America.* New York: Oxford University Press, 1993.
Smith, Huston. *The Soul of Christianity: Restoring the Great Tradition.* San Francisco: Harper, 2005.
———. *Why Religion Matters: The Fate of the Human Spirit in an Age of Disbelief.* New York: HarperCollins, 2001.
Sommerville, John. *The Decline of the Secular University.* New York: Oxford University Press, 2006.
Suenens, Cardinal Leon-Joseph. *Memories and Hopes.* Dublin: Veritas Publications, 1992.
Taylor, John V. *The Go-Between God.* Minneapolis: Fortress Press, 1972.
Teilhard de Chardin, Pierre. *Christianity and Evolution.* New York: Harcourt, 1978.
———. *The Future of Man.* New York: Harper & Row, 1959.
———. *The Heart of Matter.* New York: Harcourt, 1978.
———. *Human Energy.* New York: Harcourt Brace Jovanovich, 1969.
———. *The Human Phenomenon.* New edition. Translated by Sarah Appleton-Weber. Eastbourne, UK: Sussex Academic Press, 1999.
———. *Letters from a Traveler.* New York: Harper & Row, 1962.
———. *The Making of a Mind.* New York: Harper & Row, 1965.
———. *Mass.* Mahwah, NJ: Paulist Press, 2005.
———. Retreat Notes, Beijing, October 1945. Translated from the French in *The Way*, 44, no. 3 (July 2005.
———. *Science and Christ.* Translated by Rene Hague. New York: Harper & Row, 1968.
Tennyson, Alfred. "In Memoriam A.H.H.," in *A Collection of Poems.* Edited by Christopher Ricks. New York: Doubleday & Co., 1972.
Tripole, Martin. *Jesuit Education 21: Conference Proceedings.* Philadelphia: St. Joseph's University Press, 2002.
van Beeck, Frans Jozef. *Catholic Identity after Vatican II: Three Types of Faith in the One Church.* Chicago: Loyola University Press, 1985.
———. *God Encountered: A Contemporary Catholic Systematic Theology.* Collegeville, MN: The Liturgical Press, 1989.
Viviano, Benedict Thomas. *Study as Worship.* Leiden: E. J. Brill, 1979.
von Balthasar, Hans Urs. *Cosmic Liturgy: The Universe According to Maximus the Confessor.* San Francisco: Ignatius Press, 1993.
Whybray, R. N. *The Intellectual Tradition in the Old Testament.* Berlin: Walter de Gruyter, 1974.
Wilcox, John R., and Irene King, eds. *Enhancing Religious Identity: Best Practices from Catholic Campuses.* Washington, D.C.: Georgetown University Press, 2000.
Woods, Thomas E. *How the Catholic Church Built Western Civilization.* Washington, D.C.: Regnery Publishing, 2005.

Index

academic faculty members, 1–27; academic
communities and shared meanings, 21,
127–28; biographical snapshots, 15–21;
and the good spoken of in terms of
particular wholes, 5–7; good that each
is attempting to achieve, 1–2; personal
self-descriptions, 5–6, 21–22; personal
self-understandings of their beliefs,
21–22; statistical data on spirituality
and religious faith, 11, 21–22, 26; and
virtues of academic enterprise, 24–27;
workshops and interviews, 1–4, 10–12
academic freedom, 55–56, 140
Ad gentes, 66, 142
antinominanism, 62
Antiochene school of Christology, 107
Arendt, Hannah, 75
Aristotle, 45
Association of Catholic Colleges and Universities, 26
atheism, 136
Augustine, 41, 94

baptism in Christ, 129–31
Becker, Ernest, 114, 118
"being": nature of, 42–44; notion of, 44,
46, 58–59; as the supreme heuristic
notion, 58–59
Berry, Thomas, 79
Bettinotti, Maria, 20–21
biases and the Catholic intellectual tradition, 81–82, 85–87, 96–97
Boeve, Lieven, 33–34

canon law: canon 812, 141, 145; and charisms, 145–46; and episcopal and papal

authority, 145; and *Ex corde ecclesiae*,
141, 145–46
careerism, academic, 25, 75, 101
categorical sources of meaning, 153–55
"Catholic" as adjective/term, 70–72, 93
*Catholic Higher Education: A Culture in
Crisis* (Piderit and Morey), 159–61
Catholic intellectual tradition, 61–104; and
academic disciplines, 13, 53–54, 90–97,
100–101; the adjective "Catholic" and
term catholic, 70–72, 93; approaching
with hermeneutics of circumspection/
appreciation, 77–78; and biases, 81–82,
85–87, 96–97; and bodies of knowledge,
7–8, 83, 86; boundaries of, 66–67,
69–70; and Catholic identity of institutions, xi, 5, 37, 95, 132–35; and catholicity, 52–57; challenges in relating Church
to world/world to Church, 68–69; and
Christological doctrine, 55–57, 69–70,
71–72; and Church's defensive position,
67–68; and Church's engagement with
questions about the true and good, 78;
and the Church's history of anti-intellectualism, 78; and common sense and
theory, 84; compound nature of, 66, 67,
71–72; and conceptualism, 96–97; and
difference between theology and religion, 62–63; differentiating from the
Sacred tradition, 61, 63, 64–65, 69–70;
dimensions of, 88–89; distinctiveness
of, 65; and doctrinal poverty, xi–xii, 6;
effect on other intellectual traditions,
103; and faith, hope and love, 91–92;
faith and reason, 65; and fragmenta-